Excellent Citizens and Notable Partings

Excellent Citizens and Notable Partings

A further look at the popular series,
"Portrait of an Excellent Citizen,"
published in *The Review-Appeal,* 1966-1968,
in Franklin, Tennessee

Marcia P. Fraser and Ashleigh M. Florida
Compilers and Editors

Special Collections Department
Williamson County Public Library

Foreword by Rick Warwick,
Williamson County Historian

*A project of Williamson County Public Library and
Friends of the Williamson County Public Library*

Academy Park Press
An Imprint of Williamson County Public Library
Franklin, Tennessee

Library of Congress Control Number: 2020910350

ISBN 978-0-9970690-5-1

Book and cover design by Ashleigh M. Florida and Rebecca Tischler

Williamson County Public Library
Dolores Greenwald, Director
and
Friends of the Williamson County Public Library
Debbie Sanders Eads, President (outgoing)
Mary Herring, President (incoming)

Printed and Bound in the United States
By IngramSpark
La Vergne, Tennessee

Table of Contents

1968 Masthead , *The Review-Appeal*

Foreword

Strange as it may seem, I think obituaries are the most important and interesting reading found in our local newspapers. Over the years, I have gleaned more valuable family information from reading old obituaries than almost any other source in the Williamson County Archives and the Williamson County Public Library. Relationships of the subject of the obituary have solved many puzzles in identifying parents, siblings and vital statistics. In fact, my main reason for subscribing to *The Tennessean* today is to read the obituary columns.

With *Excellent Citizens and Notable Partings*, Williamson County Public Library has published another valuable source for anyone interested in knowing who were some of the noteworthy citizens of Franklin and Williamson County in the mid-1960s. This publication takes a project I collected for the Williamson County Historical Society's 2010 Journal, entitled *Portraits of Williamson County*, a step further. By supplying the subject's obituary, if deceased, or additional biographical information, if still living, we get a more complete picture of these notable citizens and the contributions they made to this town and county.

From 1966 until 1968, *The Review-Appeal* featured each week, *Portrait of An Excellent Citizen*, a pencil drawing of a well-known citizen. The artist Bill Duke, as attributed by his signature, managed to draw 143 local personalities. However, *The Review-Appeal* editor failed to introduce the artist at the beginning of the series and, surprisingly, ended the project without fanfare or recognizing Duke. Turns out, Bill Duke was a well-known Nashville artist and a staff artist for *The Tennessean*.

For book collectors of local history and those who are true patrons of our public library, *Excellent Citizens and Notable Partings* will be a must have addition to our personal libraries. Publications such as this further our knowledge of local history and deepens our appreciation for a place we call home.

Rick Warwick,
Williamson County Historian

"We move through places every day that would never have been if not for those who came before us."

— *Mitch Albom*

Excellent Citizens and Notable Partings
viii

Introduction

June 2020

This is a book that was waiting to happen.

While combing through an old box of items we discovered in the Manuscript Room of the library's Special Collections Department, we came across a nearly complete set of newspaper clippings entitled "Portrait of an Excellent Citizen." Needless to say, we were intrigued by this select group of local citizens, so highly regarded that each face was hand drawn by *Tennessean* staff artist, Bill Duke, and so we set out to find more. We soon discovered that the articles ran as a series in *The Review-Appeal,* a local Franklin paper, between 1966 and 1968, beginning with Joe Pinkerton on February 17, 1966, and quietly ending with Charles A. Rigsby on October 31, 1968. Neither article bore any information about the creation of the series, the artist, or its demise. We also found profiles in the series that our original collector had missed, bringing the number of entries to 143.

We wondered how the lives of these citizens played out and what their stories could tell us, so we set out to locate obituaries and other articles. After compiling additional material, it was easy to see that if we could get it into a book, it would be a valuable resource, particularly for family and local history researchers. And so our odyssey began. As we became more deeply involved in our research and in the mechanics of building a book, we decided to thread in ads of the era from *The Review-Appeal*, *The Williamson Leader*, and local Franklin directories, and also add quotations and excerpts from other local sources whenever possible.

As for those "Excellent Citizens" who are still living, we made a concerted effort to contact each one to ask for their help, or their family's help, in creating an updated entry. Sadly, for a few, we were not able to realize that goal, but, during the process, we did amass additional and original content for many of our Excellent Citizens, living and deceased.

While our focus has been solely on these 143 citizens, we recognize that there were many notable citizens of the day who were not included in the series. With that in mind, we also point our readers to other sources, such as *Who's Who in Williamson County* by Jane Bowman Owen (1935-1953), *Who's Who in Williamson County* by Nat Osborne, Jr. (1953-1956), and *Who's Who in Williamson County* by Derry Carlisle (1957-1977), all edited and republished by Rick Warwick. We also encourage our patrons to read narratives of locals who have chronicled their own lives in Williamson County during this time, and in doing so, have animated the lives of many of the citizens featured in this book. Look for works by Leonard Isaacs, Bill Peach, Bobby Langley, Jimmy Gentry, W. C. Yates and Russ Farnsworth, among others.

Today, we have "social media" and "influencers," but these men and women of the late 1960s were *influential*. Their birth years spanned the years 1870 to 1942. They were doers, and their lives reflected their interaction with, and their influence in, the community. For a time, they were all here in this place together, the stalwarts of their day.

We hope these pages provide readers with a useful resource as well as an interesting look back at Williamson County during a time we now call "The Sixties."

Marcia P. Fraser,   Ashleigh M. Florida,

Special Collections Librarian   Special Collections Assistant Librarian

Williamson County Public Library,

Franklin, Tennessee

Acknowledgements

Compiling and editing this book required concentrated effort, teamwork, and a love of local history, but the deep satisfaction we received from its creation was truly its own reward.

With the help and support of many heads and hands, we were able to produce this work. For them, we are very grateful.

Production
Dolores Greenwald, Director, WCPL
Jeffie Nicholson, Manager, Adult Services, WCPL
Rick Warwick, Williamson County Historian
Debbie Sanders Eads, President, Friends of the Library
John Davis Fraser and John Rory Fraser
Shannon Boyd McNamara
Sharon Reily
Cindy Schuchardt
Rebecca Tischler
Linda Woodside

Contributors
John S. Beasley II
John H. and Paula Zeikle Childress
Linda Sue Strickland Conrad
Susan McCall Fisher
Cindy White Gentry
Margaret Jewell Gordon
Loy G. Hardcastle, Jr. and Cheryl Hardcastle Petty
Huberta Hill, Roger Hill and Randy Hill
James William and Katherine Ladd Hood
Eunetta Mayberry Kready and Paula Ligon
Shannon McNamara
Bill Peach
Lillian Campbell Stewart
Mary Ann Gray Tate
Peggy Stephenson Wilson

Copyright Permissions
Gannett Co., Inc., for *The Review-Appeal* and *The Tennessean*
The Bailey Leopard Family, publisher, *The Williamson Leader*
Derby Jones, publisher, *Williamson Herald*
Williamson Memorial Funeral Home
The Nashville Public Library for *The Nashville Banner*
Asheville Citizen Times (North Carolina)
Beatrice Daily Sun (Nebraska)
Leaf-Chronicle (Clarksville, Tennessee)

In Appreciation

We simply would not have been able to publish this book without the cooperation of the Gannett Corporation and *The Tennessean*. We are indebted to them for allowing us to use the original articles as printed in *The Review-Appeal* and supplementary articles from *The Tennessean* and *The Review-Appeal*. Most of the content of this book is available due to their generosity.

THE TENNESSEAN
A GANNETT COMPANY

The Review-Appeal
and THE WILLIAMSON COUNTY NEWS

Journalistic Landmark

The oldest weekly newspaper in the state of Tennessee, *The Review-Appeal*, is published in Franklin. Established in 1813, it has the largest weekly newspaper circulation in the state, and the fifth largest in the entire South.

Two metropolitan newspapers supply the county its daily news fare, on a twice-a-day basis. Both the *Nashville Banner*, an evening newspaper, and the morning *Tennessean*, distribute their late editions throughout the county.

— From *Town of Franklin and Williamson County, Tennessee Directory: A Civic-Government Handbook,* 1963

Excellent Citizens and Notable Partings

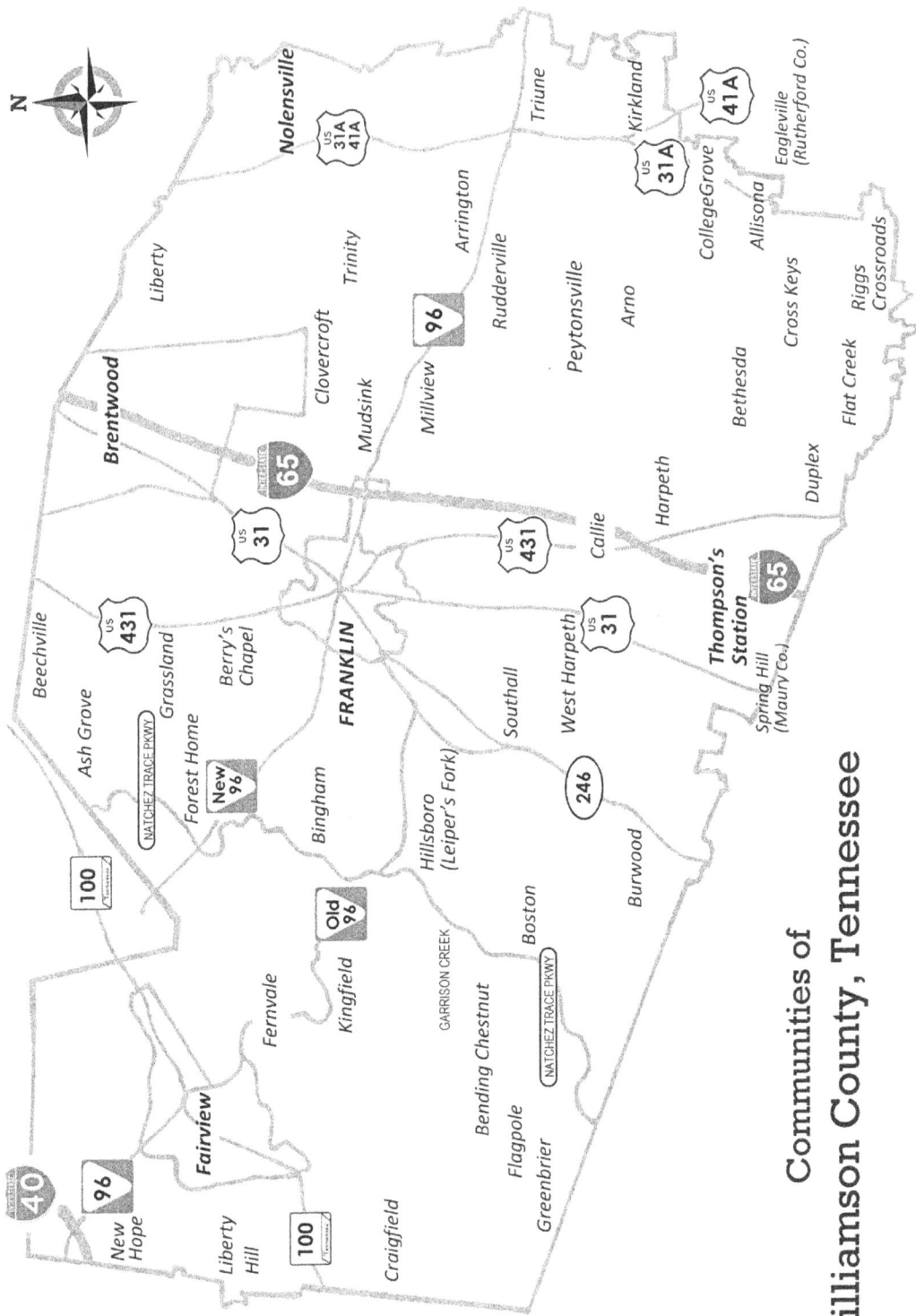

Communities of
Williamson County, Tennessee

Nolensville

Liberty

Trinity

Clovercroft

Mudsink

Brentwood

Millview

Arrington

Rudderville

Peytonsville

Arno

Triune

Kirkland

CollegeGrove

Allisona

Eagleville
(Rutherford Co.)

Cross Keys

Bethesda

Flat Creek

Riggs
Crossroads

Duplex

Harpeth

Callie

Beechville

Grassland

Berry's
Chapel

Ash Grove

Forest Home

Bingham

FRANKLIN

Hillsboro
(Leiper's Fork)

Southall

West Harpeth

Thompson's
Station

Spring Hill
(Maury Co.)

Fernvale

Kingfield

GARRISON CREEK

Bending Chestnut

Boston

Burwood

Flagpole

Greenbrier

New
Hope

Liberty
Hill

Craigfield

Williamson County Statistics and Government
1966-1968

Area in Square Miles – 593
County Population: 1960 – 25,267; 1970 – 34,330
Franklin Population: 1960 – 6,977; 1970 – 9,404

1967 County Tax rate – $3.55
1967 Total Assets – $42, 373, 688
Figures from the Tennessee Blue Book, 1967-1978

Williamson County Officers and Governing Body, 1967- 1968

County Judge – Fulton Greer
County Attorney – Tyler Berry, Jr.
General Sessions Judge – James C. Short
Clerk and Master – Ethel M. Grigsby
Circuit Court Clerk – Joe Herbert
Election Commission Chairman – Melvin P. Maxwell, Sr.
Sheriff – Earl M. "Mutt" Huff
Highway Official – Mack Osburn
Registrar – Jimmie D. Bennett
Superintendent of Schools – W. C. Yates
Hospital Administrator – Clifford L. Gardner
County Board of Health – Dr. R. H. Hutcheson
Home Demonstration Agent – Lois Crowley

Franklin's Governing Body

Mayor – Asa Jewell (1961-1969)
Aldermen serving during the years 1966-1968:
1st Ward – Frank L. Murrey, Earl Beasley,
2nd Ward – Robert N. Moore, Henry W. Hall, Ralph Duke
3rd Ward – J. P. (Pete) Gunnel, James Culberson
4th Ward – W. L. Henry, Ed Woodard, A. C. (Cliff) Frensley
Recorder – Marshall Liggett
City Attorney – Cletus McWilliams
City Treasurer – Joe Pinkerton, James William Hood
Franklin Special School District Superintendent – Emmett Strickland
Chief of Police – Lewis Morgan Hood
Municipal Planning Commission – Roy Barker (chair),
Bill Ormes, Paul Ogilvie, James Gentry, Marshall Liggett

Portrait of An Excellent Citizen

James Boyd (J. B.) Akin

James Boyd (J. B.) Akin is business manager of Battle Ground Academy and lives across the street from the school on Everbright Street with his wife, the former Miss Katherine Beckett. They have two daughters, Mrs. Janice Simms, of Donelson and Mrs. J. B. Bosch (Polly Vance) of Panama, Central America.

Mr. Akin is a charter member of the Franklin Lions Club and a member of the Franklin First Methodist Church where he is chairman of the Official Board.

As Published in _The Review-Appeal_ on October 13, 1966

JAMES BOYD AKIN
1907 - 1983

Retired BGA President J.B. Akin Dies at 75

Memorial services for James Boyd Akin, 75-year old former president of Battle Ground Academy, were Tuesday at First United Methodist Church.

Mr. Akin, who served 33 years at the Franklin preparatory school before his retirement in 1975, died Saturday at Nashville's Baptist Hospital following a long illness.

He became President and Headmaster of BGA in 1968 and continued as President from 1969 to 1973. Earlier he served as coach and Athletic Director, head of the Science Department and business administrator of the school.

The son of Burwood merchant Millard Fillmore Akin and Lulu Boyd Akin, he was born November 27, 1907. After attending Burwood School, Akin attended Battle Ground Academy as a student from 1924-26.

Akin graduated from the University of Tennessee with honors with a Bachelor of Science degree and earned Master's degrees in Science and School Administration from Middle Tennessee State University.

His 45-year career as an educator began in 1930 as a coach and teacher at Ashland City High School. At the end of the 1935 school year, he returned to Burwood to operate the family store and farm following his father's death.

Akin served as principal of Burwood School from 1936 to 1941, then spent one year as a science teacher and coach at Franklin High School.

He returned to BGA in September 1942 as teacher of Bible, Science, Physics and Chemistry. Later he became head of the school's Science Department and its Athletic Director. He coached football, basketball, baseball, track and golf.

Akin's 1944 football team was undefeated and BGA never had a losing football season during his 17 years as a coach. His basketball teams at BGA won the district championship five of his last seven years in coaching.

The school's athletic field was named in his honor in 1958.

Besides his association with BGA, Akin was widely known for his involvement with church and civic organizations. He served three terms as a director of the Williamson County Chamber of Commerce; was on the Board of Stewards of First United Methodist Church for 20 years and also served as Sunday School Superintendent; was a charter member and former president of the Franklin Lions Club, and served 10 years as director of the Williamson County United Way campaign.

In recent years, he did volunteer work for the Williamson County Public Library.

Akin was married to the former Katherine Beckett of Columbia in 1931. She survives along with two daughters, Mrs. Janice Akin Falk of Franklin and Mrs. Polly Vance Akin Bosch of Arlington, Virginia, and six grandchildren.

The family requests that memorial gifts may be made to the Williamson County Public Library or to a charity of their choice.

– The Williamson Leader, June 3, 1983

"Throughout my growing up, there were special people who influenced me or helped my family in a special way. J. B. Akin was one of them."

– Bobby Langley, *Ruby's Son*

Portrait of An Excellent Citizen

James Clayton Arnold

Living at Thompson Station in the house where he was born is James Clayton Arnold and living with him are four sisters, Misses Stella, Geneva, Mary and Ruth Arnold.

Mr. Arnold is a retired farmer. For a number of years he operated a general merchandise store and served as Postmaster at Thompson Station.

During World War I, he served in the Armed Forces in the Argonne sector and in the Army of Occupation six months after the Armistice was signed.

He is a Mason and a member of the Unitarian Church.

As Published in *The Review-Appeal* on February 22, 1968

UT benefactor Clayton Arnold Dies at 95

University of Tennessee benefactor Clayton Arnold, 95, died here yesterday.

Memorial services for Arnold, the last of 10 children, will be at 2 p.m. today at Franklin Memorial Chapel. He is survived by five nieces and nephews.

Although his life had an Horatio Alger air to it, Arnold described himself as a "stingy man who made fortunate investments."

The retired rural mail carrier of Thompson Station in Williamson County built a fortune on personal thrift and wise investments in stocks.

His only education was in a two-room rural school, but at his death more than 300 UT students had received Clayton Arnold Scholarships.

"We always have cited Clayton Arnold as our shining example of philanthropy," said UT President Edward J. Boling. "In 1963, Mr. Arnold became the first to enter into a life income agreement with UT, and his total contributions to the institution amount to well over a million dollars. He had a genuine concern for the future generations, and he wanted his money to provide good teachers for them."

Since teachers touch the lives of so many students, he decided that gifts to UT's teacher training program could help the most people.

"A person will have three or four outstanding teachers in a lifetime," he said once, "one can make a big difference in a student's future."

Mr. Arnold said he turned to UT rather than private universities because student scholarships at UT would "do more for needy boys and girls."

Mr. Arnold, who served in France during World War I, was a lifetime resident of Thompson Station area.

— The Tennessean, July 31, 1987

"I tell young people to save $1,000 as soon as they can, and invest it in mutual funds. It will triple in three years, and in 40 years that $1,000 will have grown to $81,000.

"It takes time, but young people who try do succeed. If you want to make a million, don't pray for it; go to work for it. ... I've been a miser, living within my income. And then I made fortunate investments."

— Clayton Arnold, "Not for Love ... Nor Money," by Louise Davis, *The Nashville Tennessean Magazine, June 28, 1970.*

William Casey Ashworth

Mr. Ashworth is Postmaster at the Franklin Post Office. He resides on Carolyn Avenue with his wife, the former Miss Lois Rader and daughter, Bette Lois Ashworth. He has a son, William Casey (Bill) Ashworth also of Franklin. He is minister of the Kingston Springs Church of Christ.

As Published in *The Review-Appeal* on October 27, 1966

WILLIAM CASEY ASHWORTH
1919-2000

William Casey Ashworth, 80, died Tuesday, March 7, at Maury County Regional Hospital

Mr. Ashworth considered himself a native of Williamson County, although he and his wife Lois lived in Columbia for the past several years.

From 1940-45 he served in the U.S. Air Force as a bomber pilot, leaving the service with a rank of first lieutenant. He was U.S. Postmaster in Franklin for 18 years, retiring in 1975. For many years he was very active as a preacher in the Church of Christ, preaching in gospel meetings and doing local work as well. He has served as the preacher for Hillview in Nashville, Oak Avenue in Dickson and Hickory Heights in Lewisburg, as well as several other congregations. He continued to be active in preaching by monthly appointments, even up to the month prior to his death.

He was a member of College View Church of Christ in Columbia.

He was preceded in death by his parents, Wilson and Jenny Ashworth. Survivors include his wife, Lois Ashworth; a son, Bill Ashworth of Columbia; a daughter, Bette Wolfgang and her husband Steve of Danville, Kentucky; five brothers, Harold Ashworth of Acworth, Georgia, Donnie Ashworth of Reno, Nevada, Elbert Ashworth of Hendersonville, Charles Ashworth of Eagleville and Richard Ashworth of Lyles; a sister, Virginia Jones and her husband Elton of Clarksville; and five grandchildren, Casey, Ben and Rob Ashworth, Lesley (Clay) Jackson and Lindsay Wolfgang.

Funeral services were held on Thursday, March 9, at Williamson Memorial Funeral Home with Steve Wolfgang, Donnie Rader and Dorris Rader officiating. Burial followed in Williamson Memorial Gardens. Active pallbearers were Ben, Rob, Harold, Richard, Charles and Elbert Ashworth, Clay Jackson and David Mast. Honorary pallbearers were elders, deacons and preachers of College View Church of Christ. Memorials may be made to the American Diabetes Association.

Williamson Memorial Funeral Home was in charge of arrangements.

— The Review-Appeal, March 10, 2000

"The love story of Billy and Lois is remarkable even now — they had met and dated before the war, and their relationship continued even when Billy went into service. Even though Lois suffered from active tuberculosis in a day when people would cross the street to avoid contact with her, Billy's love for her was unwavering, and they married on February 5, 1943. Fifty years later, in February 1993, a host of relatives and friends gathered in Franklin to celebrate with them a half-century of marriage."

— Steve Wolfgang, *Truth Magazine*, July 6, 2000 (published online).

Charles Mark Ballard

Charles Mark Ballard lives at 1004 Fair Street where he has resided for the past 45 years. He came to Franklin from Cookeville, Tennessee, and was employed with the Franklin Interurban Company. In later years he formed a partnership with the late N. Y. Walker and they operated Ballard-Walker Tire and Battery Company on Main Street. After dissolving this partnership Mr. Ballard opened The Ballard Machine Shop on Fifth Avenue North, which he sold to Dortch Stove Works during World War II. After that he built a shop at the rear of his home where he now operates, and is known to his many friends as a "master machinist."

He was honored by WSM when he appeared on the "Noon Show" and was presented a plaque with the inscription for "above and beyond" services rendered to WSM television, WSM radio and to his community.

Mr. Ballard served on the Board of Mayor and Alderman for a number of years and is a member of the Methodist Church. He has one son, Everett Ballard, of Louisville, Kentucky. His wife was the former Miss Viola Huddleston.

As Published in *The Review-Appeal* on July 20, 1967

CHARLES MARK BALLARD
1883 - 1972

C.M. Ballard dies, master machinist

Charles Mark Ballard retired master machinist and alderman for the City of Franklin for many years died Sunday at noon at Harris Nursing Home where he had been a patient for the past five years.

Funeral services were held Tuesday morning at Franklin Memorial Chapel with burial in Williamson Memorial Gardens. The Rev. C. H. Hunt officiated.

Mr. Ballard was recognized as a genius in machine work with metal and was frequently asked by WSM, Nashville radio station, to make particular pieces for equipment that could not be obtained elsewhere. It is legend in Franklin that WSM-TV could not go on the air in 1950 until Mr. Ballard had completed some machine work for the television equipment. Several years ago WSM officials paid tribute to Mr. Ballard and his work and presented a plaque to him during a television program.

Mr. Ballard had also done special work for Dyer Observatory in Nashville and had made a sundial for Jack DeWitt, retired WSM official who subsequently gave the sundial to Vanderbilt University. It is now on the university's campus.

Mr. Ballard had made a scale model of a steam locomotive which had attracted much attention and acclaim.

A native of Smith County, he was the son of the late John and Mary Halliburton Ballard. He came to Franklin as an employee of the old Nashville Franklin Interurban. After a short time he went to Cookeville, where he was employed with the power and light company.

He returned to Franklin for several years before he went into business for himself. He was a partner with the late N. Y. Walker in a garage here and Mr. Ballard specialized in battery work. He operated Ballard Machine Shop with interim employment as a machinist for Dortch Stove Works. At the time of his retirement five years ago he had his shop behind his home on Fair Street.

He was 89 years of age at the time of his death.

He was a member of the Methodist Church and was a Mason.

Mr. Ballard was married to Miss Viola Huddleston of Cookeville who died in April, 1961.

He is survived by one son, W. E. Ballard of Louisville; four sisters, Mrs. A. E. Kent and Mrs. M. T. Murrah, both of Carthage, Mrs. Irl Bradford of Nashville, and Mrs. Byrd Burton of Cookeville; two brothers, Ben and Emerson Ballard, both of Shelbyville; two grandchildren, and two great-grandchildren.

Honorary pallbearers were Clem Blackburn, Dan Parsons, Tyler Berry, Norman Smith, Robert Cook, Sam Ragsdale, Dr. Bob Hardy, Willie Hill, Jack DeWitt, Fleming Williams.

Serving as active pallbearers were Royland Southgate, Leon Evans, Perkins Reynolds, James Hickman, Clebert Lewis, Thomas McCall, Bill Herbert, and Jack Toone.

Franklin Memorial Chapel was in charge of the arrangement.

– The Review-Appeal, November 30, 1972

"This love for mechanical things grew with the years and the dislike for the farm also multiplied, so when he gained majority, he left home with $6 in money and a cheap suit of clothes. He never wrote home for a penny, was never hungry or broke, though he does acknowledge he has been pretty flat at times."

— Jane Bowman Owen, *Who's Who in Williamson County*, Rick Warwick, ed., originally published in *The Review-Appeal*, September, 17, 1936.

Portrait of An Excellent Citizen

Roy Edwin Barker

Roy Edwin Barker, a native of Williamson County, lives at Brentwood with his wife, the former Ruth Evelyn Horton. They have two children, Susan Luquita and Roy Edwin, Jr.

Mr. Barker represented Williamson County in the Legislature for two terms. He is a veteran of World War II, when he was wounded and is a recipient of the Purple Heart. He is a member of the American Legion, Veterans of Foreign Wars and Disabled American Veterans. He is also a Rotarian, member of the Chamber of Commerce and chairman of the Franklin Planning Commission.

He attends the Fourth Avenue Church of Christ, and is manager and vice-president of Truett-Barker Insurance Company.

As Published In *The Review-Appeal* on May 11, 1967

Roy Barker passes away at 90
By Carole Robinson

Franklin lost a pillar of its community when Mr. Roy Edwin Barker passed away Monday, March 28 at the age of 90. According to those who knew Mr. Barker well, he was a war hero; he was kind, honest, loyal, caring, generous, humble, and a fine, fine man.

Mr. Barker was born on Aug. 14, 1925 on a farm in the rural Williamson County community of Burwood during the depression. He learned the meaning of hard work at a young age.

Mr. Barker graduated from Franklin High School in 1944 and with his classmate Jimmy Gentry, he joined the Army.

"We went into the military together, we went to training at the same time, and we went overseas together, but we were separated after we reached England," Gentry said. "He was wounded shortly after we arrived but since we weren't together anymore, I didn't know until I got back."

In mid-January 1945, the Tennessee farm boy found himself in Glasgow, Scotland assigned to the Ninth Army, Company G, 334th Infantry. A month later he was fighting the Battle Behind the Battle in a small German town between the Roer and Rhine rivers. It was the last major German offensive on the Western Front. During the battle, just five weeks after arriving in Europe, Mr. Barker was seriously wounded in the left shoulder by a German machine gun. His left arm was paralyzed but when he was discharged from the hospital 22-months later, he had regained partial use of his arm.

Mr. Barker was awarded the Bronze Star, Purple Heart, Presidential Unit Citation and the Combat Infantryman Badge 1st Award.

"I remember as a very young boy, when we saw Mr. Barker my parents pointed him out as a war hero," said WAKM Radio 950 AM personality, Tom Lawrence, who had known Mr. Barker for "almost 66 years."

When Mr. Barker was discharged from the Army in 1947, he attended the University of Tennessee in Knoxville on the GI Bill and received a bachelor's degree in finance, insurance and real estate and also married his long-time friend, the late Ruth Horton. They had two children – Roy E. "Win" and Susan.

His first job was with the Aetna insurance company in Chicago. He returned to Franklin in 1953 as a special insurance agent with Aetna.

In the mid-1950s he became a partner with the Felix Truett Insurance Agency. Truett also had a real estate agency, and Mr. Barker added real estate to his resume. He remained with Truett for almost 20 years.

During that time, he became very civic minded. He was active in the Franklin Noon Rotary and the Williamson County Chamber of Commerce.

"I believe he was the longest serving Rotarian we had – more than 50 years," said his life-long friend, Ron Ligon.

He started helping with the rodeo in 1965, the year heavy rains flooded the Fowlkes Street park where the rodeo was held.

"Losing him, we lost a great Rotarian," Ligon added. "At some point we both were awarded the Legends of the Chamber award for our service to the chamber."

Mr. Barker served in the Tennessee General Assembly as a member of the Clement faction of the Democratic Party from 1961-1963 and in 1965. "We would not have Highway 96 West if not for Roy Barker," Lawrence said. "At that time it took a long time to get to Fairview. He saw to it the state built Highway 96 West."

He also "saw to it" that telephone calls to Fairview, Nashville, Nolensville and College Grove were no longer long distance.

"He brought Williamson County under the Nashville umbrella," Lawrence added. "He loved to talk politics."

During his legislative tenure he also earned a law degree from the YMCA Night Law School.

"My husband Ed and Roy were the best of friends," said Eileen Moody, widow of the late Ed Moody. "In 1958 they were co-chairs when Buford Ellington ran for governor and they were in Rotary together. Ed was president one year and Roy was president the next year. I always thought he was very nice and a good person. He was kind, loyal and he had a nice sense of humor."

In 1965 Mr. Barker made a run for the U.S. Congress but withdrew from the campaign because the other candidates were better known.

He was a delegate to the 1971 Constitutional Convention and served on the Franklin Planning Commission for more than 17 years.

Local banker Jody Bowman met Mr. Barker in the late 1960s when he needed insurance for his new GTO automobile.

"I was in my early 20s and no one else would give me insurance on that car, but Mr. Barker did," Bowman said.

In 1972 Mr. Barker bought the Truett agency and created the Barker Insurance and Real Estate Company.

"Mr. Barker was a good businessman; very conservative – he would take risks, but they were calculated," said Bowman, who attended Fourth Avenue Church of Christ with Mr. Barker. "He was a very caring man; a straight arrow and he always stood for the little man. He was honest as he could be, he was loyal to his friends and well-respected."

Mr. Barker was an active member of the American Legion Post 22 and a past post commander.

"We all enjoyed his company at the Post," said Legion Post 22 member Jim Howard. "He was always friendly; he always had a smile. You couldn't help but feel good when he was around. He enjoyed people and Rotary was his life."

His parents George and Mary Troope Barker; his wife, Ruth Horton Barker and brother John W. Barker precede him in death. He is survived by his son Roy E. "Win" (Debbie) Barker of Franklin and Susan (Danny) Bowman of Goodlettsville, Tennessee; grandchildren Troy (Heather) Bowman and Sloan (Brandy) Bowman; great grandchildren Micah, Parker, Carson, Avery, Kayla and Nathan Bowman.

"We lost a good citizen; I lost a dear friend," Ligon said. "He did a lot for others and for the community. Franklin is a better place because of him."

Mr. Barker was laid to rest Wednesday in Williamson Memorial Gardens. Memorials may be made to GraceWorks, 104 Southeast Parkway, Franklin, Tennessee, 37064 or Happy Tales Humane, 4001 Hughes Crossing #161, Franklin, Tennessee, 37064.

– The Williamson Herald, March 31, 2016

Excellent Citizens and Notable Partings

Portrait of An Excellent Citizen

Col. Fulton Beasley

Portrait Published in *The Review-Appeal* on July 28, 1966

FULTON BEASLEY
1911-1991

Franklin Auctioneer Fulton Beasley Dies

Funeral for Col. Fulton Beasley, longtime Franklin auctioneer, was Sunday, March 17, at Fourth Avenue Church of Christ, with Myron Keith and Jim Taylor officiating. Burial was in Mt. Hope Cemetery.

Mr. Beasley died Friday, March 15, at Nashville's Westside Hospital at the age of 79.

For many years, Beasley owned and operated an auction barn at the corner of Bridge Street and Second Avenue, North. On Saturday mornings, his amplified chant could be heard throughout downtown Franklin as he sold everything from household furnishings to tools.

He was a member of the Franklin Rotary Club, the Elks Lodge and Fourth Avenue Church of Christ.

Survivors include a stepson, Jerry Church of Old Hickory; step-daughter, Margie Dobler of Franklin; brother, Horace Beasley of Cummins [Cumming], Georgia; sister, Mrs. Ruby Eldridge of Chattanooga; three step-grandchildren and several nieces and nephews.

Active pallbearers were Chip Beasley, Dan Beasley, Charles Thurman, Billy Eldridge, Tommy Beasley, Waldon Smithson, Don Smithson and Glen Steakley.

Honorary pallbearers were members of the Franklin Rotary Club and the 200 Bible Class of Fourth Avenue Church of Christ.

Williamson Memorial Funeral Home was in charge of arrangements.

– The Williamson Leader, March 21, 1991

"Among Franklin's young businessmen, there is not a more popular one than Fulton Beasley, who, with J. E. Spencer, owns and operates the Sanitary Dry Cleaners establishment on North Fifth Avenue. He is liked by old and young for his pleasing, hail-fellow-well-met manner.

"Fulton was born April 11, 1911, near Boston in the second district, next to the youngest of eight children of Mr. and Mrs. Tom Beasley. When he was 18 months old, the family moved to Thompson Station ... At age six, he entered school under Miss Mary Z. Sowell. ... When he reached third grade, the family moved to Franklin and he entered school here where he remained until his graduation as president of the Franklin High School class of 50 members in 1929. ...

"Fulton is a Democrat and cast his first vote for Roosevelt and is one of his most ardent admirers. ... He has a keen sense of humor and enjoys a good joke. His broad smile and hearty laugh are two of his strong characteristics.

"From morning until night he keeps busy rustling up business, for he agrees with Lloyd Jones who said, 'The men who try to do something and fail are infinitely better than those who try to do nothing and succeed.'"

— Jane Bowman Owen, *Who's Who in Williamson County*, Rick Warwick, ed., originally published in *The Review-Appeal*, January 20, 1938.

John Snodgrass Beasley II

John Snodgrass Beasley II, a native of Franklin, lives on Fourth Avenue South, with his wife, the former Allison Tidman of Nashville. They have two children, John Snodgrass Beasley III and Eleanor Christensen Beasley.

Mr. Beasley is Associate Dean of the Vanderbilt Law School, is part owner of Pebblestone Court, and serves as a temporary organist at the First United Methodist Church. He is past president of the Nashville Symphony, president of the Coverdale Scholarship Federation and Trustee of the Association for the Preservation of Antiquities. He is also a member of the Carter House Association and the Williamson County Historical Society.

As Published in *The Review-Appeal* on May 4, 1967

Flawed Recollections of an Octogenarian

I was born in early October 1930 on the day my paternal grandmother died and was named for my surviving grandfather. Hence, the "II" on my name. He was the only physician in Hickman County, setting broken bones or suturing wounds in the office attached to his house in Centerville, or delivering babies and taking care of tractor damage in the county's hollows. His son, my father, was Earl Beasley, and he came to Franklin as a young lawyer to wed my mother, Elsie DeMoville Eggleston.

***

The Egglestons had been in Franklin almost before there was a town, and Josiah Carr Eggleston was a lawyer and judge. He was a man of huge proportion, quite tall for the time, and weighing more than three hundred pounds. His law office was in the northeast corner of the Square, between the City Offices and the old Post Hotel. He gave my grandmother, Julia Plummer Eggleston, four girls and two boys, my mother the last child before the boys followed. They lived on Third Avenue North at the northwest corner of Bridge Street in the big house with the columns, and the Interurban ran past their house headed through the farmland to Nashville. As a treat in my childhood, my grandmother would take me on a round trip, the motorman letting me play with a lever that had no function as though I were driving the streetcar. The Eggleston phone number was "9." Miss Carrie Wagner's grocery was "8."

***

After his death, my grandfather's half-brother, James Fleming Eggleston, lived in a small apartment in my grandmother's house and practiced law and banking from an office on the second floor over Trice Hardware on the Square. Tommy West, who ran West Point restaurant on the Square's northwest corner, rented a room on the second floor.

Their old cook, Aunt Tenny, had given birth to twins, whom my grandfather had named *Romulus* and *Remus*, and my brother and I grew up with "Romus" and Remus. The family was large and colorful, and a series of children's books was written about them by Christine Noble Govan, a Chattanooga author who had grown up in Franklin with the Eggleston children and found the family fascinating. Their exploits were chronicled in *Judy and Chris* (Judy was my aunt Judy and Chris, Ms. Govan), *Those Plummer Children*, and *Narcissus* (Aunt Tenny) *and the Chillun.*

The Egglestons were the backbone of the Methodist Church, and my parents took their place there as well. Our little family of three lived on Fifth Avenue South in a small house where my brother Earl was born, and in 1936 we moved to 235 Third Avenue South to a house S. E. Farnsworth built for us. Our block was the second one south from the Square, and an interesting one, indeed. In the course of my childhood and adolescence, three Vanderbilt trustees, a federal judge, a United States Congressman and the mayor of the town (my father) lived there, both sides of the street, and three suicides took place on that one block.

***

I walked to our elementary school, at Five Points across from the Post Office, where I had great teachers. Miss Mary Campbell Burnett in the first grade, Miss Helen Jordan in the second, Miss Mary Ellen Hendricks in the fourth, Mrs. Laura May Miller (Mrs. William) in the fifth, Miss Jesse Gray in the sixth, Miss Chloe Yates in the seventh. Much later, my two children were lucky enough to have those same first and second grade teachers. It was from Miss Jesse Gray that I learned to diagram sentences, one of the most useful things in a long life. In eighth grade, I went to BGA and ultimately completed high school there.

Frank Gray, the town druggist, lived next door to us toward town, and "Joe" would deliver his prescriptions from Gray Drug. Sam Fleming's mother, Miss Cynthia, lived next door to him. Fleming was one of the early men behind Third National Bank, today SunTrust, and Allison and I later were in San Francisco when he was installed as president of the American Bankers Association. Imagine – a Franklin boy president of that national association of powerful people. Our neighbor to the south was Fannie Park Small (Mrs. Faxon) on the corner. In a small apartment in part of her house lived Mrs. Alex Steele, a widow who raised four great boys there herself. The youngest one, Allen Steele, became a major executive with Life and Casualty Insurance Company, and a Vanderbilt trustee. Directly across the street lived Sara and Tyler Berry, whose daughter and grandson are responsible for the Berry Farms development on Lewisburg Pike, and to their south, on what was then the corner, the McGavock family.

***

Leonard H. Armistead owned the town weekly newspaper, *The Review Appeal*. He had married Mattie Hunter, and she and my mother had become closest friends. I can remember her arriving at our house in a cloud of dust in her black LaSalle, the dust in a whirl because the streets were not paved to the sidewalk. They had two boys, Leonard, Jr. and Hunter, both fascinating and smart. At his death, the elder son took it over. (In Franklin, for some unknown reason, it seemed that every "Leonard" went by "Bill," and his son and grandson followed in this tradition. I remember Leonard Brittain was called Bill, and when his younger brother William was born, the family had both a William and a Bill.)

L. H. "Bill" Armistead, Jr. married Alyne Queener, the beautiful daughter of a Columbia lawyer, and they bought the McGavock house where they raised another Bill (Leonard) and Bob. After their divorce, Alyne built a small house in the side yard and my recollection is that she lived there with her boys until she married Jack Massey.

My father had a musical talent, and I inherited from him a "good ear." I could hear a melody and pick it out on the piano, and by six I was playing accurate harmonies in the left hand. The organist at our church was Bess Buford, and Miss Bess let me play the organ from time to time. Later, as early as just before my teens, I would substitute for her when she was away or sick, by which time I was able to reach the pedal desk. It was thrilling to command that organ which seemed huge to me, but was in fact quite small. The pipe organ there today is a larger instrument installed much later, after the choir loft was enlarged and a Hammond was in use for some years.

***

George I. Briggs was headmaster of BGA for my first year, and Glenn Eddington succeeded him on his death. Eddington was a gifted math teacher, strict and demanding, and we learned greatly from him. At BGA I worked hard to make good grades, took "expression" from Mrs. Pryor Lillie and debated, and in my senior year edited

The Cannon Ball, our school newspaper. My father was on the board of trustees, and later I joined the board as well. Students were mostly from Franklin, though there was a dormitory which housed a number of boarders. It was a boys' school then, and in my first year or so, a military one.

***

The second world war took a great many of the men off to the service, many of whom did not come home, and rationing gasoline and certain foods became commonplace. We had a Victory Garden in the back yard, and my brother and I learned to weed bean rows. But persistent crabgrass finally caused my father to give up on that, and we put in a light on a pole and laid off a badminton court in the grass. The neighbors assembled in our yard most nights and on occasion Frank Gray would call to say he had a quart of ice cream we could have. It didn't go far, but it beat nothing. By this time, Marge and Sam Ewin had moved in next door to the Fleming house. My father was elected Mayor, partly because there were so few available men, he said. People still rode the Interurban out from Nashville to swim at Willow Plunge, but ultimately the rail was replaced with buses.

***

After graduation, I entered Vanderbilt and was there through Law School. I lived on campus, but was home in the summers and for holidays. Franklin had begun to grow from the six-eight thousand people when I was growing up, and to accelerate its change.

After law school, in mid-1954, I became a Naval officer and spent the next three plus years in the Far East, Air Intelligence Officer to a brilliant young Rear Admiral, shipboard based and homeported in Okinawa. As it later turned out, my brother Earl was posted there as well with the Marine platoon he led. For more than a year, at occasional suppers in the Officers Club when our flagship was not at sea, we would read six-week-old *Review -Appeals* which our parents would have sent out to us. Half of the family in Franklin, half in Okinawa. Remarkable!

***

I came home at the very end of 1957 and entered the practice of law with my father. Our office was directly behind the Red Grill, just off the square. Miss Mary Leila Dozier (later, Crutcher), my father's long-time secretary who practiced good law herself and knew where everything in the courthouse was, took care of us both and nurtured me as I began. I married Allison Tidman, a former Miss Vanderbilt, and we rented a house on Fair Street directly across from "the freshet" which had figured in the Govan stories. Franklin was much altered since I had left it, the main street beginning to fall into some decay when shopping patterns changed and Interstate 65 came through. I left the practice when a summons came from Vanderbilt, and began a career there which lasted more than a half century.

But we still lived in Franklin, and each day I took the Interurban – by this time a bus - to Vanderbilt. When our son was born in 1961, we bought a house of our own, our agent Billy Billington, a well-known young realtor. 335 Fourth Avenue South was the address, the dead end of the street, and a block I called "Ewin Neck." Ben, Mildred and Connie Ewin lived just south and across the street, Kathryn Ewin (Pinkerton) had owned the house we bought, Dee and Mason Ewin and their parents lived directly across the street, and their grandparents owned the big house on the corner, today an apartment building. Kate Niel Winstead, another relative, owned the grand house at the top of the hill where O'More is today. They were all Ewins, and Judge Connie Clark lives in a house one door from ours today.

***

I joined the board of the Franklin Special School District, and later the board of BGA, and I took my place at the Methodist Church on Fifth Avenue. Our second child, a daughter, came along in 1965. We lived in the house for a half century, adding to it twice after essentially re-doing it before we moved in. We built a brick terrace in the back ourselves, Allison carrying bricks around from the parking area while pregnant with our daughter, and we moved the rickety garage down to the back of the yard and set it on a concrete foundation for a little office. T. L. Still worked with us on everything we did, and he was magic! Aubrey Cole, Franklin's premier finish carpenter who had made the handsome pulpit in St. Paul's church, built our kitchen.

***

When Miss Bess moved to McKendree Manor, I took her place on an interim basis which turned to be fairly long. Some few years later, after we switched to the Episcopal Church, Allison's denomination, I did a long interim stint as organist and choirmaster at St. Paul's as well.

Meanwhile, Franklin's downtown was falling apart. The vacancies on Main Street were

multiplying and city tax funds were shrinking. I had always wanted to own a table-top store, in retrospect, a potentially foolish wish, and now seemed to be the time. Currier Goodall, a widow who lived with her niece Fanny Haynes, ran a small shop out of her apartment, and I had no wish to do such a thing as long as she was in business. But she was giving it up. No experience, of course, but youth and enthusiasm. My brother and I decided to do it, and we talked to Marge Ewin (Mrs. Sam, another of the Ewins) from our days on Third Avenue, to see if she would be interested in running it. To our great delight, she was. It would handle super-fine merchandise, peppered with some good antiques. I had a house picked out, plenty of parking, easily found, but Marge pulled for our buying the old City Offices on the square. Asa Jewell, the mayor and a friend of hers, was anxious to unload it and pressed us to consider it. It was in the increasingly vacant downtown, terrible parking, the building in advanced decay, the offices having earlier moved elsewhere, rolls of linoleum standing for sale outside, the sidewalk falling apart. We looked carefully at the building, certainly an historic one. In the front room was the place where you once paid your taxes to Miss Hettie Farr Denton, in the back, the jail cell. On the left side was the place where the fire engine parked, and upstairs, the volunteer firemen lived. Even a tiny room for female prisoners. It would take lots of money to make it work. But if it did, buying it would take it off the City's hands and put it on the tax rolls, and if the business succeeded, it could possibly spark a rebirth for downtown.

***

The three of us consulted my father for financial backing, then the four of us put together a corporation to own the building and a second one to own and operate the business, and we sought a lender. We were all credit worthy, and that was a snap.

We employed the Stills, Tom and his son T. L., as contractors, and began the months and months it took to do the extensive work. We scraped off the inside plaster to expose the old rich bricks, reconfigured the huge door to the fire engine and the front window, floored the room that had held the jail with more bricks, paved the entryway with flagstone, added shelves and cupboards, made a passageway where the women's cell had been, and installed good and proper lighting. Marge knew of a store elsewhere named "Cobblestone Court," a sound we liked but did not plan to adopt. Since we were going to replace the sidewalk outside, we decided to do it with

Excellent Citizens and Notable Partings

aggregate made from river gravel, pebbles, and named the store "Pebblestone Court." We set four small boxwoods in spaces we created for them in the sidewalk, watered from underneath with a central valve, painted the outside, put two handsome awnings over the windows, and were ready to receive merchandise in late November 1965. The postal address was something like 234 ½ Public Square, but we never used that. Instead, we gave ourselves a new address. "One Town Square." To help people from out of town find us, our radio ads all ended with "Under the awnings at One Town Square." We had the only awnings.

***

Marge had good taste, and we went for the high end. We opened with Tiffany sterling, Baccarat crystal, bone china from the best English makers, porcelain from Limoges, some very contemporary pieces from Dansk designer Jens Quistgaard, some handmade pottery from Mary Alice Hadley in Louisville, and a few good antiques. And we bought Currier's unsold stock. For some things we went to the market in Atlanta, for old Sheffield plate, to New York. We had a grand opening on December 2, 1965, just in time for Christmas, and were off and running. Even though I was Associate Dean and Professor of Law at Vanderbilt, I was at the store every morning before going to work, checking sales, paying bills and worrying about making a payroll. Marge got friends to work part-time for us – Mary Ann Crowell, Rebecca Gentry, Nell Walker, Emmie Caldwell, her daughter Cecil, others - and we were able to squeak through that first year without bankruptcy. People came out from Nashville or up from Columbia to shop with us, and in addition to advertising with The *Review-Appeal*, we advertised on Nashville radio with stylish ads and in places like Symphony programs. Franklin had some real personality and charm, and we played it up to our own, and to the town's, advantage. The store gathered speed and ran for a good twenty years, and I have just recently thrown out the filing cabinet with all the records.

***

The boxwoods, the new sidewalk, the fresh paint and stylish awnings prompted a new focus on downtown, and our investment indicated that money could still be made on Main Street. It was the first commercial restoration in downtown, and I think there is no question but that what has happened in Franklin dates from those moments.

The Williamson County Bank was a handsome old building on the southwest corner of the square. The Flemings were founders, I think, and part owners. In 1963 the bank, in an effort to be "modern," sheathed the outside in glass and aluminum, creating an ugly and nondescript building which could have been anywhere. Historic Zoning had become something of a thing in America, and it had ready application for Franklin. The antithesis of what the bank had done, it called for adaptation and preservation. A group was putting together the beginnings of the Heritage Foundation, and probably because of what we had done with Pebblestone Court, they approached me about being its first president. Sue Berry (Mrs. C. D. Berry), Ruth Kinnard, a couple of others came to my office in the Law School at Vanderbilt to "make the ask," and, of course, I agreed. I expect it was that, plus the success of Pebblestone Court, which prompted the "Excellent Citizen" selection.

***

I am enormously proud of what the Heritage Foundation has done over the years, proud of Franklin's growth and development, and grateful to have had a tiny part in it.

Allison and I moved to Nashville in 2002, after it had become nearly impossible to live in our house. We came back one summer from Maine to find the neighbors had rehabbed and added a second floor to their garage, making essentially a second house on that small plot, a violation of Codes but one too late to challenge, and traffic down South Margin made it almost impossible at times to get off our dead end. Getting back on, getting home, was often even worse. But it had been a great place to grow up, and to raise children. Riding your bicycle, or skating on the sidewalk in the summertime, long after dark, could not have been done just anywhere. And when the town was small, your parents knew you had misbehaved long before you got home. The Special School District was one of only three, I think, accredited system-wide in Tennessee in the '60s, and I assume it still is.

But change is essential, and hugely beneficial if guided properly. As Tennyson has King Arthur tell us – "The old order changeth, yielding place to new. And God fulfills Himself in many ways, lest one good custom should corrupt the world."

– John S. Beasley II
Vice Chancellor, Emeritus
Vanderbilt University
December 9, 2019

Portrait of An Excellent Citizen

John Thomas Beasley

John Thomas Beasley is one of Williamson County's prominent dairy farmers. He lives on Peytonsville Road.

His wife was the former Miss Dotty Green and they have three daughters, Ann is a junior at Franklin High School, where Sue is a freshman. Lynn attends Junior High School.

The Beasleys attend Epworth Methodist Church and Mr. Beasley is a member of the Official Board and the Williamson County Layman's Club. He is chairman of the Soil Conservation District, member of National Farmers Organization and Farm Bureau and director of the Williamson County Co-op.

As Published in *The Review-Appeal* on January 26, 1967

John Thomas Beasley, 84, died Wednesday, July 14, 2004, at Williamson Medical Center.

Mr. Beasley was born in Williamson County, son of the late Ernest Richard Beasley Sr. and Annie Elizabeth Fox Beasley. He spent his life as a farmer in Williamson County and made his home on his farm, Breezy Bend Farm, in the Millview Community. He served in the U.S. Air Force during World War II and was a member of the Franklin Civitan Club and the Williamson County Farmers Co-op, serving as a past director. He also was a member of the Farm Bureau and National Farmers Organization.

Mr. Beasley served 22 years as director of the Southern Livestock Barn and 21 years with the Williamson County Soil Conservation District, where he served as district supervisor. He was a longtime Red Cross blood donor.

Mr. Beasley was a member of Epworth United Methodist Church, where he was a past lay leader and Sunday school teacher. He was preceded in death by a brother, Vinnie G. Beasley, and three sisters, Bernice Mathis, Thelma Smith and Bernadene Farrell.

Survivors include his wife of 54 years, Dotty Green Beasley of Franklin; three daughters, Ann (Mike) Cothran of Chapel Hill, Sue (Bill) Fryer of Spring Hill and Lynn (Dusty) Rhoades of Franklin; a brother, Ernest Richard Beasley Jr. of Cedar Hill; a sister, Ernestine Beasley Wade of Franklin; four grandchildren, Rob (Renea) Cothran, Christopher Fryer, Geoffrey Fryer and Colin Rhoades; one great-grandchild, Audrey Cothran; and several nieces and nephews.

Funeral services will be held at 5 p.m. today at Williamson Memorial Funeral Home with Dr. Lenoir Culbertson officiating.

Burial will follow in Williamson Memorial Gardens.

Active pallbearers will be Mike Cothran, Bill Fryer, Dusty Rhoades, Rob Cothran, Christopher Fryer, Geoffrey Fryer, Colin Rhoades and Clayton Ingram. Honorary pallbearers are Elva Beard, Lib Beard, Evelyn Vaden, Lucy Leaster, Lottie Mayche, Beth Schuler, Billy Knight, Keith Knight, Jimmy Lillard, Danny Cotton, Ed Moody, Charlie Fox Jr., Hendricks Fox, T.C. Fox, Tom Fox, Robin Bowie, Jeff Bowie, Ken Graves, John Kinnie, Jerry Fly Jr., Monty Lankford, Charles Smithson, Dempsey Brewer, Jimmy Beard, Mike Derryberry, Scott Myers, Fred Clark, Clint Callicott, Tom Moon, Charlie Morris, Ed Pride, Bob Mayes, Dr. and Mrs. Robert Sullivan, Hugh Williams Sr., Bob Finley, Claude Beard, the Franklin Civitan Club, the Franklin High School Class of 1939 and teacher Mary Trim Anderson, the staff of Daylight Donuts and the Boxley Sunday School Class. Visitation is three hours prior to service at the funeral home.

Memorials may be made to Epworth United Methodist Church.

— The Review-Appeal, July 16, 2004

Joe Bellenfant

Joe Cowden Bellenfant lives at College Grove where he owns and operates the Bellenfant Implement Company.

Mr. Bellenfant is married to the former Miss Elynor Shaw of Chapel Hill and they have three daughters: Sherry is a sophomore at Middle Tennessee State University at Murfreesboro, Emy Jo is an eighth grader at College Grove and DeLacy is three years old.

He is a member of the College Grove Methodist Church and serves on the official board. He represents the 20th district of Williamson County as magistrate and is a member of the American Legion Post No. 5 in Nashville.

As Published in *The Review-Appeal* on October 5, 1967

College Grove Loses Familiar Face
County Official, Renaissance Man
Joe C. Bellenfant Dies at 77
By Bonnie Burch, Staff Writer

College Grove – A man of compassion, a man of boundless energy, a man who used humor to brighten up anyone's day, or a Renaissance man who could do anything he put his mind to.

These are just a few phrases that friends and family say define Joe C. Bellenfant, who died Monday at the age of 77.

A business man, Bellenfant was chairman of the Williamson County Beer Licensing Board. He also was a magistrate, a post now known as county commissioner, for many years and served on the county highway commission.

"He really had a mind for business that others couldn't even imagine," said his daughter Emy Joe Bellenfant-Bellis. "Even though he never went to college he always seemed one step ahead of everyone else."

Bellenfant was owner and operator of Bellenfant Implement Co., a tractor supply company. His empire quickly became known as the farm machinery center of the South as buyers from as far away as England and Canada took advantage of the business's big sale held the first Thursday of every month. It also helped that Bellenfant was a licensed auctioneer.

He owned Bellenfant Farms, acres of cotton across the Alabama line.

"He would sometimes drive two and a half hours to get there. Do his cotton farming work, and then turn right around and drive right back. And he did that for many years," said his daughter.

Bellenfant was also the former chairman of The Bank of College Grove.

Besides being a talented businessman, Bellenfant was well known for his generosity and love for others.

Every year, widows in the area received corsages thanks to Bellenfant. He also provided Easter baskets to local families.

A family that arrived in College Grove from Mexico 30 years ago was not the first to see the tender side of Bellenfant, who helped the family adjust to a new language and culture. The family's young son would visit Bellenfant in his home almost daily to study from the encyclopedias that lined his book shelves.

After the family moved to Texas, the young boy became valedictorian of a 500 member graduating class. Now a young adult, the boy, who many years ago traveled with his family all the way from Mexico not speaking a word of English, is driving to College Grove to comfort the family of his mentor.

Bellenfant was also a member of the People to People tour delegation that traveled on a friendship trip to Russia during the height of the Cold War. Later, the family played host to the Russian delegation on its farm in College Grove.

A charter member of the College Grove Lions Club, he was instrumental in building the College Grove Lions Club Ball Park. He was also a member of the Owen Hill Masonic Lodge 172 and Al Menah Shrine Temple.

"His parents died when he was a senior in high school," said Bellenfant-Bellis, "And the people in the community just took him in. I think he never forgot that."

A member of the College Grove United Methodist Church, Bellenfant erected the church's steeple in honor of his family.

He was a U.S. Army veteran of World War II serving in Europe, and was named Father of the Year by *The Review Appeal.*

The members of the College Grove Senior Enrichment Center also will miss one of their best Pedro players.

For the 14 years the center has operated, Bellenfant was active, whether traveling to Murfreesboro to feast on catfish monthly with fellow members or allowing the group to cut Christmas trees on his property, said the center's director Martha Wolfe.

"He was a real character. He would sign the attendance sheet G. C., which stood for garbage collector. Before we had a dumpster, Mr. Bellenfant would haul our garbage for us," said program director Peggy Phelps.

Many in the area would look for his trademark red 1990 Chevy pickup truck to know that Bellenfant was somewhere taking care of business, entertaining or helping the community.

"I know the thing I'll miss is his beautiful crystal blue eyes. He always had a twinkle in them," his daughter said.

Survivors include his wife of 56 years Elynor Shaw Bellenfant; daughters Sherry Bellenfant, Franklin, Emy Joe Bellenfant-Bellis and DeLacy Bellenfant-Layhew, and her husband, Richard Layhew, all of College Grove; brother, Houston McPherson, Atlanta; grandchildren Phoebe Fly Smith and her husband, Donald, Murfreesboro, and Stephanie Bellis and Richard L. Layhew III, both of College Grove; and great-grandchild Erich Smith.

Funeral services will be at 2 p.m. today in College Grove United Methodist Church with the Rev. Ed Coy, the Rev. Robert Cowperthwaite and the Rev. Eddie Smotherman officiating.

Interment will follow in Bellenfant Cemetery. Serving as active pallbearers will be: Marshall Cox, Jr., Gary Dickerson, Jerre Fly III, Richard Layhew, Jr., Richard Layhew III, Doug McPherson, Donald Smith, Frank Smith, Jr., Jerry Wilson, Jr. and Jim Wilson.

Honorary pallbearers are: Tab Ballou, Jack Tolbert, Jerry Wilson, Sr., Jim Walton, Lynn Wadlington, Jim Speakman, Jerre Fly, Jr., Robert Basse, Henry Davis, Gary Osburn, Mike Pearce, Urban and Joe Scales, Victor Barredo, Clyde Winters, Garrett Lawrence, Ed Moody, Earlon Tucker, G.W.F. Cavendar, Kenneth Boyce, Hugh Pate, Marshall Cox, Sr., Sam Rucker Ogilvie, H. C. Young, Ross Bigger, Phillips Holder, Mack Osburn, Gaspar B. Hipo Family, Dr. David Hall, Dr. Michael Petracek, Shac Herbert, Larry Pruitt, members of the Al Menah Shrine, members of the Williamson County Beer Board and his Pedro crowd.

Visitation with the family will be two hours prior to services today in the church. Memorial contributions may be made to the College Grove United Methodist Church or the Shrine Hospital.

Williamson Memorial Funeral Home, 3009 Columbia Avenue, Franklin, is handling arrangements.

— *The Tennessean, February 14, 2001*

39   Excellent Citizens and Notable Partings

Jimmie Dee Bennett

Jimmy Dee Bennett, a native of Williamson County, has just completed nine years as Register of Williamson County. He resides on Boyd Mill Road with his wife, the former Miss Mattie Ruth Beasley and they have one son, Jimmie Dee Bennett III, who is a member of the junior class at Franklin High School.

Having resided in the Bethesda community before moving to Franklin, Mr. Bennett is a member of the Bethesda Methodist Church, but now attends the Franklin Church of the Nazarene. He is a Legionnaire, member of the Farm Bureau and a member of the Registers Association of the State of Tennessee.

As Published in *The Review-Appeal* on September 21, 1967

Bennett Celebrates 60th Anniversary
Horseback Ride to California
By Carole Robinson, Staff Writer

Jimmy Dee Bennett is affectionately known as one of Williamson County's characters. He is a dancer, a farmer, a former register of deeds, and an actor, but his claim to fame is a trip he took 60 years ago when he heeded the call to go west.

"I was setting in a business class in San Antonio, Texas and thought, 'I'm going back home, raise tobacco and ride a horse to California," Jimmy Dee, now 84, said with that familiar twinkle in his eyes and quick smile. And that's just what he did.

"I was wild as a buck."

Right out of a 33-month stint in the U.S. Coast Guard during World War II, the young man with the wavy, blonde hair, flashy smile and Van Johnson look, was interested in acting and he was still hungry for adventure — sitting in a classroom wasn't satisfying that hunger.

When the 23-year-old arrived back home to the family farm in the Bethesda/Peytonsville community he worked in his tobacco field and he worked on getting in shape for the 2,000-mile trek on the back of a horse. For several months, he farmed and rode dirt roads for hours until he had the money, the horse and the seat that would get him to his destination.

"I rode horses all my life, but to get tough enough I rode every day. I rode a thousand miles before I even got started."

On September 8, 1946, a hot, late summer day, Jimmy Dee mounted his horse, Ramblin' Boy, a 'peppery' bay gelding — the first of 11 horses he would wear out along the way and prepared to leave Franklin. Sitting in his new saddle, with a few necessities in his saddle bags, a couple blankets, a raincoat and a some changes of clothes sent ahead in a suitcase on a Greyhound Bus to a future destination, he set out on his three-month journey.

The whole town of Franklin met Jimmy Dee in front of the courthouse on Public Square to send him off with Mayor Frank Beasley giving him a public farewell.

"That old horse just stood there and bucked," Jimmy Dee said. "He put on quite a show — I loved it, but I thought that horse was going to pitch me when I was going around the square."

Dubbed the Ramblin' Rider, Jimmy Dee headed up Hillsboro Road to Missouri to catch I-70, which would take him all the way to Hollywood. He expected to make 25-30 miles a day and planned to stay with farmers along the route.

It wasn't long before the Ramblin' Rider realized he had already become something of a legend.

"I rode up to Missouri and rode by 30-40 people picking cotton in Arkansas. They hollered out, 'Hey, you the guy that's ridin' a horse to California?'"

Newspapers charted his daily progress across the country, people lined roadways to cheer him on and locals opened their homes to him.

"Mostly I stayed with people who invited me in. People would ride out to meet me. They treated me like I was their own child or brother. One day I didn't make it to town before dark so I put flashlights on the horse's bridle and saddle."

Ramblin' Boy went lame early on.

"I left Ramblin' Boy in Jackson (Tennessee) - I got skinned on the deal. I traded at livery stables along the way and got cheated 'most every time. I bought one (horse) and rode all the way across Texas - 700 miles. Some lasted two to three weeks. One only lasted a day."

Some towns along the route greeted him with a parade and celebrity status. His wife Ruthie proudly produced a collection of news articles cut from periodicals that documented the young rider's journey.

"I ran into a sandstorm and only two days of rain on the whole trip. I slept out one night. That was by an Indian reservation. Out there on that desert that time of year, the sun would go behind a cloud and I'd nearly freeze, then it would come back out and it would be so hot I'd have to take my coat off."

"On top of the Rockies some railroad people put up a sign next to the tracks that said 'Next time try the train.'"

The Chambers of Commerce in Fort Smith, Arkansas, and Fort Worth, Texas, gave the rider a big reception, the citizens of Fort Worth gave him a horse and he met his idol - Gene Autry.

In Odessa, Texas, a young lad on a trick mule caught up with the Ramblin' Rider and joined him. Billy Ballard, a 16-year-old also with a lust for adventure, just showed up and tagged along.

"That mule wore out three horses."

By the time Jimmy Dee reached Yuma, Arizona, his 11th horse was showing signs of lameness and he was almost out of money so he crossed the California line and declared he had ridden as far as he was going to.

"I ran out of money so we put the mule and the horse on a truck and we rode the bus to California. I said, 'This is as far as I made my brags where I was gonna go and my money is about gone.'"

He arrived in California on December 8. That was one day shy of three months to the day of when he left Franklin.

Jimmy holed up with family in California for a few weeks and young Billy stayed with an aunt.

"I went to two studios. MGM gave me something to read and told me to cold read- I couldn't cold read anything. That MGM girl said 'Sorry son, you got the looks but that's not good enough.' I felt so bad. Gene (Autry) offered me bit parts, but I decided to come back and go to Peabody College. I listened to kin when I shouldn't have."

Young Billy stayed with his aunt for a year waiting for his parents to come for him and his mule.

"He wasn't going anywhere without his mule."

Since the now infamous ride, Jimmy Dee returned to farming. He also held a job at AVCO Manufacturing Company and for 28 years he was Williamson County's Register of Deeds.

That rejection from MGM didn't destroy his love for dancing and the stage. Jimmy Dee danced a bit on the television show, Hee Haw, he played a grandfather on a TV murder mystery, and became one of the founders of the Pull-Tight Players.

During a trip to the Grand Ole Opry he managed to get back stage where he ran into Gene Autry.

"He said, 'What are you doing here?' and told me to go to his office and talk to his manager, but Gene never called him, so I didn't go back. I regretted that. My biggest regret is not following through. Looking back now, most all the stars started out in Western movies. Sometimes we listen to the wrong people."

At age 84, the blonde hair has turned gray, but is still thick and wavy. Jimmy Dee is still a farmer, if only part-time. He still has horses - two walking horses. "They're supposed to be my granddaughter's, but she's too busy for them, now."

And he's still dancing.

"I work two hours and I dance two hours. I'm always show-boatin' somewhere."

His advice to other dreamers: "Follow your dream, but don't fall off the cliff doing it. There's a time when you must realize either you have it or you don't. I enjoy entertaining people around here. I don't have to have Hollywood."

— *The Williamson Herald, December 2, 2006*

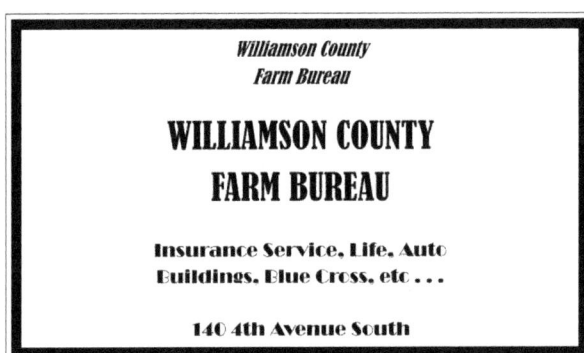

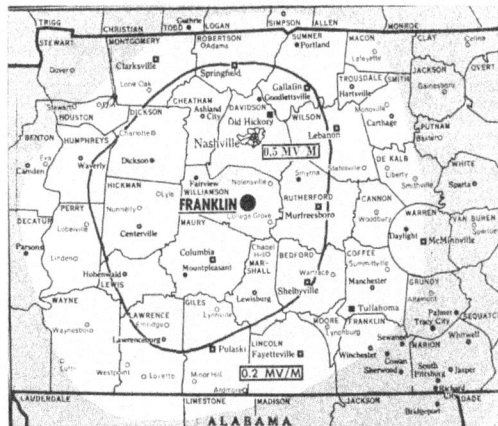

Portrait of An Excellent Citizen

Tyler Berry

Portrait Published in *The Review-Appeal* on September 8, 1966

Tyler Berry, Jr. died at 8:40 p.m. Tuesday, February 27, 1996 at Williamson Medical Center. He was born December 4, 1912 in Franklin, Tennessee. His great-grandfather, Cabell Rieves Berry was a lawyer and Speaker of the Tennessee Senate (1885-1887). His father, Tyler Rieves Berry, practiced law in Franklin; and later served as Chief Examiner for the Federal Communications Commission in Washington D.C.

Tyler Berry, Jr. attended Battle Ground Academy, graduating from Culver Military Academy. He attended Vanderbilt University and completed his collegiate studies at Cumberland University, Lebanon, Tennessee, earning his law degree and was admitted to the Tennessee Bar in 1936.

He practiced law in Franklin for almost 50 years. He was elected Williamson County Attorney in 1938 and served in that position until 1967 except when he served in World War II and for the period of 1951-1956.

At age 26, with a wife and two young children, Tyler volunteered to serve his Country in war, entering service as a private. He was commissioned in the Judge Advocate General's Corps. Later he was sent to the South Pacific where he served as an artillery officer at Corps level in the Philippines fighting. Following cessation of hostilities, he participated as an attorney in the Japanese War Crimes trials following World War II. He was discharged as a Captain.

Upon his return to Franklin following World War II, Tyler resumed the practice of law and serving as County Attorney. In addition, he served as Interim County Judge.

After moving to Rural Plains, south of Franklin, he became a successful grain and tobacco farmer, as well as raising herds of Herefords and Black Angus cattle.

At various times he held memberships in the Tennessee Bar Association, the American Bar Association, Franklin Rotary Club, The American Legion No. 0022, Veterans of Foreign Wars. He was a member of the First United Methodist Church of Franklin.

Tyler was instrumental in the formation of Carnton providing the necessary legal work to facilitate the gift from Dr. and Mrs. Suggs to the Association. He continued to serve as a Charter and Life Member of the Carnton Association, Incorporated, now known as Carnton Plantation.

He was preceded in death by his mother, Elizabeth Avalyn Berry, his father, Tyler Rieves Berry, Sr. and his first wife, the late Sara McGavock Roberts Berry.

He is survived by his wife, Nancy Ragsdale Berry; his daughter, Sara Avalyn Berry Swain and his son Tyler Berry III; his grandchildren, Devan Elizabeth Swain Smith, Great Falls Montana; Tyler R. Berry IV, Franklin, Tennessee; Kathryn Alicia Swain Krall, Lawton, Oklahoma; Timothy Whitzel Swain III, Champaign, Illinois; and Kristan Melissa Swain, Madison, Wisconsin; and three great grand-children.

Active Pallbearers: Tyler Berry IV, Timothy W. Swain III, Steve Curry, Bill Evans, John Green III, Walter Green, Jr., John Parkes Small, David Ives. Honorary Pallbearers: Sam M. Fleming, Nelson Elam, Bob Sewell, Robert White, Walter Bond, Robert Pitner, Jerre Fly, Dan Parsons, Mel Andrews, Malcolm Gibbs, Ralph Naylor and surviving Magistrates prior to 1967.

Memorials may be made to the Franklin First United Methodist Church Building Fund Historic Presbyterian Church Organ Fund, Carnton Plantation or charity of choice.

The funeral will be 11:00 a.m. Saturday, March 2, 1996 at the Franklin Historic Presbyterian Church in Franklin, Tennessee, with Rev. Bob Lewis and Rev. Mike Waldrop officiating.

Visitation with the family will be 5 to 7 p.m. Friday at Franklin Memorial Chapel and one hour prior to services at the church. Franklin Memorial Chapel, 794-1512.

– The Tennessean, March 1, 1996

BILL DUKE

James William Bond

James William Bond, the senior member of the firm J.W. Bond & Sons, lives at Bethesda where he is a purebred livestock dealer.

He is married to the former Miss Leo Grigsby and they have three sons. James. W. Bond III is County Agent at Morristown, Tennessee, Charles G. is stationed with the Air Force in Texas and Daniel S. is a sophomore at Austin Peay College at Clarksville.

Mr. Bond is a member of the Bethesda Presbyterian Church where he serves as an Elder, while his wife is a member of the Bethesda Methodist Church. Mr. Bond is a member of the Milk Producers Association, member and former director of the Williamson County Farm Bureau and the Tennessee Cattle Breeders Association.

As Published in *The Review-Appeal* on January 12, 1967

JAMES WILLIAM BOND, JR.
1906 - 1967

James W. Bond, Jr., Prominent Farmer, Dies in Hospital

James W. Bond, Jr. of Bethesda, prominent Williamson County farmer and civic leader, died Sunday night at Williamson County Hospital. He had been a patient in the hospital for several days for treatment of double pneumonia but his death was unexpected after he apparently suffered a heart attack. He was 61 years of age.

Funeral services were held Tuesday afternoon at Franklin Memorial Chapel. The Rev. Clifford A. McKay, minister of the Bethesda Presbyterian Church and the Rev. Cecil Vaughn, minister of the Bethesda Methodist Church officiated Burial was in Williamson Memorial Gardens.

A native of Williamson County, Mr. Bond was the son of the late Mr. and Mrs. James W. Bond, Sr. In 1936 he was married to Miss Leo Grigsby, who survives.

Mr. Bond was one of the county's leading dairy and livestock farmers and his three sons were reared to know the value of good farming practices. His farm operation is under the name of J.W. Bond and Sons.

He was a member of several livestock associations for registered Jersey and Polled Hereford cattle and was director of the Nashville Milk Producers Association for this area. He was also on the Williamson County Soil Conservation Board of Supervisors and was a former director of the Williamson County Farm Bureau.

In 1963 the Bond family was selected by the Progressive Farmer Magazine as Master Farm Family of the Year for the Kentucky Tennessee area, an award given only to an outstanding farm family.

Mr. Bond was magistrate from the Twelfth Civil District on the Quarterly County Court and served on the important Tax Study Committee which has studied revenue problems for this court.

He was an elder of the Bethesda Presbyterian Church.

In addition to his wife he is survived by three sons, James W. Bond III, of Morristown, Tennessee; Charles G. Bond of Vincennes, Indiana; and Danny S. Bond, a student at Austin Peay State University in Clarksville; one sister, Mrs. James Glenn of Clarksville; and two grandchildren.

Honorary pallbearers were the elders and deacons of the Bethesda Presbyterian Church, the Board of Directors of the Nashville Milk Producers Association, members of the Williamson County Quarterly Court, the Williamson County Soil Conservation Board of Supervisors, members of the Eagleville Polled Hereford Association and Dr. Harry Guffee.

Active pallbearers were Leonard Grigsby, Lewis Steele, Alex Steele, Tommy Anderson, Walter Anderson, DeWitt Wilson, Ham Paine, Ken Daniels, Blythe Bond, Douglas Graham, Malcom Gibbs, and Shearer Irvin.

Franklin Memorial Chapel was in charge of the arrangements.

— The Review-Appeal, November 30, 1967

"James and Leo Grigsby Bond and their three healthy sons live at Blue Grass Farm, consisting of 215 acres, part of an original grant of 840 acres purchased in 1809 for $2,040 by his great-great grandfather, John Bond. ... The present two-story frame house ... has for its nucleus a log room of the original house. It was in this room James' grandfather Cicero Columbus Bond, and father J. W. Bond, were born and died."

— Jane Bowman Owen, *Who's Who in Williamson County*, Rick Warwick, ed., originally published in *The Review-Appeal*, May 22, 1952.

Excellent Citizens and Notable Partings

John A. Bragg

John A. Bragg and his wife, the former Miss Jane Crane of Mt. Pleasant, Tennessee, live on Everbright Avenue across the street from Battle Ground Academy. Mr. Bragg is Assistant Headmaster of the school. They have one daughter, Becky, 11 years old.

Mr. Bragg is a member of the Franklin First Methodist Church and serves on the Official Board. He is a Mason and a Shriner.

As Published in *The Review-Appeal* on November 10, 1966

John Alden Bragg, 93, passed away
August 19, 2018

Mr. Bragg was born to the late John Roy Bragg and Chloe Adcock Bragg. His paternal and maternal ancestors were among the early settlers of Middle Tennessee, having come from Virginia and North Carolina when Tennessee first reached statehood.

His younger years were spent at his family home in McMinnville and on his father's nursery/farm, the Cumberland Valley Nurseries, where he worked as a boy. He attended McMinnville city schools, graduated from the Sewanee Military Academy and was inducted into the Army during World War II.

In January of 1944, he was sent to New Caledonia, in the South Pacific, to become a member of the 147th Regimental Infantry Group, which was attached for much of the war to the Marine Corps. Its mission was to follow the Marines as they invaded islands in the Pacific Theater and to secure each island, bringing it to garrison status.

During his time in the Pacific War, Mr. Bragg was engaged in three major battle campaigns: the Admiralty Islands, Iwo Jima and Okinawa. For this service, he was awarded three battle stars, the Combat Infantryman's Badge and the Bronze Star. In 2001, for his service in World War II, Mr. Bragg became the 11th recipient of the Dr. Joe Nunley Memorial Award, presented at Middle Tennessee State University to a distinguished Veteran of World War II who is known also for his service to others.

Returning from the war, Mr. Bragg went to the University of the South at Sewanee, graduating with honors. He was a member of the Order of the Gownsmen, of the Phi Gamma Delta fraternity and of the Red Ribbon Society. He did his graduate work at the University of Virginia and at Middle Tennessee State University.

In 1950, he joined the faculty of Battle Ground Academy as an English, Spanish and history teacher and tennis coach. In that same year, a college fraternity brother introduced him to Octavia Jane Crane of Mt. Pleasant, Tennessee, whom he married at the end of the school term.

In 1955, the couple had a daughter, Rebecca, their only child.

Mr. Bragg would spend his adult career at Battle Ground Academy, a span of 40 years. At that time, it was the longest tenure in the history of the school. After serving as teacher, department chairman and assistant headmaster, he was elected in 1969 as the Academy's ninth headmaster and held that position until he retired in 1990.

During his administration, he put the school in sound financial condition for the first time in its history, creating, with his board's approval, a substantial endowment; he changed the school from a boarding/day school operation to a day school and reinstituted coeducation after a 50-year absence. He also dramatically increased the enrollment, enlarged the faculty and staff, remodeled buildings, built new ones and introduced many new and noteworthy educational programs.

In 1988, the Tennessee Association of Independent Schools recognized Mr. Bragg for his outstanding contribution to education. In 1990, the Franklin Lions Club named him Educator of the Year, and also in 1990, Tennessee Governor Ned Ray McWherter awarded him with a citation for his "40 years of faithful service to, and in the best interests of, the highest traditions of the state of Tennessee."

In 1998, the BGA Board of Trustees dedicated the English and history building on the new campus as Bragg Hall, honoring both John and Jane Bragg.

Mr. Bragg had long sought more regional and national recognition for BGA and he succeeded in the 1960's by helping showcase the academy's annual Tug of War on NBC's Huntley and Brinkley national news program. He did so again at the Academy's Centennial Celebration in 1989, when Speaker of the U.S. House of Representatives, Tip O'Neill, gave the commencement address; all three of the major national networks covered the event in Franklin.

Continuing the school's Centennial Celebration, Mr. Bragg appeared with his student body on ABC's "Good Morning America" program, standing on the school quadrangle, shouting to the nation "Good morning America from Battle Ground Academy in Franklin, Tennessee." This was played throughout the news media in the nation.

That year, he also instituted the BGA Faculty Hall of Fame and Sports Hall of Fame.

Mr. Bragg's retirement years were spent at his Franklin home and at his home on the Tennessee River, where he enjoyed fishing and hunting, his lifelong passions. He held membership in the First Franklin United Methodist Church, where he served for a time on its board of stewards. He was a member of the Hiram Masonic Lodge Number 7, the Scottish Rite, the Al Menah Shrine, past president of the Franklin Noon Rotary Club and a Paul Harris Fellow. He also served on the Williamson County Chamber of Commerce.

Since early childhood, Mr. Bragg had been a constant reader; in later life, he read fiction, the classics, mysteries, historical novels, biographies and autobiographies; rode his motor scooter on a regular basis throughout Franklin and Williamson County; and kept up with his grandchildren's lives, but always he was interested in Battle Ground Academy, his school, where he spent his adult life.

His friend and former student, Dr. Robert Foote of Hartland, Vermont, wrote a poem on the eve of the Academy's Centennial Celebration, describing the 100 years of love and labor of its students. The following lines depict not only their feelings, but Mr. Bragg's, as well:

> When we
> Decades hence are gone
> And all we treasure
> Dissipated with our prejudice
> And son and daughter come
> To take the measure of our century,
> Let them say this: "They strove
> For honor, they hoped for grace,
> Their struggles are written
> In this rich place

He was preceded in death by his wife, Jane Crane Bragg, and sister, Virginia Roy "Joy" Bragg.

Among Mr. Bragg's survivors are his daughter, Rebecca Bragg (Marc) McNamee; grandson, David Bragg (Elizabeth) McNamee; granddaughter, Jane Crane McNamee; great-grandson, Marc Raymond McNamee; and numerous nephews, nieces and cousins.

The family wishes to express its sincere thanks to the staff of NHC Place - Cool Springs and Alive Hospice.

A celebration of life service will be conducted at 3 p.m. on August 27, 2018, at First United Methodist Church, located at 120 Aldersgate Way in Franklin, and visitation with the family will be from 12:30-3 p.m. at the church.

The honorary pallbearers are the BGA Board of Trustees, past and present, all students of classes of 1950 through 1990, all faculty and staff from the same period, Douglas and Jan Darby, Robert and Harriet Sewell, Douglas and Julie Fisher, Patricia Charron, Tom and Charlotte Cone, Bob and Gerri Steltjes, Glenn Adams, Harry Lee Billington, David Wood, Billy Grimes, Bill Cherry, Bill Armistead, Bob Armistead, Eleana McCoy, Thomas P. Bragg, Ellen Finney, Padge Beasley, Charles H. Warfield, Richard Tippens, Nick McCall, Rob Foote, Anne Rutherford, Larry Stumb, Tom Taylor, Skipper Phipps, Jimmy Patterson, Irwin McKee, Tom McKee, Warren York, John Colton, John Oxley, James Beard, Larry McElroy, Charlie Brown, William (Bunny) Akin, Bill Ramsey, Glenda Marshall, Carol Sensing, Kevin Smith, Dudley West, Anne Clark Foster, Jan Buckner Herbert, Cathy Buckner Hoover, Martha Buckner, Sheila Fleming, Jimmy Rippey, Margaret Callihan, John B. Lynch Jr., Dan Parsons and Harriett Keyes.

Memorials may be made to the BGA Endowment Fund or First United Methodist Church.

WILLIAMSON MEMORIAL FUNERAL HOME, 615 794-2289.

– The Williamson Herald, August 23, 2018

* * *

BATTLE GROUND ACADEMY

FRANKLIN, TENNESSEE

BATTLE GROUND ACADEMY is a college preparatory boarding-day school for boys, grades 7-12. Founded in 1889, the school is a non-profit, non-military institution situated on the site of the famous Civil War Battle of Franklin. With an enrollment of 285 s t u d e n t s and a faculty of 18, B.G.A. prepares young men for entry into leading institutions of higher learning and generally promotes moral, physical and intellectual growth. The twelve acre campus includes an administration-classroom building, paved tennis courts, a football stadium and several athletic fields, a gymnasium, a track, and two dormitories. The conviction that young men must revere God, love and respect their fellows and relentlessly seek knowledge has inspired the structure of the school's curriculum. In addition to the regular school year, there is an eight week summer program which includes a summer school and an athletic day camp.

Columbia Avenue   Phone 794-3812

Excellent Citizens and Notable Partings

Portrait of An Excellent Citizen

Ransom Joseph Brent

Ransom Joseph Brent was born and reared in Franklin. He received his education in the Franklin schools and is a graduate of Franklin High School. After graduation he went to work at the Third National Bank in Nashville but his working days were interrupted when he was inducted into the Air Force during World War II. He served 2½ of his four years in service in Tokyo, Japan.

Joe is now employed at the Williamson County Bank where he has been since 1952, and holds the position of 1st vice president and cashier. He is a member of the Board of Directors of the Carter House and has served as its treasurer and is also a member of the Franklin Golfing Association. He is not a member of any civic club at present but plans to become a Rotarian. He holds membership in the Graymere Country Club in Columbia.

Mr. Brent is married to the former Miss Catherine Hardison and they have two sons, Ransom Joseph Brent, Jr., a student at Franklin Junior High School and Craig Hardison Brent, who attends Franklin Elementary School. The Brents attend Franklin First United Methodist Church.

As Published in *The Review-Appeal* on May 23, 1968

Ransom Joseph "Joe" Brent Sr., 84 of Franklin, Tennessee and Bonita Springs, Florida, died Oct. 8, 2012, in Franklin, Tennessee, with his loving wife of 58 years and family by his side. Born Oct. 2, 1928, in Nashville, Tennessee, he was a member of the United States Air Force serving a tour in Japan during WWII. He was a banker for 41 years before retiring from Bank of America formerly known as Williamson County Bank where he was an executive vice president.

Mr. Brent was also an avid golfer and historian.

He was preceded in death by his parents, Louise Dudley Hassell and Henderson Cook Brent, stepfather Charles Berry Hassell, and infant daughter, Catherine Leslie Brent. Mr. Brent is survived by his wife, Catherine Hardison Brent; sons Ransom Joseph Brent Jr., Craig (Susan) Brent; grandchildren, Caroline Brent, and Alex Brent all of Franklin, Tennessee; and sister Gloria Brent Ormes of Raleigh, North Carolina.

A memorial service will be held Friday, Oct. 12, 2012 at 2 p.m. at Williamson Memorial Funeral Home; Myron Keith and Jim Taylor officiating. Visitation will be held Thursday, Oct. 11, 5-7 p.m. and one hour prior to the service at Williamson Memorial Funeral Home in Franklin.

In lieu of flowers, donations may be made to St. Jude's Children's Hospital, Memphis, Tennessee, or Avalon Hospice of Nashville, Tennessee.

Arrangements are by Williamson Memorial Funeral Home in Franklin.

— The Williamson Herald, October 10, 2012

Mrs. Bess J. Buford

Mrs. Bess J. Buford, a native of Franklin, although not a resident at the present time, is indeed an excellent lady.

"Miss Bess" as she is familiarly known, has made her home at McKendree Manor in Donelson for almost two years.

For nearly a half century Miss Bess was organist at the First Methodist Church. Most of her life was devoted to music and she has pupils far and wide who began their study of music under her supervision.

Her talents, still missed in Franklin, will doubtless now give pleasure to those around her in her adopted home.

As Published in *The Review-Appeal* on February 1, 1968

BESS JOHNSTON BUFORD
1894 - 1969

Miss Bess Buford,
Church Organist 50 Years, Dies

Mrs. Bess Johnston Buford, one of Franklin's best known musicians known by young and old as "Miss Bess," died Monday at McKendree Manor in Nashville where she had made her home since 1965.

Funeral services were conducted here Tuesday afternoon at the First United Methodist Church by Dr. E.P. Anderson of Nashville and the Rev. Stuart J. Nunnally, Interment was in Woodlawn Cemetery in Nashville.

Until her retirement a few years ago, "Miss Bess" had held a position of prominence in Franklin's music circles for more than 50 years. She had been organist at the First United Methodist Church here for that length of time and had been director of the annual "White Christmas" pageant at the church for many years.

She had also taught private lessons in piano, organ, guitar, and violin with her pupils representing three generations in some families.

She was a native of Maury County, the daughter of the late Rev. William H. and Ada Hollowell Johnston. She moved to Franklin and became a member of the Methodist Church in 1913 when her father became the pastor, a post he held from 1913 until 1915. She was 75 years old at the time of her death.

Survivors include three sisters, Mrs. H. W. Watson of Dallas, Texas, Mrs. C. B. Meade of Fort Worth, Texas, and Mrs. J. D. Farris of Clearwater, Florida.; two brothers, E. R. Johnston of Atlanta and J. D. Johnston of Asheville, North Carolina and a number of nieces and nephews.

Serving as pallbearers were Dr. R. H. Hutcheson, J. W. Greer, Jr., Stewart Campbell, Jimmy Lanier, Jr., J. B. Parks, Robert Inman, Robert Sewell, J. M. Sewell, and W. F. Little.

Franklin Memorial Chapel was in Charge.

– The Review-Appeal, June 12, 1969

"Every Wednesday night and every Sunday morning Mrs. Bess Buford played the Christian songs on the carillon chimes on the church organ at the Methodist Church and I could hear it plain as day from my front porch, and I loved it with all of my heart, and to this very day they are still being played, but now by computer. I still love it and a few weeks ago, I went by the church and told their Pastor how blessed I was to hear them again after seventy five years."

— Leonard Isaacs, *Franklin Tennessee... Nestled in the Valley of the Harpeth*

James William Burns

James William Burns, manager of the local Kroger Store, is a native of Williamson County. He has been with the Kroger Store for more than 20 years and has been manager since 1956. Interested in all civic activities of the town and county he is a member of the Civitan Club and formerly served as president. He is on the Board of Directors of the Williamson County Chamber of Commerce and the Tennessee State Vocational School.

Mr. Burns is a World War II [sic] veteran, is a member of the American Legion and Veterans of Foreign Wars. He is married to the former Miss Christine Johnson and they have three children, Patty, Jim and Vicki. They reside on Battle Avenue but are building a new home in Hillsboro Acres which they expect to move into early in May. They attend the Primitive Baptist Church.

As Published in *The Review-Appeal* on March 14, 1968

James William Burns, 88, of Franklin, passed away Dec. 24, 2018.

Mr. Burns was born in Williamson County and was a veteran of the U.S. Army during the Korean Conflict. He was a retired manager with The Kroger Company with 44 years of service. He served and stayed in Williamson County his entire Kroger career. He was also awarded Father of the Year for Williamson County in 1966.

He was very active in community events, including Civitan, Crime Stoppers, J.L. Clay Senior Citizens and the Williamson County Chamber of Commerce. He was recognized as a genuine caring man with a serving heart.

He was preceded in death by wife of 56 years, Christine Johnson Burns; parents, James Roy and Ava Anna Brandon Burns; brothers, Milton and Melvin Burns; and sisters, Lois and Edna Burns.

He is survived by son, James L. "Jim" (Renee) Burns of Murfreesboro; daughters, Pattie (Steve) Dunning of Franklin and Vickie (Jeff) Pittenger of Franklin; sister, Sybil Hickman of Franklin; grandchildren, Jessica (Brandon) Snell, Amy (Pat Pollifrone) Burns, William Pittenger, Lindsey (Jason) Wiley, Ryan (Whitney Giles) Dunning and Neal (Lyndi) Dunning; and several great-grandchildren.

Funeral services will be conducted at 11 a.m. on Friday, Dec. 28, 2018 at Williamson Memorial Funeral Home, Raymond Johnson and Gary Fewell officiating. Interment will be at Williamson Memorial Gardens. Visitation will be 4-8 p.m. on Thursday and one hour prior to the service on Friday at Williamson Memorial Funeral Home.

Active pallbearers will be Steve Dunning, Jeff Pittenger, William Pittenger, Ryan Dunning, Neal Dunning, Jason Wiley, Pat Pollifrone and Brandon Snell. Honorary pallbearers will be Donald Burns, Jerry Burns, Randy Andrews, Cary Reynolds, Dorris Heithcock, Dr. Ben Rowan, Dr. Walter Clair, Kroger Fellow Employees and Employees of Cool Springs McAllister's Deli.

Williamson Memorial Funeral Home, (615) 794-2289.

— The Williamson Herald, December 26, 2018

Elmer Ernest Byars

Elmer Ernest Byars and his wife, the former Miss Lillian Shaw of Dyersburg, Tennessee, live on the Nashville Highway, just a few miles from Franklin city limit.

Mr. Byars serves as Chairman of the Board at the Williamson County Bank. He is a member of the Rotary Club of which he formerly served as secretary. He is also a member of the First Baptist Church Franklin, the Farm Bureau and is a Shriner.

As Published in The Review-Appeal on March 23, 1967

ELMER ERNEST BYARS
1893 - 1968

E. E. Byars, Williamson Bank
Board Chairman Emeritus, Dies

Ernest E. Byars, chairman emeritus of Williamson County Bank, died unexpectedly Sunday night at his home on Nashville Highway.

Mr. Byars had gone to find a goat that was out. When he did not return, Mrs. Byars summoned Fuller Arnold, an official with the bank, to look for him. He was found on the hillside back of the house. Death was apparently the result of a heart attack.

Mr. Byars was a native of Dyer County and was the son of the late P. N. and Elizabeth Byars. He attended the public schools of Newbern, Tennessee. He was in the banking business in West Tennessee, served with the State Banking Department, and was an examiner with the Reconstruction Finance Corp. in that area before he came to Franklin to become vice-president and manager of Williamson County Bank, September 6, 1935.

He became executive vice-president of the bank in January, 1937, and was elected to the Board of Directors in 1939. He was elected president in January, 1941, and chairman of the Board in 1950. In January of this year he was named chairman emeritus.

He was honored at a luncheon given by the Board of Directors and at a dinner given by the officers and employees of the bank last December. He was presented scrolls by both groups in appreciation for his service.

Joe Pinkerton, who succeeded Mr. Byars as chairman of the Board, made the following statement:

"The Williamson County Bank and the entire community have suffered a great loss in the passing of Mr. E. E. Byars. His interest in the betterment of the community has continued throughout the years and his leadership will be greatly missed. His contribution to the growth of the Williamson County Bank has been outstanding. He came to it in the midst of the depression and, through his good management, saw it grow and increase to its present status. He was held in the very highest esteem by the directors, officers, and employees of this bank. He lived a rigid code of ethics from which there was no compromise. His life will long be a guiding beacon to those of us who will carry on after him."

Mr. Byars was named the first chairman of the Board of Trustees of the Williamson County Hospital when it was completed in January, 1958. He served as a trustee until his resignation last year.

He was greatly interested in the development of the County Center in the 1940s, and, although he was not so active as he was in the Center, he followed with keen interest the work underway now.

— The Review-Appeal, May 16, 1968

Excellent Citizens and Notable Partings

Byrd Douglas Cain, Jr.

Byrd Douglas Cain, Jr., is a native of Nashville but is fast becoming a Williamson Countian. He lives in Royal Arms Apartments in Davidson County but as soon as his house in Battlewood Estates, now under construction, is completed, he will move to Williamson County. He is married to the former Miss Sarah Ann Drinkard and they have three children, Byrd Douglas Cain III, Leslie Ann and Scott.

Mr. Cain is president of Cain Buick-Pontiac Company, Inc., on Columbia Avenue. He received his high school education at Isaac-Litton and graduated from Southwestern University in Memphis. When a young man, he worked in his father's newspaper office, but later transferred to the automobile business and is dedicated to his work. He is a member of the Tennessee Automotive Association and is an avid golfer.

He attends Franklin First Presbyterian Church.

As Published in _The Review-Appeal_ on May 30, 1968

Mrs. George Cameron

Mrs. George Cameron, born and raised in the Harpeth Community is one of Williamson County's best beloved citizens. She was before her marriage Miss Olie Edgmon, a family long prominent here.

She is a member of the New Hope Presbyterian Church, but attends the First Presbyterian Church in Franklin.

She lives with her son and daughter-in-law Mr. and Mrs. Douglas Cameron on Buckner Road. She has two other children, Mrs. Douglas Harmon and Mrs. William Moss, Jr., and nine grandchildren.

She is a former member of the Harpeth Home Demonstration Club.

As Published in *The Review-Appeal* on October 17, 1968

Mrs. Olie Edgmon Cameron

Funeral for Mrs. Olie Edgmon Cameron was Saturday at Williamson Memorial Funeral Home, with Oliver Pantall officiating. Burial was in Mt. Hope Cemetery.

Mrs. Cameron, 90, died Thursday, July 10, at Williamson County Hospital.

A native of Franklin, she was a homemaker and a member of New Hope Presbyterian Church. She was the widow of George M. Cameron.

Survivors include two daughters, Mrs. Blanche Moss and Mrs. Jane Harmon, both of Franklin; one son, Doug Cameron of Thompson Station; a sister, Mrs. Weltha Pratt of Pikeville; and nine grandchildren and nine great-grandchildren. Grandsons served as active pallbearers.

— The Williamson Leader, July 18, 1986

Popular Farmer Dies of Injuries Sustained Friday

George M. Cameron, 49, popular farmer in the Douglas community, was struck Friday night about 6:30 o'clock while walking along Lewisburg Road by an automobile driven by Claiborne King. It is stated that Mr. King attempted to stop his car to give Mr. Cameron a ride when the car skidded on the ice covered road hitting Mr. Cameron and knocking him down. Mr. King took Mr. Cameron to Dan German Hospital where it was found he was suffering from head injuries, and his death occurred Saturday morning at 3:30 o'clock.

Funeral services Sunday afternoon at 2:30 o'clock were from the chapel of Warren-Smithson by Rev. Henry P. Mobley, Jr. Interment was in Mt. Hope Cemetery.

Son of Mrs. Iva Billington Cameron and the late Don Cameron, he was born in this county and received his education in the Franklin schools. He was a member of the Franklin Presbyterian Church and a man of whom only good was ever spoken. By his quiet, unassuming disposition he was highly respected by all who knew him, and his honesty and integrity were above reproach.

Besides his mother he is survived by his wife, Mrs. Olie Cornelia Edgmon Cameron; children, Blanche, Douglas and Iva Jane Cameron; sisters and brothers, Mrs. Bessie Reynolds and Mrs. Margaret Huddleston, of Nashville; Miss Ann, William and Don Cameron, Jr., of Franklin.

Serving as pallbearers were Sam A. Hargrove, Brent Cook, Robert Jefferson, Claude Alexander, Joe Bowman and Will Moss.

Warren-Smithson in charge.

— The Review-Appeal, January 22, 1948

Portrait of An Excellent Citizen

James William Cameron

James William Cameron is owner and operator of Cameron Oil Company, on Columbia Avenue, and jobber for Shell Oil Products. He lives on Carter's Creek Pike near Burwood with his wife, Mrs. Jessie Grigsby Cameron.

Mr. Cameron has three children, Billy, of Franklin, Bobby, of San Francisco, California, and Mrs. James T. Eason of Nashville.

He is a member of the Burwood Methodist Church, serves on the Official Board and is assistant superintendent of the Sunday School. He is also a Mason, member of the Lions Club, Chamber of Commerce and Tennessee Oil Men's Association.

As Published in *The Review-Appeal* on April 13, 1967

J. W. Cameron,
Well-Known Oil Distributor, Dies

James William (Bill) Cameron of Thompson Station, well-known distributor of Shell products, age 81, died Thursday, October 14, at Williamson County Hospital. Services were conducted on Saturday, October 16, at the Franklin Memorial Chapel with the Rev. George Jones and the Rev. Tim Salyers officiating. Burial was in the Williamson Memorial Gardens.

Active pallbearers were J.W. Cameron, III, Mike Cameron, James Eason, James Huff, Bobby Russell, Randall Bryson, Don Cameron, Tim Cameron, and Tom Cameron.

Honorary pallbearers were: Dr. Fulton Greer, Dr. Jeff Bethurum, Charlie Sawyer, Fleming Williams, Wallace Stovall, Judge Fulton Greer, Leonard Grigsby, Dr. Fred Haley, and Douglas Cameron.

In lieu of flowers donations may be made to the Middle Tennessee Heart Association.

Mr. Cameron was chairman of the board of Cameron Oil Company. He was a native of Williamson County.

Survivors are: his wife, Mrs. Jessie Grigsby Cameron, Thompson Station; daughters, Mrs. James T. Eason, Nashville, Mrs. Betty Fryer, Garland, Texas; sons, Billy Cameron, Jr., Franklin, Dr. Robert M. Cameron, Campbell, California., Jim Huff, Winston-Salem, North Carolina; sisters, Mrs. Margaret Huddleston and Miss Ann Cameron, both of Franklin; six grandchildren; six great-grandchildren.

Franklin Memorial Chapel was in charge.

— The Review-Appeal, October 19, 1982

Mrs. Jessie Louise Grigsby Huff Cameron passed away on May 26, 2008. She was born in the Bethesda Community in Tennessee on March 3, 1911.

Preceded in death by her parents, Ollie Turner and Ida Alexander Grigsby; husbands, James William Huff and J.W. Cameron; son, James William Huff, Jr.; sisters, Vivienne Watson, Cleo Grigsby and brother, Leonard Grigsby; stepchildren, Martha Eason, Dr. Robert and J. W. Cameron, Jr.

Jessie was an amazing, extraordinary lady, who touched the hearts of many. After moving from the Burwood Community in 1991, she made her home in Richardson, Texas. She was a retired Williamson County teacher, a member the Arapaho United Methodist Church, and the Old Glory Chapter DAR.

She is survived by her daughter, Betty Grigsby Huff (John) Rodriguez of Garland, Texas; brother, Glenn (Sara) Grigsby of Columbia, Tennessee; grandchildren, Jaymi Huff, Dr. William Alexander (Lori) Huff, Jonathon (Kelly) Huff of North Carolina, Lisa (Russell) Morgan of Texas, J. R. (April) Rodriguez of Colorado, who serves in the military in Iraq; seven great grandchildren; numerous nieces, nephews, and great nieces and nephews. She is also survived by daughters-in-law, June Cameron of Franklin, Tennessee and Jean Cameron of Canada; step-grandchildren, Jim (Margaret), Mike (Jeri) of Tennessee, Judy (Randy) Bryson of North Carolina, Michael Stuart Cameron, Kirsten (Mark) Jewett of Washington and Jim Eason of Tennessee; and step-great-grandchildren.

Funeral Service will be held at Williamson Memorial Funeral Home, June 7, 2008 at 10 a.m., in Franklin, Tennessee, with graveside services following at Mt. Hope Cemetery.

Pallbearers will be the grandsons, nephews and great nephews.

Memorials may be made to Burwood U.M.C. or Burwood Community Center.

Williamson Memorial Funeral Home, (615) 794-2289.

— The Tennessean, June 5, 2008

SHELL

CAMERON
OIL CO.

P.O. Box 446
Franklin, Tennessee

Stewart Campbell

"My Uncle Stewart Campbell was one of the two local bank presidents, quiet, soft spoken and so very wise. I can't remember the many times when I would run up on someone ... and then hearing story after story of, "he took a chance on me when nobody else would," "he is responsible for me having this farm," or "this business," or "this house..."

— Russ Farnsworth, *Growing Up in Old Franklin*

Portrait Published in *The Review-Appeal* on July 14, 1966

STEWART CAMPBELL, SR.
1908 - 2000

Franklin – Stewart Campbell, Sr., retired chairman of Harpeth National Bank in Franklin and a World War II veteran who helped reestablish banking systems in Germany during the U.S. occupation, died Thursday at his home. He was 92.

Visitation with the family is scheduled for 1 to 3 p.m. today at Williamson Memorial Funeral Home, 3009 Columbia Ave. Graveside services are set for 4 p.m. at Mt. Hope Cemetery.

Campbell was born in 1908, son of William Winder and Anne James Briggs Campbell. He graduated from Battle Ground Academy in 1924, then attended Vanderbilt University. After a brief period with Williamson County Bank, he joined the firm of J.C. Bradford, where he remained for 10 years. At 31, he became president of Harpeth National Bank, a career interrupted in 1942 by the war, when he joined the Army Air Force, served as base adjutant at Olmstead Field, Pa., then transferred to the military government branch of the armed services. He arrived in Scotland on D-Day and spent the remainder of his term in Europe, discharged as a major in early 1946.

Back at the helm of the bank, Campbell became a leader in business and civic affairs, and was instrumental in bringing CPS, Lasko and other industries to the Franklin area.

Campbell was one of the founders in 1954 of Hillsboro Enterprises, a Nashville venture capital firm. He was a member of the Fourth Avenue Church of Christ, The American Legion, The Country Club of Franklin, Carnton Plantation Association, and formerly, the Belle Meade Country Club. He served on the board of First Tennessee Bank of Franklin, Federal Reserve Bank of Nashville, Battle Ground Academy, Mt. Hope Perpetual Care Association, and other corporations and associations.

As a strong supporter and trustee of BGA, his most recent gift to the school was the new track and field complex which bears his name.

He retired as chairman of Harpeth National Bank in 1974, but remained active in the business community.

Campbell was a descendant of several prominent Williamson County families. His mother was raised by her aunt and uncle, James and Anne Briggs Harrison, leading citizens of Franklin in the late 19th century. Harrison, founder of Williamson County Bank, was largely responsible for the construction of several city landmarks, including the Historic Franklin Presbyterian Church. Harrison's home, built in 1881, was for many years a landmark at the Five Points intersection.

The historic William H. Harrison house on Columbia Pike south of Franklin was the childhood home of Campbell's maternal grandmother, Matilda Harrison Briggs. Mrs. Briggs was 12 when the Battle of Franklin took place, and Confederate Gen. John Bell Hood used the Harrison home as his command post before the tragic battle.

Campbell's paternal grandmother, Louise Winder Campbell, was a granddaughter of Felix Grundy, U.S. Attorney General under President Martin Van Buren. Mrs. Campbell's sister, Carrie Winder McGavock, was the mistress of Carnton at the time of the Battle of Franklin, remembered for her care of the wounded during the battle and for establishing a cemetery for the fallen soldiers on the grounds of Carnton.

Campbell's paternal grandfather, Patrick Campbell, established the Harpeth Male Academy in Franklin shortly after the Civil War.

Campbell is survived by his wife, Louise Farnsworth Campbell; their four children, Mrs. John W. Clay, Jr., Mrs. Charles D. Cline, Mrs. Margaret Miller and Stewart Campbell, Jr.; seven grandchildren; a niece and nephew, William Winder Campbell and Lillian Campbell Stewart; and two great grandchildren.

The grandchildren will serve as active pallbearers. Honorary pallbearers include Charles E. Morton, John T. Flaugher, Patsy Radabaugh, W. Lipscomb Davis, Jr., Mrs. J. Michael Hayes, and William B. Ferrell of Delray Beach, Florida.

In lieu of flowers, the family requests that memorial gifts be made to Mt. Hope Perpetual Care Association, Battle Ground Academy, Carnton Plantation Association, or the charity of your choice.

– The Tennessean, August 13, 2000

Excellent Citizens and Notable Partings

Portrait of An Excellent Citizen

James Henry Chapman

James Henry Chapman has been a resident of Franklin since he was a small boy. In early manhood he was married to Miss Effie Cotton and they reside on Eleventh Avenue North. They have one son, James H. Chapman, Jr., of Charlotte, North Carolina and one daughter, Ruth Chapman Newman of Mt. View, California, and 5 grandchildren.

"Jim" as he is more familiarly known, operated Chapman's Pie Wagon on the public square for 25 years and was known far and wide for his hamburgers, steaks and home-made pies. Chapman's Pie Wagon has never ceased to be missed.

Mr. Chapman is now representative for Triopane Gas Company and his office is on Bridge Street. He is a member of the First Presbyterian Church where he has been a member of the Session since 1945, and is a member of the Men's Bible Class of which he is secretary.

As Published in *The Review-Appeal* on August 24, 1967

JAMES HENRY CHAPMAN
1895 - 1968

Jim Chapman Dies, Rites Held Tuesday

Funeral services for James Henry Chapman, 72, a prominent Franklin businessman for many years, were held Tuesday morning at First Presbyterian Church. Dr. James A. Cogswell and Dr. T. B. Cowan officiated and burial was in Mt. Hope Cemetery.

Mr. Chapman died at Williamson County Hospital Sunday. He had been in declining health for the past few months and had been a patient at the hospital for several weeks but his death was unexpected.

A native of Scottsville, Kentucky, he came to Williamson County as a boy to live with his sister, Mrs. Charlie Gray and Mr. Gray in the Bingham community and was reared in that section. He was married Jan. 14, 1917, to Miss Effie Cotton of Franklin, who survives. His death occurred on their 51st wedding anniversary. They have resided on 11th Avenue, North.

Mr. Chapman was known throughout this section for Chapman's Pie Wagon which he operated on the Public Square for about 25 years. For the past 15 years he was the manager of the Franklin office of Triopane Gas Company.

He was a member of First Presbyterian Church and was active in all phases of church work. He had been an elder of the local church for many years.

In addition to his wife he is survived by one daughter, Mrs. Eugene Newman of Mountain View, California; one son, James H. Chapman, Jr., of Charlotte, North Carolina; a sister, Mrs. Roy Lockhart of Pasadena, California; a brother, Dan Chapman of Lawton, Oklahoma; six grandchildren; and a number of nieces and nephews.

Serving as honorary pallbearers were the elders and deacons of First Presbyterian Church, employees of Triopane Gas Company, and Will Linton.

Active pallbearers were Brown Kinnard, Frank Murrey, Wilson Herbert, Joe Hendricks, Lee Dozier, Dr. Harry Guffee, Tom Herbert, and Fuller Arnold.

Franklin Memorial Chapel was in charge of arrangements.

– The Review-Appeal, January 18, 1968

"In 1917 he married Miss Effie Cotton and it was right then Madame Fortune dropped him a hat full of posies. She has stood shoulder to shoulder with him, sharing every handicap with a smile. It takes two conditions to make a man's life a success - his home and business associates. Jim was fortunate to marry one and his genial manner made the other.

"After his marriage he farmed a while and later worked in a store. One Sunday he was on his way to Nashville to hear Bill Sunday preach. He stopped at a pie wagon in front of Vanderbilt University to get a sandwich. Right there he conceived the idea of opening one in Franklin. ... From the first his business grew until within six months he was able to build a $1,000 house."

— Jane Bowman Owen, *Who's Who in Williamson County*, Rick Warwick, ed., originally published in *The Review-Appeal*, April 2, 1936.

Excellent Citizens and Notable Partings

John H. Childress

John H. Childress is a native of Franklin. He was born in the Harpeth community and received his elementary education there, going on to Bethesda High School where he graduated in the class of 1961. At present he is a Sales Representative for Jamison, Inc. Prior to going with Jamison he was with National Life and Accident Insurance Co.

John is married to the former Miss Mary Lee Jackson. They have one daughter, Rhonda Lee, 4 years old. They reside on Lewisburg Pike, and attend Cowles Chapel Methodist Church.

Active in civic affairs, John is president of the Franklin Jaycees, chairman of the Williamson County March of Dimes, and is a member of the Board of Directors of the Williamson County Chapter for Retarded Children.

As Published in *The Review-Appeal* on April 25, 1968

Not long after the article was printed in the newspaper, Jamison Upholstery gave me an opportunity to move to Florida. I thought I'd move to Florida for a few years and then move back home. As I grew and started cultivating Jamison's furniture business in Florida, I settled into life in the Sunshine State. I established Childress and Associates in the mid 70's and created a full line furniture representation company serving Florida. My work brought me to every major city in Florida, but I did not enjoy living in a big city. I gravitated back to small town life in DeLand, Florida because it reminded me of Franklin. DeLand is 20 minutes from Daytona and 40 minutes north of Orlando.

I made my career in the furniture business. I have Jamison Upholstery and Hal Jamison to thank for the start of my career. I've been fortunate to be involved with many cutting-edge parts of the furniture business. Waterbeds, massage chairs, air beds and adjustable bed bases. This has allowed me to work with many creative, imaginative leaders in the furniture and bedding industries. They say if you love what you do then you'll never work a day of your life. I believe that. I have been a partner with my wife Paula Zeikle Childress for the last 21 years. I retired 5 years ago from working but Childress and Associates is still in business.

I have been fortunate to snow ski, play golf and tennis. My wife and I bought a small horse farm 19 years ago I was able to get into cutting horses. I have been able to buy some great horses and compete in the Southeast.

I have been a member of the Florida Home Furnishings Association for over 40 years. I am also a member of the DeLand Downtown Rotary. My daughter Rhonda is married and lives in Salt Lake City, Utah with her husband Tim. She is in sales and also works with her community's city council.

– John Childress, November 2019

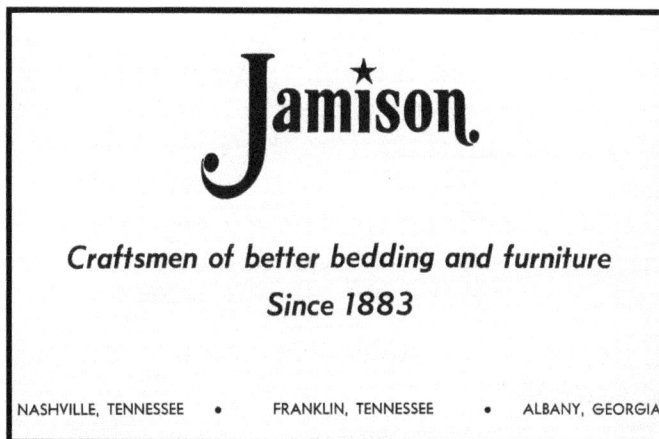

Joe Clinard

"Joe Clinard has proved himself to be an asset not just to the growing community of Fairview but to the entire county. ...Few things are undertaken in the First District that Mr. Clinard doesn't have a part in, and he participates in many activities for the benefit of the whole area. In his very young years, it might be said that Joe Clinard had a hard time settling down, but once he did, he settled well.

"Anything Joe Clinard undertakes he does enthusiastically and wholeheartedly."

— Derry Carlisle, *Who's Who in Williamson County,* Rick Warwick, ed., originally published in *The Review-Appeal,* October 21, 1965.

Portrait Published in *The Review-Appeal* on September 1, 1966

Joseph M. Clinard, Jr. (Joe), age 90.

Joe departed on his last great adventure September 28, 2009.

Born October 21, 1918 in Winston Salem, North Carolina to Joseph Marion Clinard and Mary Elizabeth Parrish, he was the oldest of nine. He was married over 53 years to the love of his life, Mary Lillian Knight of Nashville.

Preceded in death by his parents; sisters, Lenore, Jean and Nell; brothers, Jack and Jim, and survived by sisters, Dorothy Hamilton, Mary Lou Flynt; brother, Larry Clinard; his loving wife, Mary; son, Joseph M. (Jody) Clinard III and wife Marie; daughter, DeeDee Brickner and husband Steve; and grandchildren, Alan, Adriene, Julie, Ryan and Zach.

At age 65, Joe left Shelby Mutual Insurance Company after serving for 33 years as Resident Vice President, which he followed with a 19 year career as Insurance Director for Metro Nashville, where he finally retired at age 84.

He was a member of Westview United Methodist Church, AOPA [Aircraft Owners and Pilots Association], EAA [Experimental Aircraft Association], USUA [U.S. Ultralight Association], Lions Club, PTA, and the Tennessee 1752 Club (Treasurer 18 years).

A Master Mason of over 50 years, Joe was member of Fairview Lodge #776 F&AM. Joe served on the Board of Directors of Middle Tennessee Electric Membership Corporation (21 yrs.), and Shelby Mutual Insurance Company. He served on the Tennessee Joint Underwriters Association, was Chairman of The Tennessee Assigned Risk Plan, and was enshrined into the Robert E. Musto Tennessee Insurance Hall of Fame in August, 2009. He also served as Chairman of the Williamson County School Board (1968-74).

He had a lifetime love of aviation and physical fitness, holding world records in cross country flight and indoor rowing.

Services at Westview United Methodist Church, Fairview, Tennessee, Sunday, October 4th, 1 p.m. visitation, 2 p.m. Masonic Service, 2:30 p.m. Memorial Service, followed by a fellowship meal.

In lieu of flowers, the family requests memorials to Alive Hospice, Westview UMC or your favorite charity. Guestbook www.crawfordservices.com Crawford Mortuary & Crematory, (615) 254-8200.

– The Tennessean, October 2, 2009

Dr. James A. Cogswell

Dr. James A. Cogswell has been minister of the First Presbyterian Church here since July 1, 1967. Reared in Memphis, he was graduated from Southwestern College there. He did his theological work at Union Presbyterian Theological Seminary in Richmond, Virginia, where he received his doctorate in 1961. The work for his master's degree in theology was done in Princeton University, Princeton, New Jersey.

After World War II, Dr. Cogswell spent two five year periods in mission work in Japan. Following his return in 1960 he served with the Board of World Missions of the Presbyterian Church U.S. as secretary for the Far East.

As Published in *The Review-Appeal* on July 11, 1968

Editor's Note: During the research phase of this project, we discovered that Rev. Dr. Cogswell was living in a retirement community in Black Mountain, North Carolina. We were able to catch up with Dr. Cogswell when one of our Special Collections volunteers, Shannon McNamara, realized she would be traveling there that very weekend! Shannon graciously offered to check in on our subject and enjoyed a wonderful visit. At her suggestion, we reprinted Dr. Cogswell's wife's obituary, because "it so perfectly describes their life of ministry together." Here is Shannon's account of her visit with Dr. Cogswell:

"While on a visit to Black Mountain, North Carolina, I took the opportunity to visit with Dr. Cogswell at his home of almost 30 years. I was greeted warmly by the very alert and very tall 97 year old. I felt at home among the collection of books, pictures and small statues that told of a life well traveled and well lived. Dr. Cogswell's life has been devoted to serving God through the ministry of the Presbyterian Church.

"Born in Houston, Texas, Dr. Cogswell was born to a military man who had met his French wife, Cogswell's mother, in France. Dr. Cogswell went to Memphis, Tennessee schools.

The Cogswells felt called to the mission field. Language school took them to California then to serve in Japan with their young family.

"He and his family enjoyed their time in Franklin while he served at First Presbyterian in downtown Franklin.

"Dr. Cogswell was delightful to visit with and was looking forward to a family reunion in Montreat, North Carolina, this summer."

— *Shannon Boyd McNamara, Library Volunteer, June 2019*

Black Mountain, North Carolina - Margaret Elizabeth Griffin Cogswell entered the Church Triumphant on Sunday, October 28, 2012, after celebrating her 90th birthday with family on October 11. Her life was defined by devotion: devotion to family, friends, community, church, and her 67 years with her husband, the Rev. Dr. James Cogswell. Her remarkable life of service to others was founded upon an unshakeable Christian faith; an extraordinary sense of commitment, duty and discipline; and a wellspring of love that nourished all the many hearts she touched.

Born in Richmond, Virginia on October 11, 1922, Peggy (as she was known to so many) met Jim in 1940 on the steps of Westminster Presbyterian Church in Memphis, Tennessee, where they both had been reared. She studied at the Presbyterian School of Christian Education in Richmond, and after Jim's graduation from Union Theological Seminary in Richmond, they were married on June 11, 1945. They applied for missionary service in Japan under the Board of World Missions of the Presbyterian Church, U.S. While awaiting permission for new missionaries to enter postwar Japan, they served in organizing a new church in Pascagoula, Mississippi, and then pursued study at Princeton Theological Seminary in New Jersey, during which time Peggy served as secretary to the Department of Philosophy at Princeton University. After training in the Japanese language at the University of California in Berkeley, the Cogswells sailed for Japan in December 1948 with their one-year-old daughter Margaret Ann.

During their 13 years of service as evangelistic and educational missionaries, they participated in the founding of Shikoku Christian College (now Shikoku Gakuin University), taught at Kinjo Gakuin University in Nagoya, and worked in

Excellent Citizens and Notable Partings

establishing and strengthening churches on the island of Shikoku and in the metropolitan area of Nagoya.

In 1960 (now with four children) they returned on furlough to the United States where in 1961 Jim was called to serve as Asia Secretary for the Board of World Missions in Nashville, Tennessee. Along with caring for their four children, Peggy worked as secretary to the Dean of Admissions at Peabody College, then at Vanderbilt University School of Law. In 1967, Jim was called to serve as pastor of the First Presbyterian Church in Franklin, Tennessee, where Peggy served not only as a pastor's wife, but also as school secretary at Franklin Elementary School. In 1971, Jim became Director of the World Hunger/World Service Program of the Presbyterian Church, U.S., moving the family to Atlanta. During this period, Peggy served as staff for the Board of Women's Work, PCUS *[Presbyterian Church in the United States]*; secretary to the Dean of Columbia Theological Seminary; secretary at Emory University School of Nursing; and secretary for Greater Atlanta Presbytery. She also served as an elder at North Decatur Presbyterian Church. Mindful of the beautiful as well as the practical, Peggy maintained a beautiful yard at their home in Decatur and enjoyed the fellowship and entertaining of many friends.

In 1984, the Cogswells moved to the New York area when Jim was called to be Director of the Division of Overseas Ministries of the National Council of Churches. Always seeking an avenue of service, Peggy had a position at the Graduate Theological School of Drew University in Madison, New Jersey, where they lived. Following retirement in 1988, the Cogswells returned first to Atlanta (where Peggy served as secretary to Decatur Cooperative Ministry), then in 1995 to Black Mountain, North Carolina In 1999, following Peggy's heart attack, they became residents at the Highland Farms Retirement Community.

Peggy was witty as well as wise. Her subtle humor bubbled up everywhere from holiday gatherings to annual family reunions. Evening dinners at Highland Farms were not complete without Peggy's warm hello. Her accomplished children will cite her mix of tender and tough parenting as the foundation of their achievements. Peggy's children are Margaret Ann and her husband, Terry Kolb, of New York City, James Jr. and his wife, Sarah Stitt, of Ann Arbor, Michigan, Sara and her husband, Will South of Columbia, South Carolina, and Dan and his wife, Margaret Couch, of Asheville, North Carolina. She is the grandmother of six: Eli Wells of Mobile, Alabama, Anna Hodges of Greensboro, North Carolina, Will and Camille Cogswell of Asheville, David and Katherine Cogswell of Ann Arbor. She is also the great-grandmother of the newest addition to the Cogswell clan, two-year old Reid Hodges. Her two younger brothers, Roland and Thomas, predeceased her.

Throughout her life, Peggy was a devoted wife, a loving mother, a loyal friend, and a dedicated Christian who poured out her life for others. The memory of her grace, her kindness, and her unconditional love will resonate through the lives of her family and into a world always needful of those as compassionate as Peggy Cogswell.

Memorial contributions may be made to the Presbyterian World Mission Program, 100 Witherspoon Street, Louisville, KY 40202; or the Presbyterian Heritage Center, P.O. Box 207, Montreat, NC 28757. Messages of condolence may be sent to 200 Tabernacle Road, Apt. F-41, Black Mountain, NC 28711. A memorial service will be held at Black Mountain Presbyterian Church on Sunday, November 4, 1:30 p.m.

— The Ashville Citizen Times (NC), October 31, 2012

———————

See also:

— "Dr. James Cogswell," *Who's Who in Williamson County, by Derry Carlisle*, Rick Warwick, ed., originally published in *The Review-Appeal*, January 25, 1968.

James A. Cogswell, Th.D.

The ministry of Dr. Jim Cogswell made a great difference in my personal faith that had been instilled in me while growing up in the Presbyterian Church in the United States (formerly the southern branch.) As a child and adolescent during the Jim Crow era, I had taken little notice of exclusionary signs posted over public wash rooms and water closets. We were only cognizant of persons of color who cooked or provided laundry services in homes or in the very few restaurants serving the community. Before the national upheaval to obtain civil rights for all Americans in the 1960's, churches in Franklin had easily separated themselves into black and white congregations according to the prevailing mores that followed the Civil War.

Dr. Cogswell, having recently returned from the mission field in Japan, accepted the call to ministry at First Presbyterian Church at Five Points. Soon thereafter, he proceeded to contact the pastors of all churches in the downtown area in order to form Franklin's first ministerial association. In 1968, at the First Missionary Baptist Church on Natchez Street, he was one of the leaders of the Association who organized a memorial service to honor the life of Dr. Martin Luther King, Jr. It is heartening to observe how spiritual and community leaders in Franklin have continued to cross barriers and build the peaceful and just city we cherish today.

Attending the service for Dr. King enabled me to more fully understand the mandate for Christians to embrace across all social differences and to enjoy the sustaining fruits of unity and inclusiveness. Whether preaching and pastoring his flock, or baptizing young children, including my own, or playing competitive tennis with new friends, Dr. Jim courageously led us to move beyond the blinding constraints of local customs and to see for ourselves the visions described in the prophesies of Isaiah and the letters of St. Paul.

Lillian Campbell Stewart, Elder
Historic Franklin Presbyterian Church
Mayor of Franklin 1987-1989

First Presbyterian Church

5th AND MAIN   FRANKLIN, TENNESSEE

"*Enter into his gates with thanksgiving, and into his courts with praise:
be thankful unto him, and bless his name.*

Portrait of An Excellent Citizen

Haywood Clark Cole

Haywood Clark Cole, for eighteen years principal of Grassland School, lives on Hillsboro Road with his wife, the former Miss Ann Looney of Nashville now employed as a nurse with the Williamson County Health Unit.

He is the father of three daughters, Polly Anne a student at Memphis State University, Sally, a junior at TCU in Ft. Worth and Carolyn, a junior at Franklin High School.

Mr. Cole's interest centers around Grassland School activities and the Grassland Community Club. He received his Master's Degree at George Peabody College and is past president of the Williamson County Board of Education and is present treasurer of the association. He is a member of the Franklin Lions Club and has served as president, also secretary and treasurer and is now on the Board of Directors.

A member of the First Baptist Church in Franklin, he is active in the work of the church and is a Deacon.

As Published in *The Review-Appeal* on November 2, 1967

HAYWOOD CLARK COLE
1911 - 1980

Retired Educator Dies in Kentucky

Retired county school principal Haywood Cole died Tuesday following an apparent heart attack while en route to visit one of his three daughters in Louisville for the Thanksgiving holidays.

Funeral services for Mr. Cole, who was principal of Grassland school for 25 years, will be today (Friday) at 11 a.m. at Franklin Memorial Chapel, with Dr. Gaye McGlothlen, interim minister of First Baptist Church, officiating. Burial will be in Mt. Olivet Cemetery in Nashville.

Mr. Cole and his wife Ann were driving to Louisville Tuesday afternoon when he became ill and collapsed. Mrs. Cole, a registered nurse, drove to the nearest exit off the interstate, about a quarter mile away, but her husband was already dead. He was officially pronounced dead on arrival at University Hospital in Louisville.

Cole, 69, had retired in May 1974 after spending 35 years in public education, including 25 at Grassland School where he saw the facility grow from a small rural school to one of the most highly regarded schools serving the growing urban area north of Franklin.

A native of Trenton in West Tennessee, Cole held bachelor and masters degrees from Peabody College in Nashville. He had also attended the University of Tennessee at Martin and Union University in Jackson.

He was a petty officer in the Navy during World War II.

Since moving to Franklin in 1950, Cole was active in community and church life of the town. He had been a member of the Franklin Lions Club 28 years, and had held virtually every office, including that of president. He also was a former deacon in First Baptist Church, where he was a member.

Survivors include his wife, Mrs. Ann Looney Cole of Franklin; daughters, Mrs. Polly Cole Pitts of Scotts Valley, California, Mrs. Sally Cole Blank of Metuchen, New Jersey, and Mrs. Carolyn Cole Guagliardo of Louisville, Kentucky; sisters, Mrs. Mary Lou Andrews, of Aberdeen, Mississippi., Mrs. Catherine French of Memphis and Mrs. Christine Berry of Philadelphia, Pennsylvania; brother, Edward L. Cole of Jackson, and two grandchildren.

Honorary pallbearers will be members of the Franklin Lions Club, principals of Williamson County schools and members of the board of directors of Holiday Shores.

Pallbearers will be H.J. Andrews, Jimmy Wood, Jim McGlothlin, Bill McGlothlin, Jesse Frank, Herman Lovell, Hiram Beasley, James Short Sr., Dr. Kenneth Poag, John T. Beasley, Bob Bratcher, Robert Inman, Nathan Lowe, L.I. Mills and Ed Moody.

— The Williamson Leader, November 28, 1980

"In 1873, Sunnyside School was built on Hillsboro Road north of Sneed Hill where Greater Pleasant View Baptist Church now stands. In January 1911, the school moved to a new building on Hillsboro Road overlooking Moran Road and became Grassland School. It had only two rooms in which to teach grades one through ten. ... In the fall of 1950, our present building [on Bethlehem Loop] was opened with an enrollment of 240 students combining the schools of Grassland, Ballow, Forest Home and Bingham. The principal was Mr. Haywood Cole, and our library is dedicated in his memory."

— Grassland Elementary School Yearbook, 1992.

Portrait of An Excellent Citizen

Joseph Powell Covington

Joseph Powell Covington is owner and operator of Covington Feed and Seed Company at College Grove where he lives with his wife, the former Miss Pauline Thurman, and daughter, Miss Dorothy Covington.

Mr. Covington has another daughter, Mrs. Polly Ann McFarlin of Nolensville, and a son Powell Covington, Jr.

Mr. Powell attends the College Grove Presbyterian Church. He is a member of the College Grove Lions Club and the Williamson County Farm Bureau. He is a magistrate in Williamson County Court representing the 21st district. Mr. Covington is president of the Bank of College Grove and director in the Williamson County Bank of Franklin.

As Published in *The Review-Appeal* on May 15, 1967

Funeral for Joseph Powell Covington, 89, College Grove farmer and businessman, was Saturday, Oct. 10 at Williamson Memorial Funeral Home. Doy Hollman and Dr. John T. Netterville officiated with burial in Williamson Memorial Gardens.

Covington died Friday, Oct. 9 in Williamson Medical Center. He was one of the founders of the Bank of College Grove, now the Dominion Bank, and was owner of Covington Feed and Seed Co.

Covington was a native of Williamson County, a veteran of World War I, and a member of the College Grove Church of Christ.

Survivors include a daughter, Mrs. John (Polly) McFarlin, of Nolensville; son, J. P. Covington Jr., of College Grove; sister, Mrs. Della Corlette, of College Grove, and three grandchildren, J.P. Covington III, Mrs. Danny (Sara) Brown, and Mrs. Horace (Ginny) Sullivan.

Active pallbearers were J. P. Covington III, Dr. John Mann, Daniel Brown, Ralph Thurman, Horace Sullivan, Bruce Covington, Dr. Robert Mann and Ellis McFarlin. Honorary pallbearers were Dr. Harry Guffee, John U. Wilson, Matthew Harwell, Joe Bellenfant, Robert Moran, Melvin White, Frank Crosslin, Sam Waters, Sam Rucker Ogilvie, Wilson Herbert, Bill Ogilvie, Thomas Hamm, Charles Jewell, James Rigsby, Robert Wilson, Albert Wilson, Clarence Graham, Howard Smithson, Larry Hazelwood, and Robert McCoy.

— The Williamson Leader, October 23, 1987

Dr. T. B. Cowan

Dr. T. B. Cowan has served for the past year as interim supply minister of the First Presbyterian Church. A native of Scotland, Dr. Cowan retired in April, 1966, and he and Mrs. Cowan moved to Franklin to make their home. They have an apartment in John Ewin's house on Fourth Avenue South. Dr. Cowan has become interested in a number of civic activities of Franklin and is serving in the chaplaincy program of the Williamson County Hospital and on the Citizens Advisory Committee of the Welfare Department.

As Published in *The Review-Appeal* on June 22, 1967

THOMAS BEVERIDGE COWAN
1896 - 1972

Services held for Dr. Cowan

Dr. T.B. (Scotty) Cowan, retired minister of the Presbyterian Church, U.S. who has served a number of churches in Nashville and other Middle Tennessee cities on a temporary basis since his retirement, died July 2 in his native city of Dunfermline, Scotland.

He and two of his brothers left July 1 for a "pilgrimage back home." Death was caused by an apparent heart attack. He was 75. The body arrived in Nashville Sunday afternoon.

Funeral services were held Monday afternoon at 2 o'clock at the First Presbyterian Church. The Rev. T. L. Croft officiated. Burial was in Mt. Hope Cemetery.

Dr. Cowan migrated to the United States as a young man after he had served four years in the British Army in the Royal Engineers. He worked in the steel mills and coal mines of Pennsylvania before he began his college work. He received his B.A. degree at Cumberland University in Lebanon and took his Bachelor of Divinity work at both Vanderbilt and Yale. He received his master of theology at Louisville Presbyterian Seminary and two years before his retirement Berea College in Berea, Kentucky, conferred the Doctor of Divinity degree upon him.

During his college days he served the College Grove Presbyterian Church in Williamson County as a student pastor.

His first full-time pastorate was with the Third Presbyterian Church in Chattanooga. Later he was minister of the Norris Religious Fellowship in Norris, Tennessee, and Everybody's Church in Lexington, Kentucky, both non-denominational. He was minister of Union Church in Berea, Kentucky, when he retired in 1966. At that time he and his wife, the former Miss Gladys Watson, came to Franklin to live.

Among the churches he served as interim supply are Glen Leven and Hermitage Presbyterian churches in Nashville and Harpeth and First Presbyterian churches in Franklin.

While Dr. Cowan was in Chattanooga, he was chairman of the Committee of 100 which worked to bring TVA to this area.

He began reviewing books for the Chattanooga Times and he continued to do reviews for that newspaper on a regular basis until his death.

He was chosen by the National Council of Churches as one of a team of 14 ministers to visit the British Isles in an exchange program.

Soon after he came to Franklin, he began laying the ground work for a day care center that opened last fall.

Dr. Cowan gave talks and lectures for many organizations and delighted many groups with poetry and tales of Scotland while dressed in his kilt.

Surviving in addition to his wife are one sister, Mrs. Isabelle Cowan of Schenectady, New York, and two brothers, Andrew L. Cowan of Los Angeles, California and Walter S. Cowan of Albany, New York.

Active pallbearers were John Ewin, Dan Parsons, Tim Akin, Bob Boyce, C. D. Berry, Frank North, Clair Regen, Ronald Ligon, Joe Pinkerton, and Walter Carlisle.

Honorary pallbearers were the elders and deacons of the First Presbyterian Church in Franklin and members of the Franklin Ministerial Association.

In lieu of flowers the family requested that donations be made to the Elders Triumphant Fund of First Presbyterian Church.

Franklin Memorial Chapel was in charge of arrangements.

– The Review-Appeal, July 13, 1972

Excellent Citizens and Notable Partings

Herschell Eugene Crawford

Herschell Eugene Crawford is pastor of Franklin's First Baptist Church. He is married to the former Miss Mary Dierking and they live on South Third Avenue with their three small daughters, Monte, Kande, and Dina. Mr. Crawford is president of the local Lions Club. He is member of the Board of Directors of the Economic Opportunity Act, and of the Franklin Ministers Association.

As Published in *The Review-Appeal* on February 2, 1967

HERSCHELL EUGENE CRAWFORD
1919 - 1990

Funeral for the Rev. Eugene Crawford, 70, who served as minister of Franklin's First Baptist Church in the 1960's, was Monday, April 2, at Williamson Memorial Funeral Home, with Dr. Robert Crumby officiating.

Burial was in Williamson Memorial Gardens.

The Rev. Mr. Crawford died Saturday, March 31, at Williamson Medical Center.

A native of Meridian, Mississippi, the Rev. Crawford and his family had lived in Franklin 30 years after he became pastor of First Baptist Church in 1960.

After leaving the pastorate of the Franklin church in 1969, he joined the state Commission on Aging and later was director of Gerontological Services for the state Department of Mental Health.

He also taught gerontology, the study of the phenomena of old age, at Meharry Medical College for two years.

For 15 years, he had served as minister of Bethany Presbyterian Church at Ardmore in Giles County, and was a member of the Presbytery of Middle Tennessee.

He was a past president of the Franklin Lions Club and member of the City of Franklin's Affordable Housing Committee.

Survivors include his wife, Mrs. Mary Crawford; three daughters, Mrs. William (Monte) Bennett of College Grove, Mrs. Richard (Kande) McBride of Johnson City, and Mrs. Dale (Dina) Cotton of Clarksville; sister, Mrs. Ardina Keeton of Meridian, Mississippi; brother, M. E. Crawford, also of Meridian; four grandchildren, Joshua, Monica and Natalie Bennett and Katherine McBride.

Active pallbearers, were Jimmy May, Arlie Smith, Fred Wisdom, Jerry Stephenson, Dr. Henry Moses and Jimmy Lish.

Honorary pallbearers were members of Franklin Police Department, members of First Baptist Church, Dr. Robert Hollister and Dewees Berry.

Memorials may be made to the American Heart Association or the American Cancer Society.

– The Williamson Leader, April 6, 1990

"Their wedding in May, 1950, was most unusual. They were married on the "Bride and Groom" television show in Hollywood. ... In order to get on the program, both the prospective bride and groom had to fill out lengthy applications and submit pictures. The applications were studied by psychologists who made recommendations to the producers of the program. ... In addition to being given a lovely wedding, they had a honeymoon on a dude ranch in Mexico, where Mr. Crawford said they saw an entirely different way of life from anything he had ever expected to see. They were also presented many lovely gifts, including sterling silver, on the show."

— Derry Carlisle, *Who's Who in Williamson County*, Rick Warwick, ed., originally published in *The Review-Appeal*, July 7, 1950

Excellent Citizens and Notable Partings

Miss Lois Crowley

Miss Lois Crowley is home agent for Williamson County, a position she has held since February 1, 1947. In her work, she plans and supervises demonstrations and instructions in all phases of homemaking for women in more than 40 home demonstration clubs in all areas of the county.

Miss Crowley was reared in Cookeville where she attended public schools and was graduated from Tennessee Technological University. She is a member of the First Methodist Church of Franklin and is active in the work of the Wesleyan Service Guild. She is also a member of the Franklin Business and Professional Women's Club, the Nashville area Home Economics Association, which she serves as treasurer, and other professional organizations.

Miss Crowley's office is in the Agriculture Building on Third Avenue South, and she lives in an apartment in the Beckye Ann Apartments on Battle Avenue.

As Published in *The Review-Appeal* on October 26, 1967

MARTHA LOIS CROWLEY
1919-2001

Martha Lois Crowley, 82, died Sept. 5, 2001, in Oxford, Mississippi, at Baptist Memorial Hospital. Ms. Crowley was born in Cookeville to A.C. and Mabel Peek Crowley. She attended public schools in Cookeville and graduated from Tennessee Tech in 1941 with a degree in home economics. Ms. Crowley taught in Hardeman County schools and was appointed Extension Agent for Scott County in 1944.

She transferred to Williamson County in 1947 where she retired as Williamson County Extension Agent in March 1977. During her tenure in Williamson County Ms. Crowley organized and worked with 40 local home demonstration clubs. Her interest in reading was instrumental in the establishment in 1964 of the first branch library in Williamson County in Fairview - with the help of members of the Del Rio Home Demonstration Club.

In 1998, the Lois Crowley Leadership Camp scholarship was established for members of the women's clubs, now known as the Association of Family and Community Education. She was honored on May 19, 1999 with the proclamation of "Lois Crowley Day" by the Williamson County Executive's office.

Ms. Crowley was active in the Franklin First United Methodist Church where she served on boards and committees and as a volunteer. She was also active in local civic and cultural groups. She traveled extensively both in the United States and abroad. Ms. Crowley lived in Franklin over 50 years and moved to Mississippi earlier this year to be near her sister.

Survivors include her twin sister, Ruth Upchurch and husband William of Coffeeville, Mississippi; two brothers, James Crowley and wife Christine of Kingsport and Claude Crowley and wife Carolyn of Fort Worth, Texas; and several nieces and nephews.

The funeral service will be held Saturday, Sept. 8, at 11 a.m., at Franklin First United Methodist Church with the Rev. Robert H. Lewis Jr. officiating. Burial will follow in Williamson Memorial Gardens. Pallbearers will be H. Y. Beeler, DeWayne Perry, Billy Walker Sr., William Edmondson, Gene Turns, Jimmy King and Burt Upchurch. Visitation will be at the funeral home Friday from 5-7 p.m. Memorial donations may be made to the First United Methodist Church in Franklin.

Williamson Memorial Funeral Home is in charge of arrangements.

– The Review-Appeal, September 7, 2001

"Lois Crowley, Williamson County's home demonstration agent for 30 years, will retire March 1. ... Looking back over her career, she noted that the greatest changes had come in food processing. ... 'One of the biggest changes is the freezer. Women freeze foods now instead of canning, although canning is coming back,' she said. 'But when I first entered extension work, canning was the only way to preserve fruits and vegetables.'

"Miss Crowley has also seen the women's division of the Extension program grow. 'There were 26 or 27 clubs in the county when I came here. Now there are 34 clubs with 750 women enrolled,' she explained."

— "Extension Agent Lois Crowley to Retire," *Williamson Leader*, February 6, 1977

Glen Davis

Glen Davis, one of Franklin's most industrious citizens, is Science teacher at Franklin Junior High School and operates the Farm Bureau Insurance Service. He is a member of the Fourth Avenue Church of Christ, serves as Elder and teachers a class of young married couples. He has done a great deal of work with Boy Scouts. Always interested in schools he is a member of the NEA, the TEA and the MTEA, all Educational Associations.

He is married to the former Miss Mary Ruth Prosser and they have two sons. Dudley, the oldest of the two is a teacher at Lipscomb School in this county and David is a Freshman at the University of Tennessee.

The Davises live on Ralston Lane.

As Published in *The Review-Appeal* on March 21, 1968

Glen Davis, 82, died Sunday, March 3, 2002, at NHC Healthcare of Franklin. Mr. Davis was born in Marshall County to the late William Marvin Davis and Lily Vance Finley Davis and made his home in Franklin. He served in the United States Navy. He was a retired insurance agent with the Williamson County Farm Bureau and Tennessee Farmers Mutual Insurance Company and was a teacher with the Franklin Special School District. He served many years as an elder of Fourth Avenue Church of Christ and gave many dedicated years of service as a local scout leader with the Boy Scouts.

Survivors include his wife, Mary Ruth Davis of Franklin; two sons, Dudley (Sara) Davis of Franklin and David (Grace) Davis of Texarkana, Texas; a brother, Finley Davis of Cornersville; and five grandchildren, Wilson, Will, Ruth, Alice and Kim Davis.

Funeral services will be held today, March 6, at 1 p.m., at Williamson Memorial Funeral Home with Myron Keith, Tom Riley and James Fiveash officiating.

Burial will follow in Williamson Memorial Gardens. Active pallbearers will be James Fiveash, Buddy Mills, Bill Anderson, Mike Sullivan, Bobby Vines, Robert McKay, Bryant McMillan and Lanny McPeak.

Honorary pallbearers are Ralph Duke, Bob Hardison, Howard Gamble, Waldon Smithson, Johnny Davis, Mitchel Wright, Everett Bizwell, Billy Walker, Bryan Ehresman, Scott Fitzgerald, John Green, Glenn Little, Hal Crowell, John Moran, Jewell Brinkley, William Gentry, Tom Harlin, Fred Issacs, Leon Hayes, Marion Robinson, N. Y. Walker, Marion Holder, John McCord, David Gentry, Glenn Crowell, John Fisher, Moody Barrentine and John Sims.

Memorial donations may be made to the Benevolent Fund, Fourth Avenue Church of Christ, 117 Fourth Avenue North, Franklin 37064. Williamson Memorial Funeral Home is in charge of arrangements.

– The Review-Appeal, March 6, 2002

Portrait of An Excellent Citizen

Woodrow (Woody) Dickerson

Portrait Published in *The Review-Appeal* on June 30, 1966

T. W. Dickerson, Civic Leader, Dies Rites at 10 A.M. Today

Thomas Woodrow Dickerson, well-known photographer and civic leader, died unexpectedly Tuesday night at Williamson County Hospital. He had been confined to his home by illness Tuesday but was rushed to the hospital that night after apparently suffering a heart attack and he lived only 30 minutes.

Funeral services will be conducted this (Thursday) morning at 10 o'clock at Franklin Memorial Chapel. The Rev. John C. Hight will officiate and burial will be in Williamson Memorial Gardens.

Loy G. Hardcastle, president of the Chamber of Commerce, issued the following statement yesterday:

"Woody's passing is a great loss to this community and to the state of Tennessee. He has given much to all of us and he will be sorely missed by his legion of friends and business associates. I mourn his untimely departure."

Mr. Dickerson, 51, was born in Gallatin and was the son of the late David W. and Lena McGlothlin Dickerson. He began work in photography as a young man under a Gallatin photographer and he also worked with his brother, D. E. Dickerson of Shelbyville. He came to Franklin to open a studio about 19 years ago.

He was a member of the Tennessee Professional Photographers Association and served as its president in 1960-61. He was also a member of the National Professional Photographers Association and its honor society, whose membership was limited to only top representatives of the profession.

Mr. Dickerson had won numerous state and national awards for his work and in 1964 won the national award for best photographer in Tennessee. He was one point short of having the number required for classification as a master photographer and has prints submitted now for consideration for that point.

He was an active member of the Rotary Club and the Williamson County Chamber of Commerce and had served as president of both organizations. He was a member of the First Methodist Church.

During World War II Mr. Dickerson was in the United States Navy assigned to duty as an aerial photographer. He was based in Norfolk, Virginia, and in the Panama area.

In 1948 he was married to Mrs. Virginia Bradley Jones, who survives.

In addition to his wife he is survived by two daughters, Mrs. C. Kenneth Frost of Lynville and Mrs. Faye Williams of Memphis; a son, William S. Jones; six grandchildren; one sister, Mrs. Martin Collier of Nashville, and two brothers, D. E. Dickerson of Shelbyville and J. W. Dickerson of Memphis.

Members of the Rotary Club will serve as honorary pallbearers.

Active pallbearers are Tom Moody, Bob Sewell, J.W. Greer, Jr., Loy G. Hardcastle, Charles Gunter of Shelbyville, Ed Moody, Howlett Vaughn, J.B. Parks, William H. Miller, and Albert Ragsdale.

Franklin Memorial Chapel is in charge.

– The Review-Appeal, July 28, 1966

Col. R. L. Duncan

Veteran Duncan Has Been Part of Much American history
By Al Koontz, Sun Managing Editor

On first impression, one might get the idea Rudolph Duncan has witnessed a lot of American history in his 95 years. But Duncan has been more than a witness: he has lived an important part of that history.

The Lincoln man, in Beatrice Friday and Saturday for a meeting of the Nebraska Pearl Harbor Survivors Association, was in the Army Air Corps at Wheeler Field in Honolulu when the Japanese attacked on December 7, 1941.

That might be enough history for any one person to live through. But Duncan is also a veteran of World War I action in Europe. And before that, he served during the Mexican Border Campaign of 1915-17, chasing Pancho Villa along the U.S.-Mexican border.

Duncan, who was born on a farm outside of Nebraska City on July 10, 1895, moved from the state when he was 7. He enlisted in the Navy at age 19. Because the Navy provided communications for the Army at that time, he served as a railroad telegrapher during the chase for the famous Mexican bandit.

"We never could find him," said Duncan.

Continued on next page

Portrait Published in *The Review-Appeal* on March 24, 1966

His Navy service found him in Europe a short time later, fighting for the Allies in World War I. He was again in communications, providing a link between Brest, St. Nazaire, and other towns on the east [west] coast of France.

And in July 1918, Duncan was on the USS San Diego, a first class armored cruiser, when it was sunk by enemy fire in the Atlantic.

At Pearl Harbor, Duncan was a major in the Army Air Corps, and was signal officer for the 14th Pursuit Wing, Hawaiian Air Force. He was responsible for operation of equipment on about 50 fighter planes at the field, and for the operation of equipment on the field.

Duncan, though, says two things bother him about the readiness of U.S. forces. One had to do with the bunkers built to protect the U.S. planes. For five days prior to the attack, and on the morning of the attack, the planes were left out of their bunkers.

"The Japs just came along and got them all, except one squadron which was at a remote area for training purposes," he said.

"That's one thing that bothers me. Why weren't those planes bunkered?"

Duncan said his commanding officer was told not to bunker the planes or do anything "to alarm the populace."

Another question, said Duncan, concerns the radar detection of the attack. Radar stations phoned in that lots of planes were approaching. But they were told they were B-17s flying in from the mainland. But Duncan said the B-17s would have never been on that course unless they were lost.

"So that's the two questions I have, and I think they are very important things." Said Duncan. "I don't think we'd have won the battle if all our planes had been active, because we only had five squadrons and the Japanese had such a superior force. But it would have helped a helluva lot," he said.

– The Beatrice Daily Sun (Nebraska), May 6, 1991

Duncan – Col. Rudolph L., 97, 2001 S. 48th St., died Monday (5-17-93). Born Nebraska City. Retired colonel, U.S. Army Signal corps.

Member, Pearl Harbor Survivors Association, American Legion post 3, VFW Post 131, Sesostris Temple of the Shrine, Sesostris Legion of Honor, Southeast Shrine Club, Institute of Electrical and Electronic Engineers. Former president, Chamber of Commerce, Franklin, Tennessee. Former chairman, Easter Seal Foundation, Florida.

Survivors: wife, Laura J.; son, daughter-in-law, Ray and Suzanne Ortega, Lincoln; sister, Leah Miller, Hamburg, Iowa; grandchildren, Tammy, Corinne, Benjamin Ortega, all Lincoln; niece.

Services: 9:30 a.m. Thursday, Roper & Sons Mortuary, 4300 O St. Visitation: 10 a.m. Wednesday until services, mortuary. Memorials to Shrine Crippled Childrens Hospital or the Easter Seal Foundation.

– The Lincoln Star (Nebraska), May 19, 1993

Evelyn Duncan drowns in swim

Mrs. Evelyn Alexander Duncan, a former Williamson County resident home for a visit, drowned Thursday morning in a pond on the Nelson Elam Farm on Stillhouse Hollow Road.

Mrs. Duncan, 67, and her husband, Col. R. L. Duncan, Satellite Beach, Florida, were staying at the farm while the owners were on a trip. Authorities said she had been swimming in the pond when her husband discovered her death about 8:45 a.m.

Col. Duncan is a former executive secretary of the Williamson County Chamber of Commerce. Also surviving is a brother, Henry P. Alexander of New Hampshire.

Services were held at 2 p.m. Friday at Franklin Memorial Chapel, with the Rev. Edward K. Beckes officiating. Burial was in Williamson Memorial Gardens.

– The Williamson Leader, September 4, 1977

Portrait of An Excellent Citizen

Josiah Carr Eggleston

Josiah Carr Eggleston, more familiarly known as "Joe," is a native of Franklin. He received his high school education at Battle Ground Academy and graduated from Vanderbilt University with a degree in business administration and was a member of the Sigma Chi fraternity. He is employed at the Harpeth National Bank. He holds the office of Vice President with the bank and is Councilman of the Junior Bankers section of the Tennessee Bankers Association.

Mr. Eggleston is a member of the First Methodist Church and has served as secretary of the Official Board.

Vitally interested in civic affairs of the town and county, he serves as president of the Williamson County United Givers Fund, is a member of the Lions Club of which he is presently serving as treasurer and is a director of the Carter House Association.

He lives on Ewingville Drive with his wife, the former Miss Judy King, of Brentwood, and four-year-old daughter, Patricia.

As Published in *The Review-Appeal* on February 15, 1968

Mr. Josiah "Joe" Carr Eggleston, age 83 of Franklin, Tennessee, passed away on March 24, 2015. He was a longtime member of Franklin First United Methodist Church.

Mr. Eggleston graduated from Battle Ground Academy and Vanderbilt University where he was a member of Sigma Chi Fraternity. He retired from Harpeth National Bank, USF&G and the Crisis Call Intervention Center.

He was preceded in death by mother, Sophronia Mayberry Eggleston and father, Edmund Waller Eggleston. Survived by wife of 57 years, Judy Eggleston; daughter, Trish Eggleston Stiles; sister, Marietta Eggleston Burleigh; granddaughter, Wesley Hunter Stiles; first cousins, Eunetta Mayberry Kready, John Beasley and Earl Beasley; nieces, Fontaine Pearson and Kathryn C. Swords; nephews, Doug Carpenter and Stephen Carpenter.

Visitation will be 4 to 7 p.m. on Tuesday, March 31 at Williamson Memorial. Memorial services will be held 10 a.m. on Wednesday, April 1, 2015 at Franklin First United Methodist Church with visitation one hour prior, Dr. Lynn Hill officiating. Interment, Mt. Hope Cemetery. Honorary pallbearers: John M. Green Jr., David Wood, Robert Burleigh, Jack Schmidt, Brent Sanders and Bill Yates. Memorials may be made to Franklin First United Methodist Church.

Williamson Memorial Funeral Home and Cremation Services. 615-794-2289.

– The Williamson Herald, March 25, 2015

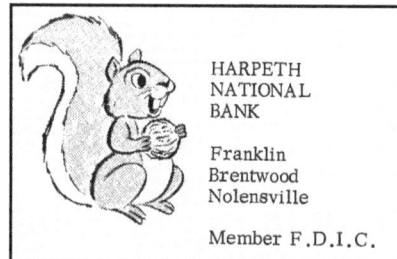

HARPETH
NATIONAL
BANK

Franklin
Brentwood
Nolensville

Member F.D.I.C.

Franklin - Judy Eggleston, age 83 of Franklin, Tennessee, went home to be with the Lord on Friday, December 8, 2017.

Judy was born in Nashville, Tennessee, on March 11, 1934, daughter to the late Frank and Ethel King.

She was an accomplished equestrian who traveled all over showing and competing in many horse shows. Graduated from Hillsboro High and studied at Stephen's College. Retired from Oak Hill School.

A longtime member of First United Methodist Church, Franklin, helped in starting Carnton Club, member of Charlotte Beasley/Minnie Pearl Tennis Group.

Preceded in death by husband, Joe C. Eggleston. Survived by daughter, Trish E. Stiles; granddaughter, Wesley Stiles and fiancé Eric Warren; great grandchildren, Jacob and Tyler Cate Warren. Sister-in-law, Marietta Burleigh, and many nieces and nephews.

Honorary pallbearers are Carnton Club Tennis Group, Charlotte Pearl Tennis Group, Supper Club, Ceacy Hailey, Eunetta Kready, Robert Burleigh, Doug and Stephen Carpenter, Kathryn

Swords, Fontaine Pearson, Peggy Crockett, Lex and Barbara Ables, Brent and Mamie Sanders, John and Louise Green, Dave and Margie Wood, William and Peggy Randolph, Dr. Jack and Joan Schmitt *[Schmidt]*, Mary Ann Crowell, Col. Bill and Peggy Yates, Marie Jordan, Lance Jordan, Dr. Bill and Sis Holliday, Bob and Margaret Martin, Bill and Barbara Grimes, Ruth and Charles Cherry, Mark and Emily Tulloch, Joe Crockett, Joe and Lisa Boyd, Scott and Leigh Ann Underwood, Charlie and Joyce Stiles, Stephen and Melissa Warren.

The family will receive friends Monday, December 11, 2017 from 5:00 PM - 7:00 PM at Williamson Memorial Funeral Home.

Memorial service will be held Tuesday, December 12, 2017, at 11:00 AM with an hour visitation prior to service.

Thanks to Brookdale and the friends she made there and Casey Lamb with BlueSky HouseCalls who took care of her.

Memorials to First U.M.C of Franklin or charity of choice, in loving memory of Judy Eggleston.

– Williamson Memorial Funeral Home

Excellent Citizens and Notable Partings

William Bryan Ehresman

Mr. Ehresman lives at Arrington, Tennessee with his wife the former Miss Woodson Johnson. He has one son, Bryan, of the same community. Mr. Ehresman is engaged in dairy farming, and is a member of the Williamson County Farm Bureau. He attends the Arrington Church of Christ.

As Published in *The Review-Appeal* on December 1, 1966

William B. Ehresman, 88, died September 4 at Harpeth Terrace Convalescent Center in Franklin.

Services will be Friday at 2 p.m. at Waller Chapel in Nolensville with O. P. Baird officiating. Burial will be in Woodlawn Cemetery.

Mr. Ehresman was a native of Nebraska and a retired dairy farmer.

Survivors include a son, Bryan Ehresman; granddaughter, Mrs. Paula E. Harris, both of Triune.

Honorary pallbearers will be the Elders and Deacons of Arrington Church of Christ and Elders and Deacons of College Grove Church of Christ.

Nephews will serve as Active Pallbearers.

– The Review-Appeal, September 6, 1985

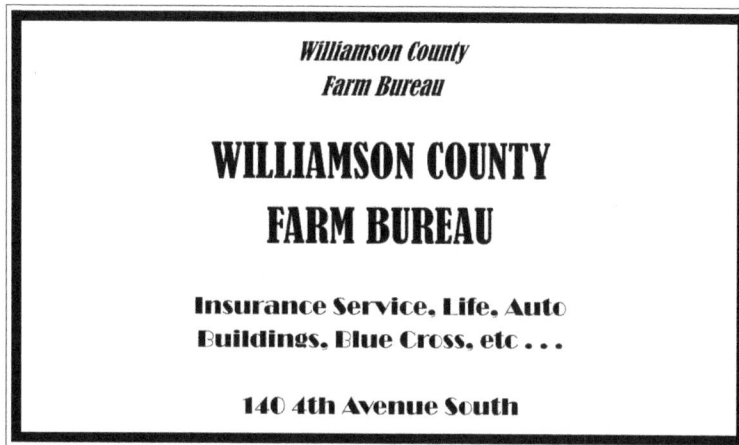

Mrs. Ehresman Succumbs At 72

Mrs. William B. Ehresman of Triune died May 30 at a Nashville hospital after a short illness. She was 72 years of age.

Mrs. Ehresman was the former Woodson Johnson, daughter of the late James K. and Ardeen McCanless Johnson. She was born and raised in the Triune area and attended David Lipscomb College in Nashville.

Mrs. Ehresman was a member of the Arrington Church of Christ.

She is survived by her husband, Mr. Ehresman; a son, Bryan Ehresman; a granddaughter, Paula Marie Ehresman, all of

Triune; sisters, Miss Bessie Johnson and Mrs. Hiram Holtsford, both of Lawrenceburg; brothers, James E. Johnson of Chattanooga and Truman Johnson of Triune; several nieces and nephews.

Services were held at the Waller Chapel in Nolensville Monday at 1:30 p.m. by Gilbert Shaffer of Lewisburg and William Vermillion. Interment was in the Woodlawn Cemetery and nephews served as pallbearers.

Waller and Company was in charge of the arrangements.

– The Review-Appeal, June 4, 1970

Mrs. T. Y. English

Mrs. T. Y. English is truly one of Williamson County's excellent citizens. A native of Williamson County, she is the daughter of J. B. and Addie Sweeney Parks and prior to her marriage to Mr. English in 1908 she was Miss Bessie Parks. Mrs. English lives in the house on Columbia Pike where she and Mr. English went to housekeeping when they married. She loves farming and since Mr. English's death in 1963 she has kept the farm and enjoys it. She spends a great deal of her time raising chickens and flowers and sews, specializing in little girls' dresses.

Mrs. English taught school in Williamson County for twenty-seven years. Living with her is her daughter, Miss Agnes English, who also taught school in Georgia for a number of years but has retired to be with her mother. Church work is one of Mrs. English's sincere interests. She is a member of the Franklin First United Methodist Church, an active member of the Women's Society of Christian Service and taught in the primary department of the Church School for many years, and is now a member of the Women's Bible Class. She is also a member of the Woman's Christian Temperance Union and the Douglas Home Demonstration Club.

Despite the fact that she is 86 years of age she is active, alert and interested in all affairs of the county, state and nation.

As Published in *The Review-Appeal* on August 29, 1968

MARY ELIZABETH PARKS ENGLISH
1882 - 1974

Funeral services for Mrs. Bessie Parks English were held at 3 p.m. Sunday at Franklin Memorial Chapel by the Rev. Eugene Gober and Tom Wallace. Mrs. English, 92, died Sept. 21 at a local nursing home.

A native of the county, she was the daughter of the late Joseph Barnett and [Addie] Ophelia Sweeney Parks and the widow of T. Y. English.

She was an active member of the First United Methodist Church and worked on the hand-made items for the annual bazaar in recent years.

Survivors include a daughter, Miss Agnes English, and several nieces and nephews.

Interment was in Mt. Hope Cemetery.

Pallbearers were Fulton Greer, Dr. Fulton Greer, Robert Russell, Freelin West, Bill Herbert, Robert Pitner, Reedy Edgmon, Robert White, Carl Smithson, Jerry Church, Fulton Beasley, Harvey Parks, Horace Edgmon and Joe Holshouser.

Franklin Memorial Chapel was in charge of the arrangements.

– The Review-Appeal, September 26, 1974

Terrill Yokley English

Franklin, Tennessee — Terrill Yokley English, 86, died yesterday in Harris Convalescent Home here.

Services will be held at 2 p.m. today at Franklin Memorial Chapel. Burial will be at Mount Hope Cemetery.

English was a native of Giles County .

He was a Methodist.

Survivors include his widow, Mrs. Bessie Parks English, and a daughter, Miss Agnes English, Dalton, Georgia.

– The Tennessean, March 18, 1963

Portrait of An Excellent Citizen

Robert Chester Finley, Jr.

Robert C. Finley, Jr., is a prominent farmer of Buckner Lane and is magistrate for the 11th Civil District. He was a charter member of the Williamson County NFO *[National Farmers Organization]* and is now serving as president of the local chapter. He is also treasurer of the Sixth District NFO, and was recently named first secretary for the state organization. He serves as key community man for the ASCS *[Agricultural Stabilization and Conservation Service]*.

He is a member of the Board of Trustees and assistant Sunday School superintendent of the Thompson Station Methodist Church. Mr. Finley is a member of the Farm Bureau and the Franklin Rotary Club. He is originally from Finley in Dyer County and has lived in Williamson County for seven years. He is married to the former Miss Gerry Pentecost and they have one son, Jim.

Mr. Finley attended the University of Tennessee and served in the Coast Guard in World War II.

As Published in *The Review-Appeal* on April 18, 1968

Robert Chester Finley, Jr.
1919 - 2006

Bob Finley

Lamasco, Kentucky – Graveside services for Bob Finley, 86, of Lamasco will be at 11 a.m. Thursday in Lamasco Church Cemetery with the Rev. John Reilly officiating.

Mr. Finley died at 1:12 p.m. Monday at Hilltop Nursing Home in Kuttaway.

He was a member of Ogden Memorial United Methodist Church in Princeton, Princeton Elks Club and the American Legion. Mr. Finley was a graduate of Dyersburg High School and the University of Tennessee.

Surviving are his wife, Gerry P. Finley; one son, Jim Finley of Lamasco; and two grandchildren, Ashley Finley and Taylor Finley, both of Lamasco.

He was preceded in death by five sisters and one infant brother. His parents were Robert Chester Finley Sr. and Effie Wheeler Finley.

Friends may call after 4 p.m. today at Morgan's Funeral Home in Princeton.

Expressions of sympathy may take the form of contributions to Ogden Memorial United Methodist Church, 305 W. Main St., Princeton, KY 42445; or the United Methodist Children's Home, P.O. Box 749, Versailles, KY 40383.

– The Paducah Sun (Kentucky), August 9, 2006

"Mr. Finley grew up in Finley, Tennessee, a small town in Dyer County which was named for his grandfather. When he bought the land here, he didn't realize what a choice piece of property he was getting. He purchased two adjacent farms, the Beaumont Anderson place and the O. O. Porter property. He knew he was getting good rich soil but after he had farmed it a while he realized that the farms all around him had rocky areas. With the exception of one small area he doesn't have a rock on his property.

"Bob Finley's roots are in the soil. He was reared on a farm and his ambition has always been to own a large acreage of land all in one tract with his house on the tract.

Now he has achieved that goal for since January 1, 1961, he has owned 500 acres south of Buckner Lane ... and they built a lovely home and Bob Finley can see the house from any field he owns."

— Derry Carlisle, *Who's Who in Williamson County*, Rick Warwick, ed., originally published in *The Review-Appeal*, January 7, 1966.

Mrs. S. M. Fleming

Four score and ten years ago tomorrow, March 24, 1877, to be exact, Cynthia Graham Cannon was born in Williamson County and she has lived here for 90 consecutive years. From this very date Franklin and Williamson County have been better places in which to live because of the radiant sunshine she has brought into our midst.

She was married to Sam M. Fleming May 1, 1903 and to their union were born three children. Mrs. Andrew Mizell, Mrs. Rudolph Farrar, and Sam M. Fleming, Jr. Her husband, who died a number of years ago, was one of the most prominent and influential citizens of Williamson County.

However, it is Miss Cynthia whom we salute and to whom we are today paying tribute. A woman of strong character and principles, she is never hesitant to express her firm convictions on any subject. She has in the past, and even today, given wise counsel to scores of people in all walks of life throughout the county. She has never been too busy to help a friend or acquaintance and today she is active and ready to visit the sick and those in sorrow. Her home is always open to everyone.

Miss Cynthia is a devout Christian and for more than fifty years has been active in the First Presbyterian Church in Franklin. She is a most charitable woman but nevertheless believes that people should work for their living and live within their means. She is extremely intolerant of laziness and of those who refuse to use their talents to the maximum. Conversely her charities include scores of people who have suffered misfortune and ill fate beyond their control.

The Review-Appeal salutes the "Number One Lady Citizen" of Franklin and Williamson County, extends to her our best wishes with the sincere hope she will continue to enjoy good health plus all of the good things in life which she so richly deserves.

As Published in The Review-Appeal on March 23, 1967

CYNTHIA GRAHAM CANNON FLEMING
1877 - 1969

Mrs. Sam Fleming
County's 'First Lady Citizen' Dies

Mrs. Sam M. Fleming, acclaimed as Franklin and Williamson County's "Number One Lady Citizen," died Monday afternoon at the age of 91 at Medicenter in Nashville where she had been a patient in recent months. She would have observed her 92nd birthday Monday, March 24.

Funeral services were held Tuesday afternoon at Franklin Memorial Chapel. Dr. James Cogswell, pastor of First Presbyterian Church of Franklin, and Dr. Walter R. Courtenay, minister of First Presbyterian Church of Nashville officiated. Burial was in Mr. Hope Cemetery.

Mrs. Fleming was the former Cynthia Graham Cannon and was affectionately known as "Miss Cynthia." She was the descendant of pioneer families of Williamson County, members of whom were prominent in the history of this county and the State of Tennessee.

Her great-grandfather, Newton Cannon, and her great-uncle, Aaron V. Brown, both served as governors of Tennessee. Her father, Newton Cannon, joined the Army of the Confederacy at the age of 15 and served as a sergeant under General Nathan B. Forrest. He was paroled with the famed general at Gainesville, Alabama, 30 days after the surrender at Appomattox.

Her mother was the former Jennie B. McEwen, daughter of Col. John B. McEwen, whose family was also prominent in the settlement of the county.

Mrs. Fleming was educated in Franklin's schools and was graduated from the old Belmont College [for Young Women], forerunner of Ward-Belmont.

In 1903 she was married to Mr. Fleming, whose family was also pioneer stock here.

All Williamson Countians and indeed her countless friends elsewhere suffered an irreparable loss in the death this week of Mrs. S. M. ("Miss Cynthia") Fleming.

This newspaper has previously referred to Miss Cynthia as the "Number One Lady Citizen" of Franklin and Williamson County, and in this time of sadness we reaffirm that designation and remind ourselves that this rare, gracious and strong lady left a mark on all who were privileged to know her.

She would have been 92 years of age next Monday, March 24, and *The Review-Appeal* had planned to send her a telegram expressing fond congratulations on her long and inspirational life. We shall miss her next Monday and in the years to come.

Miss Cynthia was a woman of tremendously strong character who believed in helping those who were ill or had suffered misfortune. Her warm heart and generosity come immediately to mind any time her name is mentioned. Yet she was a strong-willed lady who had no patience with laziness or weakness of character.

One of the human failings she disapproved of most strongly was the failure of a person to use his talents to the maximum. Miss Cynthia certainly used her talents wisely and generously.

She was active in the First Presbyterian Church of Franklin for more than 50 years and was in every sense one of the finest products of pioneer values. Her lifetime and her influence spanned large portions of two centuries.

As a child she saw the heartbreak and poverty of the Reconstruction Era which lingered on in 1877 at the time she was born. Her family had fought valiantly for the Confederacy and she learned at an early age the pride and dignity that go with having done the best you can, though you may not have won.

In a very real sense Miss Cynthia was a product of the soil. From the earliest days her family had been landowners, proud of this region, optimistic about its future.

She saw the Spanish-American War, World Wars I and II, the Korean War and the still unsettled Vietnam War and she saw good times and bad. Her firm Christian faith supported her through them all and remained an inspiration to the last.

Her husband, Sam M. Fleming, Sr., was a successful and highly respected businessman, one of the county's outstanding citizens, and while many younger residents will not remember him, they are aware of the lasting mark that he made on this area. The character and integrity of this outstanding couple are perhaps best illustrated in the successful lives of their three children, Mrs. Rudolph Farrar, Mrs. Andrew Mizell, and Sam M. Fleming, Jr.

Any parents would take pride in children who became respected, substantial, worthwhile adults and unquestionably Miss Cynthia took special pride in the national and international banking fame achieved by her only son. No one can doubt that she was a continual source of inspiration to him throughout the years.

Few of us are granted so many years – 92 of them – in one county that we love and few of us could achieve so much if granted those extra years. In Miss Cynthia's case they were not nearly enough years for her type was a great and lovely sort of person who comes along but rarely. She will always be missed by those who knew her. – J.H.A.

– The Review-Appeal, March 20, 1969

Excellent Citizens and Notable Partings

Cliff Frensley

Cliff Frensley is owner of Dad and Lad Men's Shop and Frensley's Fashions on Main Street. He lives at 203 Avondale Drive with his wife, the former Miss Betty Dye and two children, David, 10 and Ann, 9. Mr. Frensley is a member of the First Methodist Church and is one of the Trustees. He is a treasurer of the Franklin Rotary Club and is a member of the Board of Mayor and Aldermen of the Town of Franklin.

As Published in *The Review-Appeal* on December 22, 1966

Former State Rep. Cliff Frensley dies, visitation Sunday, service Monday

Former State Representative A. C. "Cliff" Frensley, age 77, of Brentwood, died Nov. 12, 2010.

A retired clothier in Franklin for 45 years with National Stores, Dad and Lad, and Frensley Fashions, Frensley first entered politics as a former alderman in Franklin and then was state representative for 10 years from 1978-1988.

He was a former president of Franklin Noon Rotary Club, founder of Williamson County Republican Party, past president of the Williamson County — Franklin Chamber of Commerce and legislative liaison for Tennessee Department of Labor.

He was preceded in death by his wife, Betty Frensley and brother, Walker Frensley.

He is survived by his son, David Frensley, Hermitage, Tennessee; daughter, Ann Frensley Damron, Nashville; grandchildren, Tiffany Frensley and Luke Damron; brothers, Bill Frensley and John Wallace Frensley; and sister, Imogene French.

Funeral service will be conducted 10 a.m. Monday, Nov. 15, 2010 at First United Methodist Church of Franklin, Dr. Lynn Hill officiating. Interment Williamson Memorial Gardens. Active pallbearers will be Bill Browne, Grant Frensley, Ben Vernon, Mike Harkreader, Luke Damron, Andy Miller, Ralph Brown, Anthony Lowry, Steve Sheehan and Scott Whitson. Honorary pallbearers will be Elbert Heithcock, Doug Ladd, Mike Jones and Larry Beasley.

Memorials may be made to the Building Fund of First United Methodist Church, 143 5th Ave. S., Franklin, Tennessee 37064.

Visitation will be 4-8 p.m. Sunday at Williamson Memorial Funeral Home and one hour prior to service at the church.

— The Williamson Herald, November 13, 2010

Mrs. Edward A. Fryer

Mrs. Edward A. Fryer, a resident of Beech Creek Road, is the magistrate for the Seventh Civil District of Williamson County and is the first woman to be elected to the Quarterly County Court. She is librarian at Montgomery Bell Academy and teaches in the Graduate School of Library Science at George Peabody College. She is active in a number of organizations and was a charter member of the Friends of the Williamson County Public Library. She has served as president of that organization and is also on the Board of Directors for the Public Library. She is an active member of Harpeth Presbyterian Church. The former Miss Libby Zerfoss, she is the daughter of Dr. and Mrs. T.B. Zerfoss, Sr., of Nashville. She is the mother of two children, Miss Martha Leslie Hailey and Bill Fryer.

As Published in *The Review-Appeal* on September 7, 1967

ELIZABETH LESLIE ZERFOSS FRYER
1922 - 2005

Elizabeth Leslie Zerfoss Fryer, Williamson [County], September 24, 2005; Born September 14, 1922 in Nashville, daughter of Drs. Kate Savage and Thomas B. Zerfoss. Wife of the late Edward Allen Fryer.

Survived by her children, Martha Hailey DuBose of Wartrace, Tennessee, and William S. Fryer of Spring Hill, Tennessee; grandchildren, Kate DuBose Tomassi of Hoboken, New Jersey, Polly DuBose of Sydney, Australia, Christopher Fryer, and Geoffrey Fryer, both of Franklin Tennessee; and brother, Dr. Thomas B. Zerfoss II of Nashville.

An alumna of Vanderbilt University, with a master's degree in library science from George Peabody College, she worked for the Nashville Public Library and was head librarian at Battle Ground Academy, Montgomery Bell Academy, and Franklin Road Academy.

She was also active in local and state politics the first woman county court member in Williamson County and first woman president of the Magistrates Association of Tennessee, first female appointed to the Tennessee Alcoholic Beverage Commission, and first woman president of the National Conference of State Liquor Administrators.

She served on the U.S. Department of Education's Appeal Board and was appointed to the National Advisory Council on Women's Education Programs by President Ford in 1976.

She was a member of Delta Delta Delta Women's fraternity, Junior League of Nashville, DAR, YWCA, and Centennial Club.

A dedicated supporter of women's issues, especially related to education, she received the Molly Todd Cup for service to the community from CABLE women's business and professional organization.

She was a member of Harpeth Presbyterian Church.

Services will be held at 11 a.m., Thursday, September 29 at Mount Olivet Funeral Home, with visitation beginning at 10 a.m.

In lieu of flowers, contributions may be made to the Peak-Zerfoss Memorial Scholarship Fund. Bedford Loan & Deposit Bank. P.O. Box 276, Bedford KY 40006 (attn.: Dawnice Westrick). Mount Olivet Funeral Home and Cemetery (615) 255-4193.

– The Tennessean, September 28, 2005

"In Libby Zerfoss Fryer's youth, a lady's name was supposed to appear in the paper only three times — when she was born, when she married and when she died.

"Fryer, 72, has had a lot more publicity than that, as the first woman elected to the Williamson County Court and first on the state's Alcoholic Beverage Commission.

"Yet no one would question her being a lady."

— Lisa Benavides, "Hurrah and Vote for Suffrage; Documentary to Chronicle State Role in Vote Fight," *The Tennessean*, October 8, 1994.

Clifford Leroy Gardner

Clifford LeRoy Gardner has been administrator of the Williamson County Hospital since 1957. He and his wife, the former Miss Amelia Jameson, live in Maury County and Mr. Gardner commutes to the hospital every day.

Mr. Gardner is a member of the Franklin Rotary Club and the Williamson County Chamber of Commerce. He serves as Red Cross Chapter Chairman and is a director in the UGF *[United Givers Fund]*.

He attends the Fourth Avenue Church of Christ in Franklin.

As Published in *The Review-Appeal* on June 1, 1967

CLIFFORD LEROY GARDNER
1907 - 1970

C. L. Gardner, Hospital Head 12 Years, Dies

Clifford LeRoy Gardner, administrator of the Williamson County Hospital for twelve years, died unexpectedly at his home in the Beech Grove community in Maury County Thursday morning, Dec. 3. He was 62 years of age.

Mr. Gardner began working with the hospital during the construction of the original building in 1957 and was administrator until he retired April 30. The operation of the hospital was acclaimed one of the most successful of the area, and Mr. Gardner guided its expansion and growth through one major addition to the building and several departmental and laboratory extensions. He continued in an unofficial capacity after his retirement to assist in present construction of a major addition to the building.

Before coming to Williamson County, he was assistant administrator of the Maury County Hospital for several years and prior to that time he was associated with the Home Owners Loan Corporation of Memphis.

He was a native of Williamson County, the son of the late David A. and Rosa Horton Gardner. He was a member of the Church of Christ and a veteran of World War II, having served with the Army in the European Theatre. He was a member of the Franklin Rotary Club and served as president in 1964.

He is survived by his wife, Mrs. Amelia Jameson Gardner; three sisters, Mrs. Cecil Allen and Mrs. Jerry Summers, both of Nashville, and Mrs. Herman Adair of Madison; four brothers, W. H. Gardner, Emerson Gardner and Grady Gardner, all of this city, and Herman Gardner of Nashville; and several nieces and nephews.

Funeral services were conducted Friday at 2 p.m. at the Oakes and Nichols Funeral home chapel in Columbia by Houston Marshall and Myron Keith. Interment was in the Alexander Cemetery. Active pallbearers were Ed Eubanks, Bill Akin, Frank McBride, J. C. Inman, James Brewer, Paul Ellis, Seth Sparkman, Charles McMeen, G. T. Curry and Bobby Russell. Oakes and Nichols Funeral Home was in charge of the arrangements.

– The Review-Appeal, December 10, 1970

"After his discharge [from the U.S. Army], Mr. Gardner returned to the States and started farming. His wife, the former Amelia Jameson, had been making her home with her parents on their farm on the Carter's Creek Pike near Sparkman's Store in Maury County. They couldn't find anyone to run the farm for them so Mr. Gardner said he would just take over. He was forced to stop in 1953 because of heart trouble, and it was then he started at the hospital in Columbia."

— Derry Carlisle, *Who's Who in Williamson County*, Rick Warwick, ed., originally published in *The Review-Appeal*, June 13, 1957.

Excellent Citizens and Notable Partings

Dr. Raymond Albert Gathmann

Dr. Raymond Albert Gathmann is a veterinarian and has practiced in Williamson County for the past 28 years. He was born and educated in Iowa. He served in the United States Air Force during World War II, and was discharged with the rank of Major. Following his discharge he came to Franklin where he met and married Miss Bertha Mai [Maye] Johnson. They have three children, Rita, William and John, and reside in West End.

Dr. Gathmann is a Rotarian and has served the local club as secretary and president. He is also a member of American Legion Post No. 5, Hiram Lodge No. 7 of the Masonic Order and is past president of the Tennessee State Veterinarian Medical Association. He is past senior warden of St. Paul's Episcopal Church of which he is a member.

As Published in *The Review-Appeal* on August 17, 1967

RAYMOND ALBERT GATHMANN
1912-1998

Raymond Albert Gathmann died Sunday, May 24, at Williamson Medical Center.

Dr. Gathmann was a resident of Franklin and was a Veterinarian. He was a member of St. Paul's Episcopal Church and was an Army Veteran of World War II.

He was a graduate of Iowa State College of Veterinary Medicine, past president of Franklin Noon Rotary Club, past president of the Tennessee Veterinary Medical Association, a life Member of the American Veterinary Medical Association, and a 50-year member of the Franklin Hiram No. 7 Masonic Lodge.

Survivors include his wife, Mrs. Bertha Maye Johnson Gathmann of Franklin; one son, William Albert Gathmann of Antioch; one daughter, Rita Rae Gathmann of Franklin; and sister-in-law, Mrs. A. C. Gathmann of Jefferson City, Missouri.

Funeral services will be held on Wednesday, May 27, at St. Paul's Episcopal Church in Franklin with the Rev. Robert Cowperthwaite officiating.

Burial will be in Mount Hope Cemetery. Visitation will be one hour prior to the time of service at the church.

Active pallbearers will be William Carter Conway, Joe Baugh Jr., John Amos Baugh, Frank Fessey Baugh, William B. Rainey and Livingfield More. Honorary pallbearers will be Franklin Noon Rotary Club, members of the Tennessee Veterinary Medical Association, Coffee Club, Malcolm Gibbs, Col. Hensley Williams, Bob Ewin, Bob White, Lamar Poovey, Steve Lawrence and Bryan Ross.

– The Review-Appeal, May 27, 1998

Veterinarian Raymond Albert Gathmann began his practice in Williamson County in an era of dusty back roads, big farms and midnight calf deliveries. "There was a little cowboy in him," said district attorney Joe Baugh, who was Gathmann's godson. '"I can remember him out in the fields having to rope a cow or two." "He was the Dr. Guffee of veterinarians," said Baugh, referring to Dr. Harry Guffee... "Not only did he go up and down the back roads of the county, but he would go to the back end of farms to treat a cow or deliver a calf." Baugh said. "I still am amazed by the care and time he showed to every animal he ever treated for us.'

His career in Williamson County, interrupted by World War II, spanned 55 years during which time he served tenures as president of the Tennessee Veterinary Medical Association and president of the Franklin Noon Rotary. "There's no telling how many freebies he did," said county historian Rick Warwick.

— "Gathmann was Vet with a Little Cowboy in Him," *The Tennessean*, May 26, 1998.

Editor's Note: Dr. and Mrs. Gathmann and their family lived in the beautiful historic home originally named Boxmere on West Main Street in Franklin. They purchased it in 1953, and it was home to the Gathmanns until July of 2017, when their daughter, Rita Rae Gathmann, died. The home was also notable for the old red oak which stood as a witness to the Battle of Franklin. The old tree has since been lost to disease and time and was removed in 2005.

Excellent Citizens and Notable Partings

Portrait of An Excellent Citizen

Mrs. Z. B. Gentry

A resident of Franklin for more than sixty years is Mrs. Z. B. Gentry who lives on Third Avenue North. She is a native of Maury County, but came to Franklin to live when she was married to Mr. Gentry, and was for many years an employee of the Southern Bell Telephone Company. Mrs. Gentry was, before her marriage, Miss Gertrude Butner. Despite her 81 years, she remains active and does her household chores daily. Her large family of children and grandchildren, most of whom see her every day, keeps her young in spirit and ever interested in current events. The boys in her family, sons and grandsons, all played football in high school and she is frequently seen attending the games at local schools.

Mrs. Gentry has three daughters and four sons. They are Mrs. Hardy (Jessie Lee) Lavender, of Nashville, Mrs. Joe (Louise) Binkley, Mrs. Baxter (Dorothy) Ewing, both of Franklin, Dan Gentry, who followed in his father's footsteps and is an employee of the South Central Bell Telephone Company, William who is with the Franklin Laundry, and Jimmy and Bobby Gentry, members of the faculty of Battle Ground Academy. She has 20 grandchildren and nineteen great grandchildren. Mrs. Gentry attends the Fourth Avenue Church of Christ.

As Published in *The Review-Appeal* on August 22, 1968

GOLDIE GERTRUDE BUTNER GENTRY
1888 - 1980

Morning services were held Saturday for Goldie Gertrude Butner Gentry who died at 92 on March 13 in Applewood Nursing Home.

Mrs. Gentry, who previously resided on Hillsboro Road in Franklin, was the widow of the late Z. B. Gentry and a native of Coffee County, Tennessee. She was a member of the Church of Christ and a housewife.

Mrs. Gentry has three daughters living in Franklin: Mrs. William (Louise) Binkley, Mrs. Baxter (Dorothy) Ewing, and Mrs. Wilbur (Frances) Binkley. Another daughter, Mrs. Hardy (Jessie Lee) Lavender, lives in Nashville. All four sons live in Franklin, William M. Gentry, Dan T. Gentry, James C. Gentry, and Bobby Gentry. She has 20 grandchildren and 28 great-grandchildren and six great-great-grandchildren.

Myron Keith and Rev. Stuart Nunnally officiated at the funeral service and interment was in Mt. Hope Cemetery. Pallbearers were Jack Lavender, and David, Danny, Zeb, Jim, Allen, Scott, and Bob Gentry.

Honorary Pallbearers were Claude Alexander, Jr., Elbert Heithcock, Richard Sullivan, Dr. Eugene Walcott, Dr. Robert Sullivan, Dr. Oscar Noel, Lonnie Burchett, Waldron [Waldon] Smithson, Congressman Robin Beard, Marshall Liggett, Joe Pinkerton, Bill Garrett, Ralph Duke, Jamie Locke, William Miller, John McCord, William B. Brown, Bobby Evans, Henry Cannon, Carlton Flatt, Grady Sweeney, Charlie Reed, Charles Culbertson, W. C. Yates, C. B. Harmon, Eddie Harmon, Cliff Frensley, Jack Lunn, Robert Sewell, J. M. Sewell, Robert Richardson, Thomas W. Coke, Hudson Alexander, Henry Greene, Owen Rains and the elders and deacons of the Fourth Avenue Church of Christ.

Franklin Memorial Chapel made all arrangements.

— The Review-Appeal, March 18, 1980

"The first War Department telegram I ever saw delivered came by bicycle up Fifth Avenue, in front of the Methodist Church. We were living on the next block, and Mama had a blue star up for my brother David. Those people who had a blue star in their window would pray, 'Please don't stop here.' ... He passed our house and turned up by Mrs. Josephine Wirt, who lived on the corner. ... Everybody knew then that something had happened to Mack Terry.

"Not too long after that telegram came to the Terry's house, another telegram was brought to Franklin. It was springtime, and people were out in their yards. They saw the messenger coming, and they watched him come up to our house and stop. David had been on a bridge over the Minturno River in Italy. He had been stringing communications wire when the Germans shelled the bridge. He died on April 29, 1944, on the way to the field hospital. He was twenty-one years old. ... Mama took down the blue star she had put in the window for David and replaced it with a gold star, which signified his death. ... The anguish that Mama went through happened to mothers all over America, and they never received the recognition they should have gotten."

— An American Life, by Jimmy Gentry

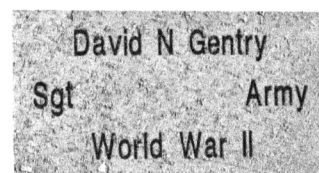

UNITED STATES

GOLD STAR MOTHERS

3¢ POSTAGE 3¢

David N Gentry
Sgt   Army
World War II

Portrait of An Excellent Citizen

Henry Goodpasture

Henry Goodpasture lives in the Sixth District. His home "Old Town" on Old Natchez Trace, is one of the historic sites of Williamson County. He is an attorney with offices in Nashville. Mr. Goodpasture is a past president of the Kiwanis and Optimist clubs and serves on the Board of Trustees for a number of institutions and organizations, including the Children's Museum, Salvation Army, Monroe Harding Children's Home, and Camp NaCoMe. He is the current president of the Tennessee Historical Society. He is a member of Westminster Presbyterian Church which he serves as elder and teacher of an adult Sunday School Class. Mr. Goodpasture and his wife, the former Miss Virginia Puryear, have two sons, Jim, who lives at home, and Dr. McKennie Goodpasture of Richmond, Virginia.

As Published in *The Review-Appeal* on April 20, 1967

Henry Goodpasture, 101,
Memorial Services Monday
By Sheila Burke, Staff Writer

Henry Goodpasture, a Nashville attorney for 55 years who helped lead the creation of the Harpeth Valley Utilities District, died Thursday. He was 101.

Mr. Goodpasture served on the Williamson County Court. He also was involved in the organization of the utility district, which today provides water to much of Williamson County and parts of Davidson County.

Mr. Goodpasture also served on the governing boards, and sometimes as president, of civic groups, including the Nashville Chamber of Commerce, Nashville Optimist Club, Cumberland Science Museum, Salvation Army, the Monroe Harding Children's Home, Downtown Nashville Kiwanis Club, Tennessee Historical Society, the English Speaking Union and the Centennial Club.

He and his wife, Virginia Puryear, lived for more than 30 years in Williamson County in the historic home "Old Town" on the Old Natchez Road.

Much of Mr. Goodpasture's energy went into the Presbyterian Church U.S. which is now part of the Presbyterian Church (U.S.A.)

He was a member of the Westminster Presbyterian Church in Nashville, where he taught Bible class and served as an elder. He was a key elder in the construction of three Presbyterian churches in Nashville: Westminster, Second, and St. Andrews.

A graduate of the law school at Cumberland University in Lebanon in 1928, he practiced law with the firm Goodpasture, Carpenter, Dale, Woods and Sasser.

Survivors, in addition to his wife, include: sons, Henry McKennie Goodpasture, Richmond, Virginia, and Jim Goodpasture, Frankfort, Kentucky; two grandchildren and a great-grandchild.

Memorial services will be at 11 a.m. Monday at Westminster Presbyterian Church. Roesch-Patton-Austin-Bracey and Charlton Funeral Services is in charge.

In lieu of flowers, donations may be made to The Jim Goodpasture Fund for Ministries in behalf of Persons with Mental Retardation and Their Families, Union Theological Seminary-PSCE, 3401 Brook Road, Richmond, Virginia 23227.

— The Tennessean, November 6, 1999

* * *

* * *

Bobby J. Goodwin

Bobby J. Goodwin is Mayor of the City of Fairview. He lives at Fairview with his wife, the former Miss Lonia Allen, of Lyles, Tennessee, and their two children, Robert Anthony, age 8 and Teresa Gail, age 7, both student's at Fairview Elementary School.

Mr. Goodwin is a member of the Fairview Church of Christ where he is teacher of the 7th, 8th and 9th grades in Sunday School. He is a past president of the Fairview Lions Club and now serves as secretary. He is also a member of the Booster Club, First District Democratic Club, Parent-Teacher Association and the Planning Commission.

As Published in *The Review-Appeal* on March 30, 1967

Bobby J. Goodwin, age 83 of Clarksville, passed away on Monday, February 23, 2015, at Gateway Medical Center.

A celebration of life service will be held at 11 a.m. Thursday, February 26, 2015 at the chapel of McReynolds-Nave & Larson Funeral Home with Bro. Steve Kirby and Bro. Roy Goodmiller officiating.

Burial will follow at Harpeth Hills Memory Gardens, Nashville, Tennessee.

The family will receive friends from 4-8 p.m. on Wednesday and from 10 a.m. until the hour of service on Thursday at the funeral home.

Bobby was born on December 9, 1931, the son of the late Harris Lee Goodwin, Sr. and Gertrude Boone Goodwin. In addition to his parents he is preceded in death by his brother, Harris Goodwin Jr., and his sister Charlene Zoet.

He was a U.S. Army Korean War Veteran in the 73rd Tank Battalion. He was a member of Shiloh Church of Christ for 40 years where he served as a deacon. Bobby was a Sunday School teacher at Shiloh Church of Christ and Fairview Church of Christ.

He is survived by his wife of 57 years, Lonia Goodwin; sons, Tony Goodwin and his wife Rita, and Rick Goodwin; daughter, Teresa Walt and her husband Bill; granddaughters, Megan Mangone and her husband Alex and Paisley Goodwin; grandson, Jazz Goodwin; sisters Billie Spencer, Patsy Mangrum, Brenda Hardin; and Jenelle Pinkerton; very special nieces and nephews.

Family and Friends will serve as pallbearers.

Arrangements are in the care of McReynolds-Nave & Larson Funeral home, (931) 647-3371. NaveFuneralHomes.com

— The Leaf-Chronicle (Clarksville), February 25, 2015

Frank Gray, Jr.

Frank Gray, Jr., has served as judge of the United States District Court for Nashville, Columbia, and Cookeville since he was sworn in November 27, 1961, following appointment by the late President John F. Kennedy. He was Mayor of Franklin for 14 years prior to his appointment. Judge Gray's wife is the former Miss Faye Anders of Asheville, North Carolina, and they reside on Lewisburg Avenue. He is a member of First Presbyterian Church where he is an inactive elder and for a number of years was a member of the Franklin Rotary Club.

As Published in *The Review-Appeal* on December 29, 1966

WILLIAM FRANK GRAY, JR.
1908 - 1978

Retired U.S. Judge Frank Gray, 70, Dies

Retired U.S. District Court Judge Frank Gray Jr. died of cancer today in Williamson County Hospital.

Judge Gray, 70, had been hospitalized intermittently in Nashville and Franklin since June.

After nearly 16 years on the federal bench, Judge Gray had assumed senior status in 1977, giving him a reduced caseload and allowing him to select the cases he wished to hear.

Thomas A. Wiseman Jr., a Nashville attorney, was sworn in last week to succeed him.

Services will be held at 3p.m. Thursday at First Presbyterian Church in Franklin. The Rev. Ned Beckes, pastor of First Presbyterian, and Dr. Kenneth Phifer of New Orleans will officiate.

Burial will be in Mount Hope Cemetery, Franklin.

The body is at Franklin Memorial Chapel. It will be at the church for an hour before the time of services.

Judge Gray, a resident of Franklin, was admitted to Vanderbilt Hospital on June 29 for treatment of a brain tumor and lung cancer. He returned home about a month ago but continued trips to Vanderbilt for cobalt treatment.

About three weeks ago, he took a turn for the worse and entered Williamson County Hospital. About a week ago, he developed pneumonia. He remained hospitalized until his death about 4:15 a.m.

The former Franklin mayor was appointed a judge of the Middle District of Tennessee in 1961 by President John F. Kennedy. He became chief judge of the Middle District in 1970.

Judge Gray's most publicized opinion in recent years was his ruling that Tennessee State University and the University of Tennessee at Nashville must merge to correct racial imbalances and constitutional violations. But the opinion of which he was proudest, he said in a 1977 Nashville Banner interview, was the one that struck down as unconstitutional Tennessee's residency requirement for voter registration.

The opinion, which Judge Gray wrote for a three-judge panel, was affirmed by the U.S. Supreme Court in 1972.

He said his most memorable case was his association with some phases of the trial of International Teamsters Union President, Jimmy Hoffa.

"I tried a lot of pre-trial motions before the case went to Chattanooga, and I tried some of those who were indicted for tampering with a jury."

Judge Gray became chief judge when U.S. District Court Judge William E. Miller was elevated to the 6th U.S. Circuit Court of Appeals. The vacancy was filled by Judge L. Clure Morton.

Judge Gray gained a reputation for criticizing lawyers and witnesses when he felt they deserved it.

He was known for handing out stiff sentences to convicted drug dealers. He said he didn't hesitate to give a substantial sentence to "a genuine drug-pusher who is in it solely for the profit motive."

Judge Gray was regarded by most people in the legal community as a fair judge. "I've certainly tried to be fair," he said, "if this means you have a feeling of compassion for the victims of crime, and for some offenders."

Before becoming judge, he was mayor of Franklin for 14 years and was active in politics for many years.

Judge Gray was named outstanding mayor of Tennessee in 1957 by the Tennessee Municipal League, which he served as a director.

The Franklin native and son of a druggist plunged into politics while the ink was still damp on his law school diploma and before he was old enough to vote.

After graduation from the former Cumberland University Law School in Lebanon in 1928, he campaigned for Al Smith, the democratic nominee for president.

"We Democrats carried Williamson County for Al Smith when most of the other counties went the other way," he once recalled proudly.

Judge Gray bowed out as mayor after the late U.S. Senator Estes Kefauver and former U.S. Senator Albert Gore recommended his appointment as judge to President Kennedy.

His mayoral administration was extremely active in the recruitment of industry.

When Judge Gray took over as mayor in 1947, the town had only one antiquated fire truck, no sewage disposal plant, few well-paved streets and an inadequate water supply. City offices didn't own a single typewriter and had only one hand operated adding machine.

When he left office, Franklin had a modern sewage disposal plant, modern fire equipment, an adequate water supply, and many miles of paved streets and many other improvements.

Judge Gray had served as chairman of the Municipal League's Committee on Fringe Areas for three years. The committee pushed through several laws in the legislature dealing with the problems of urban growth.

That legislation included the 1955 annexation law and the 1957 metropolitan government enabling act.

After that first taste of politics in 1928, Judge Gray became an auditor in the state comptroller's office in 1933. Then he went to work for the former Federal Resettlement Administration in 1936.

As an employee of the agency's investigation division, he was stationed in Birmingham, then in Chicago and Washington.

In 1940, he returned to Birmingham as special agent in charge of the resettlement agency's office there.

Eager to start practicing law, Judge Gray resigned his federal job in 1944 and opened his law office in Franklin.

"I returned in time to be named as an elector for President Roosevelt's last race," he once said.

In 1960, Judge Gray was named campaign manager of Kefauver's successful race against Andrew T. "Tip" Taylor in the Senate primary.

It was while in Washington that he met the former Miss Faye Anders. They were married in 1941. She died in 1975.

Judge Gray married the former Mrs. Norma Winters in 1977.

He was a member of First Presbyterian Church.

Survivors besides his wife include a brother, Warren P. Gray, Nashville, and two nieces.

Memorial contributions may be made to the memorial fund of First Presbyterian Church or to cancer research at Vanderbilt Hospital.

– The Nashville Banner, September 6, 1978

"What I remember most about Uncle Frank is that he loved to entertain children with magic tricks. Even in his position as judge, he would often quell fears or help a child feel more relaxed by finding a quarter behind his or her ear, or by making something disappear." When asked where he learned how to perform such magic tricks, she quickly added, "He gave credit to Mr. E. J. Jordan, who was the general manager of the Belle Meade Theatre and ran a Saturday afternoon Happiness Club for children at the theater."

— Mary Ann Gray Tate, niece, February 23, 2020.

Rites Today for Mrs. Gray in Franklin

Service for Mrs. Faye Gray, wife of U.S. District Court Judge Frank Gray, Jr., will be at 2 p.m. today at the First Presbyterian Church in Franklin, conducted by Dr. Kenneth Phifer of New Orleans and the Rev. Timothy Croft.

Burial will be in Mount Hope Cemetery in Franklin. The body is at Franklin memorial Chapel.

Mrs. Gray died yesterday at St. Thomas Hospital after a long illness.

Mrs. Gray, a native of Asheville, N. C., was a daughter of Mr. and Mrs. Theodore Anders. She was graduated from the North Carolina State College for Women, and was employed in Washington, D. C., before her marriage to Gray in February 1941.

She was a member of the First Presbyterian Church and had been active in church work since moving to Franklin.

She was a founder of the Pull-Tight players in Franklin and was a member of the Allied Artists [Arts] Club, the Friends of Cheekwood, the Friends of the Williamson County Library and the Carter House chapter of the APTA [Association for the Preservation of Tennessee Antiquities].

In addition to her husband, she is survived by two sisters, Mrs. Thomas O'Neal of Washington and Mrs. Frank C. Glenn of Asheville.

The family has requested that, in lieu of flowers, donations be made to the special scholarship fund of the First Presbyterian Church in Franklin or to a charity.

Pallbearers will be James L. Buford, Walter O. Carlisle, Charles M. Gore, Asa H. Jewell, Marshall Liggett, Cletus W. McWilliams, William H. Miller and William R. Ormes.

— The Tennessean, November 20, 1975

Judge Gray's Mother Dies

FRANKLIN, Tenn. — Mrs. Frank Gray, Sr., 82, the mother of U.S. District Judge Frank Gray, Jr., died yesterday afternoon in Williamson County Hospital.

The body is at Franklin Memorial Chapel.

Services will be at 3 p.m. today at the First Presbyterian Church of Franklin, with the Rev. James A. Jones III officiating. Burial will be in Mt. Hope Cemetery.

Mrs. Gray was the former Mary Hall Phillips, a native of Columbia, Tennessee, and the daughter of the late William and Rebecca Carpenter Phillips. She was a graduate of the University of Nashville, now Peabody College.

She and Mr. Gray were married in 1907, and had made their home in Franklin since that time. He is the owner of Gray Drug Company.

Mrs. Gray was a member of First Presbyterian Church, and was active in the work of the women of the church. She was an active member and former president of the United Daughters of the Confederacy, Daughters of the American Revolution and the Magazine Club.

Survivors, in addition to her husband and Judge Gray, are another son, Warren P. Gray of Nashville, two grandchildren and one great-grandchild.

— The Tennessean, December 2, 1964

"Grandfather, Frank Gray, Sr., was a man of few words, a good listener, and was very supportive of new businesses opening on Main Street. He loved collecting cigar boxes to give to children as pencil boxes.

"He erected the Gray's Drug neon sign in 1956, against my grandmother's protestations that it was 'entirely too large.' But the sign is still here today and somewhat of a landmark in downtown Franklin."

— Mary Ann Gray Tate, granddaughter, February 23, 2020.

Portrait of An Excellent Citizen

William Frank Gray

Mr. Gray, a druggist for the past 62 years, is the senior partner in Gray Drug Company, with two stores in Franklin. He lives on Battle Avenue. His wife was the former Miss Mary Hall Phillips, and they have two sons. Frank, Jr., is Federal Court Judge, and Warren Gray is a senior vice president and cashier of the Third National Bank. Mr. Gray is a member of the First Presbyterian Church where he has served as an elder for 32 years. He is also a member of the Lions Club.

As Published in *The Review-Appeal* on March 9, 1967

Frank Gray, Druggist 62 Years, Dies

Frank Gray, Sr. one of Franklin's and Williamson County's most prominent citizens who was given a testimonial dinner, October 7, 1965, by the Williamson County Chamber of Commerce for his 60 years in business and community service, died Tuesday night at Baptist Hospital where he had surgery last Friday.

Funeral services will be held this (Thursday) morning at 10:30 at First Presbyterian Church. Dr. James A. Cogswell, minister of the church, and Dr. Kenneth Phifer of New Orleans, a former minister of the church, will officiate. Burial will be in Mt. Hope Cemetery.

Mr. Gray was a native of Williamson County and was the son of John Black Gray and Elizabeth Blythe Core Gray. In April 1907, he was married to Miss Mary Hall Phillips of Columbia, who died in December, 1964.

Mr. Gray, Franklin's oldest active businessman, had been in the drug business for 62 years and until a few months ago worked some of each day at the Main Street location of Gray Drug Company of which he was senior partner.

He was a charter member of the Lion's Club and in 1965 was named "Lion of the Year."

Mr. Gray was a member of the First Presbyterian Church and was an elder emeritus. He served the church as an officer for many years.

He was a director of Harpeth National Bank and was a member of the Board of Trustees of Battle Ground Academy.

Survivors include two sons, Frank Gray, Jr., U.S. District Judge, and Warren P. Gray of Nashville, senior vice-president of Third National Bank; a sister, Mrs. Eugene Hunter of Franklin; two granddaughters, Mrs. William M. Tate, Jr. and Mrs. John D. Lentz of Nashville, and one great-grand child.

Honorary pallbearers will be elders and deacons of First Presbyterian Church and officers and directors of Harpeth National Bank.

Active pallbearers will be William H. Miller, Ralph Duke, William J. Garrett, James C. Maupin, Dennis Johnson, David Cook, William Walton and Randall Wyatt.

In lieu of flowers, donations may be made to First Presbyterian Church's scholarship fund and the American Cancer Society.

Franklin Memorial Chapel is in charge.

– The Review-Appeal, September 7, 1967

Curtis C. Green

Curtis C. Green has lived in Franklin since he was 5 years old and is a graduate of Battle Ground Academy. He lives on Columbia Avenue with his wife, the former Miss Seval Jordan. He is owner of Roberts & Green Real Estate and Insurance Company on Main Street.

Civic minded and interested in development, he is a member of the Franklin Real Estate Board, Williamson County Planning Commission and the Board of Equalization. He is also a member of Franklin Lions Club.

Mr. Green attends the Fourth Avenue Church of Christ and serves as deacon and treasurer.

As Published in *The Review-Appeal* on November 23, 1967

CURTIS CLINGMAN GREEN
1904 - 1991

Veteran real estate agent Green dies

Funeral for Curtis C. Green, 87, long-time Franklin real estate broker, church and civic leader, was Monday, October 21, at Williamson Memorial Funeral Home, with Myron Keith officiating Burial was in Mount Hope Cemetery.

Mr. Green died Saturday, October 19, at Williamson Medical Center after being in declining health for several years.

Born in Lynnville, his family moved to a farm on Lewisburg Pike when he was a child, and he spent most of his life in Williamson County, first as a farmer and then as one of Franklin's early real estate brokers.

He attended the old Harpeth Elementary School on Henpeck Lane, and later rode a pony to classes at Battle Ground Academy. He recalled several years ago for friends that he had to pay a toll at a tollgate on Lewisburg Pike, near the present Carnton Country Club golf course, as he rode the pony to school.

He was married to the former Seval Jordan, who died 18 months ago.

As a farmer, Mr. Green was regarded as "successful and progressive," according to a long-time business associate Richard Jordan, a nephew of Mrs. Green. He farmed 200 acres of land, operated a dairy farm with a herd of Jersey cows, and grew small grain crops, including barley, oats and crimson clover.

His entry into real estate came largely through his wife, who was working as a secretary to the late Walter Roberts in the firm of Roberts & McGavock on Main Street. When Roberts' partner died, he offered the Green's partnership positions with the firm in the mid-40's. Since that time, the firm has been known as Roberts & Green.

Green and Jordan, who joined his aunt and uncle in the firm in 1949, were instrumental in some of Franklin's largest land transactions prior to the community's boom years in the late 1970's and 80's.

Mr. Green sold developer Wilson Herbert 200 acres of land at Highway 96 east and Interstate 65 in the 1960's that today is the focal point of Franklin's shift toward the interstate. The land, farmland when it was sold, is the site of Alexander Plaza shopping center, Holiday Inn, BP Petroleum, Royal Oaks subdivision and Royal Oaks Apartments.

He also sold land for an early shopping center on Hillsboro Road, constructed by Coronado Builders for K-Mart store and other tenants.

Mr. Green and Jordan also were in construction together, and they built the West Meade commercial and professional complex on West Main Street and 50 to 100 houses in the 1960's.

They were also principals in establishing the Battlefield mobile home park in an effort to bring affordable housing to the community.

The two were also instrumental in Dr. W. D. Sugg's purchase of the Carnton mansion and land from Mrs. Van McGavock and transfer of the property to the Carnton Association, which has preserved and restored the one time Civil War battle site, hospital and cemetery.

As a member of Franklin's Fourth Avenue Church of Christ, Mr. Green served as treasurer of the church and chairman of the church's benevolent fund for many years.

He also was a member of the Franklin Lions Club, and held a number of offices in the civic organization.

Mr. Green is survived by a sister, Mrs. Elsie Green Scivally of Columbia and several nieces and nephews.

Active pallbearers were Bobby Mosely, Jim Petway, Billy Walker Sr., Bryan Ehresman, N. Y. Walker, Joseph Bowman, Glen Davis, Richard Sparkman, Lance Jordan and Clyde Redford.

Honorary pallbearers were members of the Franklin Coffee Club and elders and deacons of Fourth Avenue Church of Christ Benevolent Fund.

Memorials may be made to the Fourth Avenue Church of Christ Benevolent Fund.

– The Williamson Leader, October 24, 1991

Excellent Citizens and Notable Partings

Portrait of An Excellent Citizen

J. W. Greer

Portrait Published in *The Review-Appeal* on February 24, 1966

Former bank official dies

Final rites for John William Greer, Jr., who rose from office boy to board chairman of Harpeth National Bank, were Friday at Franklin Memorial Chapel.

The Rev. Eugene Gober and the Rev. Stewart Nunnally officiated. Burial was in Mt. Hope Cemetery.

Mr. Greer, a resident of Kittrell Road, died Wednesday night in Williamson County Hospital following an extended illness. He was 66.

A native of Williamson County, Greer was born on Sept. 13. 1907, a son of the late Dr. John W. Greer, Sr. and Bessie Mayberry Greer.

He attended Battle Ground Academy, and was graduated from the former Branham and Hughes Military Academy, Spring Hill.

He was married on Jan. 23, 1935 to the former Florence Taylor of Johnson City.

Greer retired January 1 as board chairman of Harpeth National Bank after 47 years with the bank. He continued to serve on the bank's board of directors.

He was president of Harpeth Insurance Agency; a former director of Great Commonwealth Insurance Co., Dallas; past director of Harpeth Rentals, and a charter member, past president and past secretary of the Williamson County Chamber of Commerce.

Greer also was a charter member and past president of the Franklin Rotary Club; a Farm Bureau member and a member of the Williamson County Heritage Association.

He was listed in La Societe Internationale de Who's Who in the South and Southwest; Who's Who in Tennessee; Who's Who in Banking; Who's Who in Commerce and Industry, and Tennessee Lives.

Greer was a member and treasurer of First Franklin United Methodist Church, where he also served as a trustee and steward.

The family has asked that donations be made to the building fund of the church in lieu of flowers.

Survivors include the widow; a son, John W. Greer III, Franklin; a daughter, Mrs. Tyree Vance III, Brentwood; one brother, Judge Fulton Greer, Franklin, and two sisters, Mrs. Robert Pitner, Franklin, and Mrs. Lester Miller, Richmond Kentucky.

Pallbearers were J. C. Anderson, Dan Hagerty, Ed Moody, Judge Wallace Smith, Michael Connally, Bob Sewell, Judge Jim Warren, Paul Hinson, Lewis Aita and Cortez Isaacs.

Honorary pallbearers were directors and officials of Harpeth National Bank and members of the Franklin Rotary Club.

– The Williamson Leader, August 4, 1974

Portrait of An Excellent Citizen

Judge Fulton Mayberry Greer

Fulton Greer, County Judge of Williamson County, lives on Columbia Highway with his wife, the former Miss Lila Dodson. They have three children, Captain Fulton Greer, Jr., now stationed in Colorado Springs, Colorado; Juliet Greer, a teacher in the high school at Dyersburg; and Lila, a sophomore at the University of Georgia. The Greers attend the Thompson Station Methodist Church where Judge Greer is a member of the Official Board.

As Published in *The Review-Appeal* on January 19, 1967

FULTON MAYBERRY GREER, SR.
1909 - 1989

County mourns death of public servant of 30 years

Friends of Fulton Greer, Wednesday, mourned the death of the man who served Williamson County in various capacities for nearly 30 years.

Greer, 79, died Tuesday following a brief illness after a career as a farmer, as county magistrate from 1948-1966 and as county judge for the next eight years.

"Fulton was my favorite client of all time," said Circuit Court Judge Henry Denmark Bell who served as county attorney while Greer was county judge, the equivalent of today's county executive. "We were with each other on a daily basis for four years."

When Greer served as judge, he not only concerned himself with fiscal and political matters, but also presided over the County Court with jurisdiction over probate and other matters.

"The great thing about Fulton was that, in political office, he was not deceptive at all. Most politicians when they talk to their lawyer are inclined to try to give you the facts so that the lawyer will tell the client what he wants to hear. Fulton Greer was easy to represent because you knew he would give you all the facts that he wanted an opinion on," Bell said. "He was good-natured, a very nice man."

County Executive Robert Ring remembered Greer as a man "who knew the art of government and taught it."

"Fulton Greer was county judge when I first ran for the County Commission," Ring said.

"During my second year he asked me to serve on the Budget Committee. I learned more about how government should be run, and how to treat people from that gentleman than almost anybody. I appreciate the opportunity he gave me to learn."

Ring called Greer "a pretty easy-going kind of guy who appointed committees and let the committee make its own decisions."

"What he did do was provide us with all the information we needed to make those decisions. And he went above the call of duty to help me out my first years on the Quarterly Court as they called it (the County Commission) then," Ring said.

For J.C. Anderson, a lifelong friend, and a man who served on the County Court with him, Greer had "the courage of his convictions."

"I remember once, before I was on the court, that there was debate over a pay raise in the Circuit Court Clerk's office. There was a great deal of argument over it. It was a really hot item. When they voted on it, Fulton was the only one to vote no. He felt pretty low about it, but in my estimation he did the right thing. He was that way. He did what he thought was right," Anderson said.

Greer raised sheep and wheat on his farm and one of his neighbors, Brown Cannon, called him "a good farmer, a good judge and a good neighbor."

"There are not many people of whom you can say Williamson County was a better place because of them," Cannon said. "But Fulton was one of them."

According to Ring, Greer will have a lasting memorial in the new 33 acre Fulton Greer Park located on Hillsboro Road in a bend of the Harpeth River.

"There are a lot of people across this county who wanted to honor Fulton Greer for his years of public service," Ring said. "We believe this is a fine way to do it."

Greer was a graduate of Battle Ground Academy, a member of Hiram Lodge No. 7, the Franklin Rotary Club and a member of First United Methodist Church.

Funeral services were 2 p.m. Thursday at First United Methodist Church with Rev. Art Robins and [Rev.] Jerry Mayo officiating. Burial was at Mount Hope Cemetery.

He is survived by his wife, Mrs. Lila Dodson Greer, daughters, Lila Bickley and Juliet Randolph, and a son, Fulton Greer Jr., all of Franklin. He is also survived by two sisters: Mrs. Robert (Elizabeth) Pitner of Franklin, and Mrs. Lester (Nancy) Miller of Richmond, Kentucky, and six grand-children.

Active pallbearers were: Brown Cannon, Wheeler Woodruff, Lloyd Linton, Charlie Fox Jr., Fleming Williams, Bill Dodson, and Malcolm Gibbs.

Honorary pallbearers were: The Franklin Rotary Club, Wallace Stovall, Tyler Berry Jr., Judge Henry Denmark Bell, Robert White, Blythe Hatcher, Howell Patton, J.C. Anderson, Robert Sewell, John Jordan, Jack Davis, George Harris, Dr. Oscar Noel.

The family requested that any memorials be made to charity.

Williamson Memorial Funeral Home was in charge of arrangements.

– The Review-Appeal, February 3, 1989

Blythe Grigsby

Born and reared in Williamson County, Blythe Grigsby was educated in the Franklin Schools and grew up in the house where he now lives with his wife, the former Miss Ethel Matthews, who is Clerk and Master.

Mr. Grigsby is a real estate broker with offices on Fourth Avenue South and has recently been selected "Man of the Year" by his colleagues in the realty business. Prior to entering the real estate business, Mr. Grigsby served for two terms as County Court Clerk of Williamson County. He is a member of the Church of Christ and the local, state and national Real Estate Board.

As Published in *The Review-Appeal* on March 28, 1968

BLYTHE GRIGSBY
1908 - 1973

Blythe Grigsby, well-known retired real estate agent and former Williamson County official, died Sunday night at Williamson County Hospital. He had been hospitalized since he suffered a massive heart attack at his home May 19.

Funeral services were held at Franklin Memorial Chapel Tuesday afternoon. Myron Keith and Rev. Tim Croft officiated, and burial was in Mt. Hope Cemetery.

Mr. Grigsby was a lifelong resident of Williamson County, and at the time of his death resided in the house in which he had been born. He was the son of the late John B. and Susie Hoover Grigsby. His father was a well-known auctioneer. He attended Williamson County schools and the University of Tennessee for two years.

He was elected county court clerk for Williamson County for a number of years. He retired in March on his 65th birthday from the real estate business. He had operated his own company, Blythe Grigsby Real Estate Company, for many years.

He was a member of the Church of Christ and was active in the Williamson County Real Estate Board.

In 1934 he was married to the former Miss Ethel Mathis [Matthews] who survives. She serves as clerk and master for the county.

Other survivors include five sisters, Mrs. Nathan Sawyer of Franklin, Mrs. J. E. Windrow of Nashville, Mrs. Fred Pangle of Ashtabula, Ohio, Mrs. Cathey Tansil of Sharon, Tennessee, and Mrs. Martyn Hayes of Memphis.

Honorary pallbearers were members of the Williamson County Real Estate Board and the Williamson County Bar Association.

Active pallbearers were J. E. Windrow, Nathan Sawyer, Lex Ables, Pat Hayes, Charles Grigsby, Robert Grigsby, Jack Grigsby and Harry Grigsby.

— *The Review-Appeal, May 31, 1973*

"Blyth's grandfather, Booker Grigsby, came to this county from Virginia and settled at Bethesda on an 800-acre tract. A son, Ollie, lives in the house where Booker and his wife, Mary Sprott Grigsby, reared 11 children, four of whom are still living and make their home on parts of the original farm, J.O., O.T., and Charlie Grigsby and Mrs. Cora Grigsby Bond. This grandfather was a Confederate soldier and saw service in several major battles, among them being Bull Run and Gettysburg."

— Jane Bowman Owen, *Who's Who in Williamson County*, Rick Warwick, ed., originally published in *The Review-Appeal*, April 13, 1939.

Portrait of An Excellent Citizen

Dr. Harry Jasper Guffee

Born and reared in Williamson County, Dr. Harry J. Guffee has spent most of his life in Franklin, and is now chief of surgery at the Williamson County Hospital. Dr. Guffee received his high school education at Battle Ground Academy and graduated from the school of medicine at Vanderbilt University in 1939. Soon after graduating he became connected with German-Rice Hospital, where he was associated with the late Dr. T. C. Rice. During World War II, he served with the United States Army spending 2 years in Europe and received wounds in the Battle of the Bulge. At the time of his discharge he was a Major. He is married to the former Miss Dorothy Brady and their children are Mrs. John (Betty Jane) Barringer, of Memphis, Harry Guffee, Jr. of Birmingham, Michigan, Dottie Guffee, a student at Auburn University, Auburn, Alabama, and Johnny Guffee of Franklin, and 2 grandchildren, Josephine and John Barringer, Jr.

Dr. Guffee loves horses and most of his spare time is spent attending shows and participating in rodeos. He is vice-president of the National Cutting Horse Association, the American Legion and Veterans of Foreign Wars. He is also a member of the Board of Trustees of Battle Ground Academy and the Franklin First Methodist Church. He served on the Franklin City School Board for 8 years and was presented a plaque at the time of his resignation for splendid services rendered.

As Published in *The Review-Appeal* on May 2, 1968

Dr. Harry J. Guffee, 83, died Saturday morning at Williamson Medical Center. Dr. Guffee was born and raised in Franklin and, after graduating from Battle Ground Academy (BGA), had a dream of becoming an engineer.

A motorcycle accident which took his brother Paul's life dramatically altered his perspective. Feeling that more should have been done to help his brother, Guffee decided to become a doctor and make a difference.

He entered Vanderbilt in 1930 to pursue a degree in medicine. During his undergraduate years, he also played football and captained the Vanderbilt 1934 team. He was selected in 1990 to be a member of BGA's Sports Hall of Fame.

During World War II, he served as a doctor for the injured troops at The Battle of The Bulge.

He was shot and captured by the Germans. They placed him in an isolation cell because he could not give them information they felt he held as a captain in the military. He told his children that he survived only by thinking about his home and family.

Dr. Guffee began his practice in Franklin in the late 1940's when only four doctors served Williamson County. His son Johnny remembered, "A typical day for him would be to eat breakfast with his family, operate until noon, then see between 60 and 100 patients every day. After the evening meal, he made house calls until 11 p.m."

Dr. Guffee and his wife, Dorothy, raised five children, Betty Jane Barringer, Harry Jr., Paul, Johnny and Dottie Morton. His three sons attended BGA and Dr. Guffee returned himself to serve for years as a volunteer athletic team doctor.

Love of community motivated Dr. Guffee. He and Dorothy were active members of the First Methodist Church.

Graveside services will be at 11 a.m. Monday, March 18, at Mount Hope Cemetery with the Rev. Robert Davis officiating.

Active pallbearers include: Harry J. Guffee Jr., John B. Guffee, John W. Barrringer, John B. Guffee Jr., Charles Ernest Morton IV, Robert Guffee Morton, and John W. Barringer, Jr.

Memorials may be made to the Guffee-Brown Stadium at Battle Ground Academy, 1314 Columbia Avenue, Franklin. Visitation with the family will be 4 p.m. to 6 p.m., Sunday, March 17 at Williamson Memorial Funeral Home.

– The Review-Appeal March 17, 1996

Rodeo Brings Back Memories of Dr. Guffee
By Hudson Alexander

If you go back to the earliest days of frontier medicine, even back to a time when Dr. John Sappington set up the first medical practice here, around 1802, you'd discover hundreds of physicians who dedicated their professional lives to helping the people of Williamson County.

And one of the most popular of all time, among that group, would be Dr. Harry Guffee.

According to family legend, it was only by a stroke of fate that the Guffee family ever settled in Williamson County. Dr. Guffee's grandfather was moving his family from East Tennessee to Texas, so the story goes, when his wife suddenly went into labor while passing through Franklin.

They stopped, intending to stay only long enough for the baby to be born -- but they never left.

Harry Jasper Guffee was born in 1913. He attended the Franklin schools and later graduated from Battle Ground Academy. He had always planned to study architectural engineering at Georgia Tech. But, once again, a stroke of fate intervened: those plans were drastically altered when his brother, Paul, was killed in a tragic motorcycle accident. Guffee vowed that he would dedicate all his energies toward helping those in need of medical care.

Guffee began his college studies at Vanderbilt University in 1930. During his undergraduate years, he was noted as an outstanding student-athlete. He played both offense and defense on some of the best Commodore football teams ever coached by legendary field generals Ray Morrison and Dan McGugin. He was captain of the 1934 Vandy football team.

Determined to make good on his pledge to pursue the field of medicine, Guffee then entered the Vanderbilt Medical School. After his second year of study, he was married to the former Miss Dorothy Brady of Springfield. In 1939, he received his medical degree. And the following year, 1940, he returned to Franklin, where he entered into a medical practice with Dr. Dan German and Dr. Tandy Rice at the Dan German Hospital on Fourth Avenue South.

World War II interrupted Guffee's early medical career. He hadn't much more than gotten started, when he suddenly found himself in the 84th U.S. Infantry Division, assigned to a specialty medical unit called the Blackout Express Convoy. This unit made regular trips to assist soldiers wounded at the front line. At Normandy, where thousands of American soldiers were killed storming the beaches, Guffee was with a group of about 100 soldiers who were taken prisoner.

The weeks that followed really took their toll on Guffee. He lost down from 180 pounds to only about 118 pounds. But he was lucky to have survived at all. The 84th Division started the war with 3,500 men; when it ended, Guffee was one of only 32 survivors.

After the war, Dr. Guffee once again returned to Franklin, where he resumed his medical practice with Dr. Tandy Rice at the Dan German Hospital. And for the next 30 years, he maintained one of the most successful family medical practices in Williamson County.

In 1962, Dr. Guffee began sharing a medical office, on Carter's Creek Pike, with Dr. A. Joel Lee. They were assisted for many years by Lottie Haffner, whose nursing career dated back to the days of the Dan German Hospital.

They made a great medical team back in those days.

Many old-timers still hold fond memories of Dr. Guffee. He was a unique man: he was a very skilled surgeon, but he also possessed an uncanny ability to ease the fears and apprehensions for his patients. He is also remembered for the house calls he made to the rural parts of the county, where patients could not be reached by automobile. On these occasions, he would hook his horse trailer to his Jeep. He'd drive as far as he could, and then continue on horseback, with his medical bag slung across the saddle. There were times when he would even deliver babies in backwoods cabins -- some with dirt floors.

Every year when the Franklin Rotary Club holds their annual rodeo, I can't help but think of Dr. Guffee. The rodeo was always one of his favorite projects. For many years, he especially enjoyed the calf-roping competition. And, as long as he was able, Dr. Guffee enjoyed leading the rodeo parade on horseback through the streets of downtown Franklin.

By the time Dr. Guffee retired from his active medical practice in 1975, it was estimated that he had delivered 4,342 babies in Williamson County. I was one of them, along with my brother and two sisters.

Dr. Harry Guffee died, following a lengthy battle with Alzheimer's disease, on March 16, 1996. He was buried at Mount Hope Cemetery.

– The Williamson Herald, May 10, 2006

WELCOME

PARDNER

Support Your World Famed

ROTARY RODEO

Friday-Saturday, May 5th-6th

—

Remember The Bloodmobile
Friday, April 28th

Dan Hagerty

Dan Hagerty is a member of the personnel of the Harpeth National Bank where he is executive vice-president and cashier.

Mr. Hagerty is married to the former Miss Evelyn Burrow of Franklin. They live on the Hillsboro Road. He is a member of the Franklin Rotary Club, is treasurer of the Williamson County Chapter of the American Red Cross and attends the Fourth Avenue Church of Christ.

As Published in *The Review-Appeal* on May 25, 1967

Dan Hagerty of Franklin, retired banker, dies at 69

Funeral for Dan Hagerty, retired Franklin banker and longtime civic and church leader, was Tuesday, Dec. 27, at Williamson Memorial Funeral Home, with Myron Keith, Jim Taylor and Paul Brown officiating.

Burial was in Williamson Memorial Gardens.

Mr. Hagerty died December 26 at his home on Fourth Avenue North.

He was chairman of the board of the former Harpeth National Bank (now First Tennessee), and past president of the Franklin Rotary Club in which he was a Paul Harris Fellow. He also served as president of the Franklin Jaycees in earlier years.

He was a member of the Franklin Industrial Board, Brentwood Country Club and Fourth Avenue Church of Christ.

He is survived by his wife, Mrs. Evelyn Burrow Hagerty of Franklin.

Active pallbearers were Jim Burrow, Doug Burrow, Hyde Harper Jr., Jim Morgan, Stewart Campbell Sr., Ronald S. Ligon, Hoyt Doak, Jr. and Hyde Harper III.

Honorary pallbearers were elders and deacons of Fourth Avenue Church of Christ,

members of Franklin Rotary Club, Monday Nighters, Paul H. McGinness, Thomas Greer, James Anglea, John Robinson, Mrs. Billy Reynolds, Mrs. Ruth Tindall, Dr. James Callaway, Doug Fisher, Harry Purvis, Jon Kinnard, Don Mullican, Ed Moody, John Moran, Jim Hudson, Herbert Ferguson, Melvin Roach, John Simmons, Charlie King, John Doak and Tyler Berry Jr.

Memorial gifts may be made to the American Heart Association or American Cancer Society.

– The Williamson Leader, January 6, 1989

YOU ARE ALWAYS WELCOME
AT THE

HARPETH NATIONAL BANK

Franklin, Tennessee

"A Good Bank in a Good County"

Branch offices: Brentwood and Nolensville

Member Federal Deposit Insurance Corporation

"And finally ... he proposed to Miss Evelyn Burrow, of Franklin... and plans were made for their betrothal. But soon it became apparent that his good friend, Hoyt Doak, Jr. and Evelyn's sister, Jean, had the same intentions. But to confuse the issue even more, so did Evelyn's brother, Doug, and Miss Jean Petway. So — you guessed it, plans were made on October 31, 1948, for Franklin's first triple wedding to take place."

— Jane Bowman Owen, *Who's Who in Williamson County*, Rick Warwick, ed., originally published in *The Review-Appeal*, February 1, 1951.

Loy G. Hardcastle

My father, Loy G. Hardcastle, Sr., truly helped to make Franklin a better place in which to work and raise our families. He was elected president of the Memphis Zone Dodge and Chrysler Dealer Advisory Council and the distinguished National Dealer Council for Chrysler Corporation. It was as a member of this group that he was instrumental in hiring the iconic Lee Iacocca to take over as head of Chrysler Corporation when it was on the brink of disaster. This hiring took place in December of 1978. My father died one month later, in January of 1979, and thus was not afforded the opportunity to witness the resurgence of Chrysler Corporation or reap the benefits that were to come through the leadership of Mr. Iacocca.

He was active in the Masonic Lodge, the Cedar Creek Yacht Club, a Shriner and a director on the board of the United Way of Williamson County. He served as president of both the Franklin Lions Club and the Chamber of Commerce. A devoted family man, he was also a deacon of Fourth Avenue Church of Christ.

— Loy G. Hardcastle, Jr.

Portrait Published in *The Review-Appeal* on March 3, 1966

LOY GEORGE HARDCASTLE, SR.
1914-1979

Franklin automobile dealer, Loy Hardcastle Sr., dies Sunday

Loy George Hardcastle Sr., an active Franklin business and civic leader for over 30 years died early Monday morning at Williamson County Hospital following a heart attack late Sunday.

Funeral was Tuesday at 2 p.m. at Franklin Memorial Chapel with Myron Keith and Rev. George Jones officiating. Burial was in Williamson Memorial Gardens.

A native of Red Boiling Springs in Jackson County, Hardcastle was the son of the late Thomas Luther and Cora Alice Luther [see note]. He moved to Franklin in 1947 and opened the Dodge Chrysler dealership on Main Street, where it remains today. In 1958, he bought a dealership in Columbia.

From the beginning, Hardcastle exemplified an interest in Franklin through his involvement in the Williamson County Chamber of Commerce, which he helped reorganize in the mid-1950's. He served as president and on the board of directors for a number of years.

Hardcastle was also active in the Franklin Lions Club, where he served as a president. In addition, he was a member of the Franklin Industrial Development Board.

He was elected to the board of directors of the National Dodge Advertising Council and was also a member of the National Dealer Advisory Council. At the time of his death, he was chairman of the Memphis Zone Dodge and Chrysler Dealer Advisory Council. He had received "Distinguished Dealer" awards for both the Franklin and Columbia dealerships.

He was a Shriner and a member of the Masonic Lodge and the Cedar Creek Club. He was also on the board of the United Givers Fund of Franklin and Williamson County.

A member of the Fourth Avenue Church of Christ, Mr. Hardcastle was married to the former Marjorie Andrews of Spring Hill.

Survivors, in addition to his widow, include two daughters, Mrs. Dennis (Cheryl) Petty of Brentwood and Miss Alice Hardcastle of Franklin; two sons, Loy G. Hardcastle, Jr., and Stan Hardcastle, both of Franklin; two sisters, Mrs. R.L. Jones Sr., of Madison and Mrs. Doy Jones of Oakland, Tennessee; one brother, B. D. (Dock) Hardcastle of Goodlettsville and two grandchildren.

Serving as honorary pallbearers were members of the Cedar Creek Club, the Franklin Lions Club and employees of Hardcastle Motor Company in Franklin and Columbia.

Active pallbearers were Jim Stephenson, Paul Pigg, Ed Kaeser, Jr., David Hall, Robert Hooten, R. L. Jones, Lonnie Burchett and Ralph Duke.

Franklin Memorial Chapel was in Charge of arrangements.

– The Williamson Leader, January 13, 1979

Note: This paragraph should have read, "Hardcastle was the son of the late Thomas Luther and Cora Alice Hardcastle." Loy G. Hardcastle, Jr.

* * *

* * *

Excellent Citizens and Notable Partings

Prof. Henry Hardison

"He believes in the youth of today. His motto to them is 'Only the best is good enough,' and he tries to bring this out in every individual he comes in contact with.

"To point out his concerns for humanity, Mr. Hardison and a group of men bought what is now called Rucker's Park, opened and supervised a playground for the youth of Franklin. This was before Warren Park opened, and children were forced to play in lots or on the streets because there was no place else to play."

— "Helping Others Way of Life for Franklin's Hardison," *The Williamson Leader,* April 4, 1976.

Portrait Published in *The Review-Appeal* on August 3, 1966

HENRY L. HARDISON
1918 - 1984

Tribute paid to Henry Hardison
retired educator, commissioner

A standing-room only crowd jammed into Shorter Chapel African Methodist Episcopal Church to pay final tribute Wednesday to retired Franklin educator and veteran county commissioner, Henry Hardison, who died Sunday at this home of an apparent heart attack.

Mr. Hardison, who was serving his third four-year term on the Williamson County Commission, was characterized by the Rev. James Arnell as "a man who loved his God, who loved his family and who loved his community."

Arnell cited the thousands of lives Hardison touched as a teacher for 35 years and the hundreds of others he helped.

Hardison was laid to rest in Meadowlawn Memorial Gardens in his native Maury County.

The only black member of the county commission, Hardison represented the county's 11th District – composed primarily of residents within the city of Franklin.

Hardison was a friend of both black and white in his role as a teacher and commissioner. He was instrumental in winning the appointment of Mrs. Mary Mills as the first black trustee of Williamson County Hospital. He also was a champion of education issues coming before the commission and served on a number of community-related boards, including the Williamson County Library, Williamson County Counseling Center, Williamson County Red Cross, Williamson County United Way, Franklin Housing Authority, Senior Citizens Center and Columbia State Community College.

Less than two weeks ago he received a plaque recognizing his service as a member of the board of directors of the Tennessee Vocational Training Center, a training and rehabilitation facility for the handicapped.

Hardison also was a member of a recently appointed committee named to make a recommendation as to the future use of the present Williamson County Hospital building, which is to be vacated in 1985 when a new hospital is completed.

Best known as an educator and friend of youth, Hardison retired two years ago after 35 years as a classroom teacher, including 29 years in the Franklin Special School District. He was a basketball coach at Johnson School for 10 years when the school had students from grades one through eight, and he later taught civics and math at Franklin Junior High School.

He was a graduate of College Hill High School in Columbia and held bachelor and master's degrees from Tennessee State University.

Before joining the Franklin school system, he taught in Maury County and Nashville schools.

Hardison also was especially interested in providing adequate recreation facilities for youth of the black community. He donated land for a park in the Rucker subdivision and obtained assistance from the City of Franklin to equip it.

He also worked on behalf of the black community to obtain water for a group of property owners living at the fringe of the city limits who did not have adequate water supplies.

He was a trustee of the Shorter Chapel AME Church, a veteran of World War II, and a former vice-chairman of the Williamson County Democratic Party.

Over the years, Hardison received a number of awards for his role as an educator and community leader. They include Teacher of the Week by The Williamson Leader in 1974; Educator of the Year by the Franklin Lions Club in 1976; certificate of appreciation for outstanding support to public education by the Williamson County Education Association, 1978; WCEA Humanitarian Award, 1979; Franklin Teachers Association Humanitarian Award, 1981, and Chamber of Commerce Helping Hand Award, 1982.

Survivors include his wife, Mrs. Fanny Hughes Hardison; one son, Clarence Hardison; one sister, Mrs. Annie Ruth Jones, and one granddaughter, all of Franklin.

— The Williamson Leader, January 6, 1984

Excellent Citizens and Notable Partings

Portrait of An Excellent Citizen

Matthew Thomas Harwell

Mr. Harwell is executive vice-president of the Bank of College Grove in College Grove, Tennessee. He is married to the former Miss Ina Blankenship. They have one daughter, Mary Ann (Mrs. Briggs) Smith. Mr. Harwell attends the College Grove Methodist Church and is a member of the College Grove Lions Club and the College Grove Water Utilities District.

As Published in *The Review-Appeal* on September 29, 1966

MATTHEW THOMAS HARWELL
1911 - 1991

**Former College Grove banker
Matthew Harwell dies at 80**

Funeral for Matthew Thomas Harwell, 80, former president of the old Bank of College Grove was Sunday, March 24, at Williamson Memorial Funeral Home, with the Rev. LeNoir Culbertson and the Rev. Chester Stephens officiating. Burial was in Williamson Memorial Gardens.

Mr. Harwell died March 22.

A native of Bell Buckle, Harwell was the son of a Methodist minister, the Rev. Wyatt L. Harwell, and Wilma Beasley Harwell.

He graduated from Giles County High School in Pulaski, where he and his wife, the former Ina Blankenship, were classmates.

Harwell once said he "never lived any place more than four years" due to the mobility of his father's profession.

After working for the Jewell Tea & Coffee Co., in Alabama, Harwell came to College Grove in 1938 and established an insurance agency.

Three years later, he joined the Bank of College Grove as bookkeeper and assistant cashier. He was one of two employees of the bank at the time. Both salaries totaled $2,500 a year.

"I was the janitor, bookkeeper and assistant cashier all at the same time," he recalled earlier.

Assets of the small rural bank totaled $200,000 when Harwell joined the institution, but they had grown to $14.3 million by the time he retired as president in July 1977. The bank had offices in both College Grove and Franklin.

Bank of College Grove was later acquired by U.S. Bank of Nashville and Nashville City Bank before merging with Dominion Bank of Virginia.

Harwell was a long-time community leader in College Grove. He was a charter member and former president of the College Grove Lions Club and former treasurer of College Grove United Methodist Church.

Survivors besides his wife are a daughter, Mrs. Briggs (Mary Ann) Smith of College Grove; brother Merritt M. Harwell of Nashville; three sisters, Sarah Harwell Stammer of Lewisburg, Wilma Harwell Smotherman of Murfreesboro and Anna Harwell Reed of Nashville; three grandchildren and one great granddaughter.

Active pallbearers were Charles B. Smith, T. Wyatt Smith, Jerry R. Flippen, Chester Harwell West, Bobby Reed, Larry Lewter, Wayne Hobbs, Tommy Russell and William Reed.

Honorary pallbearers were members of College Grove United Methodist Church Men's Bible class; Melvin White, Dr. Joseph Willoughby, Dr. Thomas Jantz, Sam R. Ogilvie, Edward (Buddy) Cromer, Larry Hazelwood, Jerry Wilson, Harry Taylor, William (Billy) Ogilvie, Charles Rigsby and Roy Barker.

Memorials may be made to the American Heart Association or College Grove United Methodist Church.

– The Williamson Leader, March 28, 1991

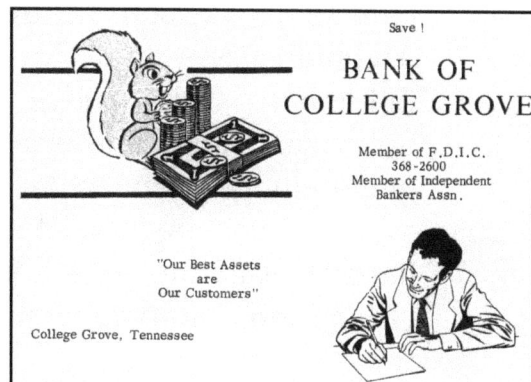

Save !

BANK OF COLLEGE GROVE

Member of F.D.I.C.
368-2600
Member of Independent
Bankers Assn.

"Our Best Assets
are
Our Customers"

College Grove, Tennessee

Portrait of An Excellent Citizen

Judge John Hughes Henderson

John Hughes Henderson is serving his first term as Circuit Court Judge. He lives on Lewisburg Avenue with his wife, the former Miss Margaret B. Heron. They have two children. John H. Henderson, Jr., lives in Corinth, Mississippi. Their daughter, Peggy, now Mrs. Frederick Ross Gentry lives in Columbus, Ohio. Judge Henderson attends St. Paul's Episcopal Church and is a member of the Vestry. As Circuit Judge, Judge Henderson is serving practically the same circuit which he served as Attorney-General of the 17th Judicial District for 20 years. He was the first president of the Williamson County Library Board and is still a member.

As Published in _The Review-Appeal_ on February 9, 1967

JOHN HUGHES HENDERSON
1902 - 1989

Judge John H. Henderson

Funeral for retired Circuit Judge John Hughes Henderson, 86, was Monday, March 6, at St. Paul's Episcopal Church, with the Rev. Robert Cowperthwaite officiating. Interment was in Williamson Memorial Gardens.

Judge Henderson, who served eight years as a circuit judge and 20 years as district attorney general, died Saturday morning at Williamson Medical Center following an apparent heart attack the evening before.

A native of Franklin, Henderson was a member of a pioneer Williamson County family whose members are in their second century of practicing law in the community.

Henderson's father, John H. Henderson, was a Franklin attorney, member of the board of mayor and alderman, president of the Tennessee Bar Association, and a special state Supreme Court judge.

His brother, Captain Tom Henderson, was an assistant state attorney general and Franklin lawyer, and also received widespread acclaim for his participation in a move to kidnap the German Kaiser during World War I.

Judge Henderson also had a distinguished legal career.

After completing undergraduate school at the University of Tennessee, he earned a law degree from Yale University in 1926 and returned to Franklin to enter a law practice with his brother's firm.

In 1930, Henderson was appointed district attorney general of the 17th judicial circuit by then-Governor Henry Horton, and he was elected to the position in a contested race in August.

Henderson ran twice without opposition and held the position for 20 years.

He entered private law practice again in September 1950, then was elected judge of the 17th judicial circuit in a race against incumbent Wallace Smith in August 1966. Henderson served eight years as the only judge of the circuit.

After his retirement in 1974, Henderson served as a special judge in several cases and joined his son, John H. Henderson Jr., in the private practice of law in Franklin.

Survivors include his wife, Mrs. Margaret Heron Henderson; daughter, Mrs. Margaret H. Macpherson; son, John H. Henderson Jr., and four grandchildren, Laurel G. Aiello, Heather L. Gentry, John H. Henderson III and Lloyd T. Henderson, all of Franklin.

Active pallbearers were T. J. Aiello, Tom P. Henderson Jr., Tom P. Henderson III, Iain S. Macpherson, Edward T. Steele, Lewis M. Steele, L. E. Tarver and Victor H. Wilson.

Honorary pallbearers were members of the Williamson County Bar Association, Tennessee Bar Association and Tennessee Judiciary.

Williamson Memorial Funeral Home was in charge of arrangements.

– The Williamson Leader, March 10, 1989

"The monument was placed in the middle of the Square some years before I was born. My understanding was the man soldier on top was Mr. Pleas Smith. ... Now whether he was or not I am not sure. I understand that when the monument was about to be raised, it was laying in the Square with ropes and so forth around it to raise it up, some individualistic farmer drove a wagon and team over one of the ropes and broke a hinky out of the hat, which is still there."

— "The Reminiscences of Judge John H. Henderson, Spring 1980," *Williamson County Historical Society Journal, #33*, Rick Warwick, ed., 2002.

Portrait of An Excellent Citizen

Mrs. Thomas P. Henderson

Mrs. Thomas P. Henderson is a charter member of several of Williamson County's most active organizations. She was the first president of the American Legion Auxiliary here and still devotes much time and effort to its work and projects. She and her husband, the late "Captain Tom," initiated the establishment of the Carter House as a memorial to the Battle of Franklin. Through her efforts the Williamson County War Memorial Public Library came into being and she is still a member of the Library Board. She is a member of several other civic organizations and is a member of St. Paul's Episcopal Church. Mrs. Henderson lives on Lewisburg Road and is the mother of two children, Mrs. H. P. Minton of Franklin and Tom P. Henderson, Jr., of Nashville.

As Published in *The Review-Appeal* on July 6, 1967

LUCILLE CARTER HENDERSON
1883 - 1974

Mrs. Henderson, leader many years, dies

Mrs. Thomas Perkins Henderson, who was a leader in many civic projects undertaken in Williamson County for nearly half a century, died Sunday in Williamson County Hospital. She had been in declining health in recent months.

Funeral services were held Monday afternoon at St. Paul's Episcopal Church. The Rev. Charles Fulton officiated, and burial was in Mt. Hope Cemetery.

Mrs. Henderson was the former Miss Lucille Carter of Richmond, Virginia, and was affectionately known throughout Williamson County as "Miss Lucille." She was the widow of Capt. Thomas Perkins Henderson, well-known attorney and civic and political leader who died in 1966. She was educated at Hollins in Roanoke, Virginia, and moved to Nashville in the early years of this century. She taught there at St. Cecilia Academy and at the State School for the Blind.

She was one of the founders of the American Legion Auxiliary and was active in all its work for many years. She also was one of the organizers of the Williamson County War Memorial Library and served as a member of the Board of Trustees until 1968. She was a member of the Carter House Association, the Association for Preservation of Tennessee Antiquities, Old Glory Chapter of the Daughters of the American Revolution, and the Williamson County Historical Society.

In her earlier years she was interested in the work of the Democratic Party and served as a delegate to the Democratic National Convention in 1932. She helped reorganize the State School for the Blind during the time Gordon Browning served as governor.

She was a communicant of St. Paul's Episcopal Church.

Survivors include a son, Thomas P. Henderson, Jr., of Nashville; a daughter, Mrs. H. P. Minton of Franklin; five grandchildren; and seven great-grandchildren.

Active pallbearers were H. P. Minton, Jr., Thomas Minton, Tom Henderson III, Dr. Arville V. Wheeler, Douglas B. White, Jr., and John Henderson.

In lieu of flowers the family asked that contributions be made to St. Paul's Episcopal Church or to the Williamson County Memorial Library.

Franklin Memorial Chapel was in charge of arrangements.

– The Review-Appeal, January 31, 1974

VISIT THE
CARTER HOUSE
A Memorial To Those Who Died
In The
BATTLE OF FRANKLIN
November 30, 1864

Excellent Citizens and Notable Partings

Joe Rucker Hendricks

Joe Rucker Hendricks was born in Franklin where he was educated and lives in the family residence with his sister, Miss Mary Ellen Hendricks. Joe is manager of Beasley's Store on Main Street. He is a member of the Fourth Avenue Church of Christ and the Masonic Lodge. He is a lover of flowers and grows beautiful blossoms all during the Spring and Fall seasons. He also likes photography, and during the years that he was connected with Mr. Jim Chapman in Chapman's Pie Wagon on the Square he photographed practically all of the daily customers and has an album containing same. Joe is the son of the late Joseph G. Hendricks who was deputy Clerk and Master with offices in the Williamson County Courthouse for many years.

As Published in *The Review-Appeal* on September 14, 1967

Joe Hendricks succumbs at 72

Joe Rucker Hendricks, 72 year-old well-known retired Main Street businessman, died Sept. 8 at Harpeth Terrace Nursing Home after an extended illness. He was manager of Beasley's Department Store until his retirement in 1970 and before that was an employee of Chapman's Pie Wagon which was located on the Square.

A native of Williamson County, he was the son of the late Amanda Overbey and Joseph G. Hendricks. He was a Mason and a member of the Fourth Avenue Church of Christ.

He had two main hobbies, taking snapshots of the regular customers as they would leave the pie wagon, a Franklin institution of past years and growing flowers, mainly daffodils. He was well known for his custom of giving blossoms to his friends.

Survivors include five sisters, Miss Mary Ellen Hendricks, Mrs. Charlie (Elizabeth) Fox, Sr., and Mrs. L. W. (Virginia) Evans, all of Franklin, Mrs. Roy (Rosa) Willis of Goodlettsville and Mrs. J. Frank (Kathryn) Ewing of Lake Oswego, Oregon.

Myron Keith and George M. Wade officiated at the final rites at 2 p.m. Saturday at Franklin Memorial Chapel. Interment was in Mt. Hope Cemetery.

Pallbearers were Lemech W. Evans and nephews, Charlie Fox Jr., Charlie Fox III, Joe Hendricks Fox, Tom Fox, Larry Hicklen, Earl Chism Davis Sr., Earl Chism Davis II, Wayne Hendricks Davis, Roy Turpin Willis, Gerald Fisher, John Frank Ewing Jr., Andrew McGavock Ewing, Winston Miller, Thomas Hillier, Robert Herman Hendricks Jr., Kevin Scott Hendricks, and Mark Hammand.

Franklin Memorial Chapel was in charge of the arrangements.

– The Review-Appeal, September 8, 1977

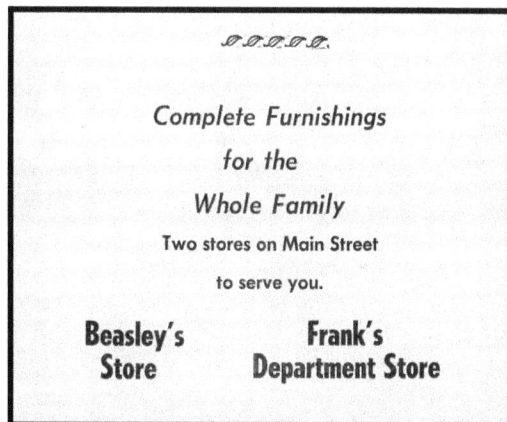

J. J. J. J. J.

Complete Furnishings

for the

Whole Family

Two stores on Main Street

to serve you.

Beasley's Store   **Frank's Department Store**

"Joe was born in the Williamson County Jail in 1905 while his father was keeper under the late Sheriff W. S. Rucker and this accounts for the Rucker in his name."

— Jane Bowman Owen, *Who's Who in Williamson County*, Rick Warwick, ed., originally published in *The Review-Appeal*, July 11, 1940.

BILL DUKE '68

Wilson Herbert

Wilson Herbert was born in the Clovercroft Community of Williamson County, son of Mary Wilson Herbert and the late Joseph Erwin Herbert. He lives on the Clovercroft Road, within sight of his birthplace and resides on the farm with his wife, the former Ann Ruffin of Memphis. They have two children, Wilson (Shac) Herbert, Jr., who is in the business with his father, and Marianne, a Junior in the University of Tennessee at Knoxville. The Herberts will celebrate their 25th wedding anniversary next March.

He is a graduate of Franklin High School, and spent three years with the U.S. Army Air Force during World War II. He attended the University of Tennessee, Nashville Branch, and has been in the insurance business since 1949. He is president of Herbert Insurance Service, Inc. and Wilson Realty Company. He is also president of Adams, Downey and Herbert, Inc., developers of Royal Oak Subdivision presently under construction on Highway 96 at I-65.

Mr. Herbert has a long record of civic activity. He was a member for 15 years of the Williamson County Jaycees, and served as its president. He is president of the Franklin Lions Club, and has recently been named to the Board of Directors for Goodwill Industries. He was a charter member of the Williamson County Heart Council and served as president for many years. He is presently serving as Vice-President of the Tennessee Heart Association and is a national delegate to the American Heart Convention to be held in Miami in November. He is a director in the Williamson County Chamber of Commerce and represents the Chamber of Commerce in the Middle Tennessee Planning Conference. He is also a member of the Methodist Laymen's Club. He has been a member of the Williamson County Court for eight years as magistrate for the 14th Civil District. He is a member of Trinity United Methodist Church.

As Published in *The Review-Appeal* on October 10, 1968

SHEDIE WILSON HERBERT
1925-2000

Herbert dies at 75
County native had dramatic impact on business community
By Mindy Tate

Wilson Herbert, recognized as one of Williamson County's business legends, died Friday, September 8, after a battle with pancreatic cancer.

Herbert, 75, was humble about his accomplishments, requesting of family and friends before his death that his life be marked by no great tributes or eulogies, no long obituaries with accolades.

The official obituary issued by Williamson Memorial Funeral Home made no mention of his business experience, his many honors or his service to the community.

But the number of his contributions and his impact on the community make it difficult not to spotlight Herbert, known by many as the barbecue man.

"Wilson was an ambassador for Williamson County wherever he went," said County Executive Clint Callicott, who said Friday he had known Herbert since high school.

Perhaps Herbert's greatest ambassadorial duties stemmed from his association with the Highway 96 East/Interstate 65 business district.

"In my mind, he was the person I knew as the first economic developer of Franklin," said Mayor Jerry Sharber, who met Herbert when he bought his first home in the city from the man.

"I guess you could say he sort of brought me to Franklin," Sharber said.

Herbert owned many businesses in that area, including Wilson Realty, the Country Store, Herbert AAA Log Homes, Holiday Lanes Bowling Center, Holiday Wines and Liquors and the one in which he met the most people, Herbert's BBQ.

Because most of the businesses were located within one block of the I-65 interchange, Herbert met many people traveling through, extending southern hospitality and a hearty welcome to Williamson County to everyone he met.

"I think Wilson Herbert exemplified what Williamson County has always been about and that is warmth, vision and credibility," Callicott added.

"He never met a stranger and he showed kindness to all. He is going to be missed."

It was Herbert's kindness which endeared him to many. Food From Herbert's BBQ – even after he sold the business in 1997 – would often be delivered by Herbert to area funeral homes to families grieving the loss of a loved one.

He frequently visited the sick or shut-ins and quietly supported numerous charities and causes, but often on the condition of anonymity.

"To me, if you ever found someone was in need, a family or an individual, Wilson would be one of the first to step forward," Sharber said. "He didn't expect anything and he didn't want anything. He just wanted to help people."

Born February 6, 1925, in the Clovercroft Community, Herbert was one of three sons born to Joe Erwin Herbert and Mary Wilson Herbert. He was proud to be a sixth-generation Williamson Countian and was proud to tell people that he had lived much of his life within seven miles of where he was born.

During World War II, he was a member of the U.S. Air Force, but returned to Franklin to begin his business and civic career.

In 1955, he opened a general insurance business on Fourth Avenue South, to which he added a real estate business soon afterwards. In 1972, he opened the Country Store on Highway 96 East, where McDonald's stands today.

"It was the first business out there besides a couple of service stations," Herbert said in a 1999 interview. "It was a whale of a business."

Holiday Wines and Liquors opened in 1981, while Herbert's BBQ opened in 1986.

During the time he owned Herbert's BBQ, he entertained adults and children alike by driving his red Buick convertible in parades while wearing a pig mask.

The list of his civic involvements was lengthy, including membership in the Franklin Jaycees, the Franklin Lions Club and the Williamson County-Franklin Chamber of Commerce, which he served as president. He was honored by the Franklin Noon Rotary Club as a Paul Harris Fellow, the highest honor bestowed by Rotary, for his support of the club, although he was not a member.

He also served as a magistrate on the Williamson County Quarterly Court.

Herbert was a lifelong member of Trinity United Methodist Church.

Williamson Memorial Funeral Home is in charge of arrangements. Private graveside services are set for Monday at Mount Hope Cemetery.

Visitation with the family will be Saturday, September 9, and Sunday, September 10, from 3-9 p.m. Prayer services will be held at 8:30 p.m. each night.

– The Review-Appeal, September 9, 2000

Editor's Note:
Ann Ruffin Herbert Floyd died on June 3, 2020, in Franklin, at the age of 93.

Excellent Citizens and Notable Partings

Portrait of An Excellent Citizen

Rev. John C. Hight

"Mr. Hight doesn't just dabble in photography — he is an expert. He has a right good-size box of ribbons which he won at the State Fair for his exhibits and one year won the grand award in the black and white amateur exhibit. He has also had several winners in the annual newspaper snapshot contest and twice won the grand award in the local contest, once in the children's division and the other time in the animal class. He does all his own developing."

— Derry Carlisle, *Who's Who in Williamson County,* Rick Warwick, ed., originally published in *The Review-Appeal,* December 17, 1964.

Portrait Published in *The Review-Appeal* on June 2, 1966

JOHN CHESTER HIGHT
1927 - 2004

John Chester Hight, Age 77, November 1, 2004. Born May 25, 1927 in Memphis, Tennessee. Preceded in death by parents, James A. Hight, Sr. and Mary White Hight.

Survived by wife of 54 years, Betty Robinson Hight; three daughters, Jean (Cliff) Hepper, Brentwood, Judy (John D.) Robnett, Pembroke Pines, Florida, and Nancy (Alan) Sanders, Paducah, Kentucky; son, John Phillip (Jami) Hight, Nashville; ten grandchildren and one great-grandchild; two brothers, James (Clarice) Hight, Memphis and Jack (Elizabeth) Hight, Villa Rica, Georgia.

The Rev. Dr. Canon Hight graduated from the University of Memphis and received a Master of Ministry from Vanderbilt University. He completed graduate studies at The University of the South, Sewanee, Tennessee.

As a Methodist Minister, he served churches in the Nashville area.

He was ordained an Episcopal Priest in 1968 and served Christ Church, Memphis, St. Barnabas, Tullahoma, Tennessee, and Good Shepherd, Knoxville, and retired as Canon Pastor of St. John's Cathedral, Knoxville.

A Memorial service will be held at 1 p.m. Saturday, November 6, 2004 at St. George's Episcopal Church, Nashville.

Friends will be received following the service. Interment will be in the Memorial Garden of St. John's Cathedral, Knoxville at a later date.

Memorial gifts may be made to Alive Hospice, Saint Thomas Foundation or the National Parkinson's Foundation. Mount Olivet Funeral Home, 1101 Lebanon Rd., (615) 255-4193.

– The Tennessean, November 4, 2004

"Young, husky fellow, still growing in ministerial work. Made a trip to England and returned with a series of photographs showing interesting England. His wife was a fine secretary that worked in the County Educational office. She was also a good minister's companion."

— *Tales of a Tennessee Yeoman*, by W. C. Yates

Portrait of An Excellent Citizen

Homer Roger Hill

Homer Roger Hill is a dairy farmer of Old Hillsboro Road and is magistrate for the Sixth Civil District. With deep concern and interest in affairs of the county, he serves on the tax study committee, the agriculture committee, and is chairman of the court's airport study committee. He is a member of the Farm Bureau and the local chapter of the NFO [National Farmers Organization], in which he has held several offices.

A member of Bethlehem Methodist Church, he has served as chairman of the official board and has led many important committees of the church. He is a member of the Tennessee Historical Society.

The son of Mr. and Mrs. Howard Hill, he is married to the former Miss Maye Tomlin and has two sons, Roger, 11, and Randy, 7.

He graduated from Franklin High School and served in the Naval Reserve.

As Published in *The Review-Appeal* on March 7, 1968

Homer Roger Hill
By Huberta Hill Perkins,
with Roger Hill and Randy Hill

Homer was born June 10, 1928, in Maury County, Tennessee. His parents were Howard Homer Hill and Lillie Anglin Hill. He was their fourth child, but the first boy. His father was native to Maury County, but his mother was from Williamson County. His older sisters, who are now deceased, were Hazel Groom, Hester Gardner and Helen Powers. Homer later had a younger brother, Hubert (deceased) and sister, Huberta Perkins. By now, you get the pattern of these names — it was even suggested at the time of Huberta's birth that she should be called "Hit's Enough!"

Homer's family moved to Williamson County before the younger children were born. He grew up on a 250-acre dairy farm on Old Hillsboro Road in the Bingham Community. They also raised tobacco, corn, hay, fruit and a very big garden. Homer attended Bingham Elementary School along with his brother and sisters. One year, all six were students there.

In 1942, he enrolled in Franklin High School, joining his sister, Helen. Homer played football and was a member of the winning team in 1946. They beat every school except Columbia, which was the last game of the season. By that time, many on the team were injured, including Homer.

Before Homer's last year in high school, his dad asked him what he wanted to do that summer. His answer was, "I want to build a house." His dad replied that he had a lot on East Fowlkes Street on which he could build. Many boys on the football team helped him build this house, and it is still there — a beige house just off Columbia Avenue.

After graduation from high school, Homer was active in many areas. He took over the dairy on the farm. He ran a flower shop for a while. He was a painter and he spread phosphate on many farms in the area.

Homer had been spending a lot of time with a young lady in Franklin. His parents were planning to move to a farm, which they had purchased in 1947, on Nashville Pike, so Homer bought their Old Hillsboro Road farm and on October 16, 1949, he married Maye Tomlin. Maye was working for National Life Insurance Co. in Nashville and Homer was running a large dairy and raising tobacco on that farm.

Homer and Maye added two precious boys to their family. First came Homer Roger, called Roger, and four years later, Randall Wray, called Randy. Maye became a stay-at-home mother. Later, Randy added two daughters, Heidi and Holly.

As time went by, Homer and Maye decided the farm across the road would better meet their needs. It bordered the Harpeth River and this would make it possible for him to irrigate his crops. They soon built a house more suitable for their family. Both boys attended Battle Ground Academy and various colleges.

After a time, Homer decided to retire from the large dairy. Too much work! He sold the cows and all but thirty-eight acres of the farm and bought Country Side Hardware on Hillsboro Road. He and Maye operated the store for several years, and soon decided it, too, had to go. Too much work! He told my daughter, Margaret, that if he had to retire the third time, it would likely kill him.

Homer got his real estate license in the early 80's. He worked with Wilson Realty Group, along with his nephew, Tim Hill and his wife, Ann. They designed and built the houses at Station South and he sold them. Homer also built rental apartment houses.

He was active as a county commissioner for several years in the 60s, 70s and 80s. The county added a new jail during that time.

He was active in the establishment of the Liberty Bank in Franklin and served on its board for several years.

In 1939, the order to rebuild the Natchez Trace was given. Years later, when this was to be carried out, Homer knew where the original Trace was on the farm across the road, and the markings for the new Trace were off. He worked with a neighbor, Jim Leeson, U.S. Rep. Richard Fulton, 5th District, and U.S. Rep. William Anderson, 6th District, to change the location. The route of the Trace was successfully relocated to the correct location and completed in 1994. (As a side note, Anderson was appointed by Admiral Rickover to be the second commanding officer of the first nuclear submarine to be placed into service, the USS *Nautilus* and was its commander from 1957 to 1959.)

Homer had an interesting life. He lost his beloved Maye on August 3, 2013, after almost 64 years of marriage. He now resides at Belvedere in Franklin. His boys and their families still live on the home place on Old Hillsboro Road.

Note: Homer Roger Hill died on August 26, 2020, in Franklin, Tennessee.

Paul Ellis Hinson

Paul Ellis Hinson, for many years one of Williamson County's prominent farmers, is now retired and lives on Battle Avenue in Franklin with his wife the former Miss Mary Stokes of Erin, Tennessee. He received his education at Wentworth Military Academy in Lexington, Mo.

Mr. Hinson is one of the directors of the Harpeth National Bank and has been a member of the Board of Trustees of the Williamson County Hospital since its organization. He was a charter member of the Rotary Club but at present is not a member.

During his farming years he was an active member of the Farm Bureau and at one time served as magistrate of the Eighth Civil District of Williamson County. He is a member of the First Presbyterian Church.

As Published in *The Review-Appeal* on March 16, 1967

PAUL ELLIS HINSON
1899 - 1980

Paul Hinson, well-known retired farmer, dies

Paul Ellis Hinson, well-known retired farmer of Franklin, died Monday morning, November 24, at Williamson County Hospital after a brief illness. He was 82 years of age.

Funeral services were held Wednesday morning at Franklin Memorial Chapel. The Rev. Edward K. Beckes officiated, and burial was in Williamson Memorial Gardens.

Mr. Hinson was born in Houston County and was the son of the late Early and Margaret Halliburton Hinson. He lived in Texas and Oklahoma in his early years and was educated at Wentworth Military Academy in Lexington, Missouri.

He moved to Franklin in 1923 and began a farming operation here. He retired when he sold his farm on Hillsboro Road in 1960 and he and his wife moved to Franklin. Mr. and Mrs. Hinson moved to Georgia for three years but returned to Franklin about two years ago and lived on Church Street.

Mr. Hinson was a devoted and active member of First Presbyterian Church and was a member of the Men's Bible Class and an elder emeritus. He was a former member of the Franklin Rotary Club and was on the original board of directors of Williamson County Hospital. He was also a retired director of Williamson County Bank.

Survivors include his wife, Mrs. Mary Stokes Hinson; a cousin, Mrs. Dan Roberts, both of Franklin; and nieces and nephews.

Serving as honorary pallbearers were members of the Men's Bible Class, Albert Ragsdale, James Stanfill, Mel Cornwell, Ray B. Peebles, Nathan Sawyer, John Hendricks, Sr., Elmer Boswell, James Warren, Jim Ogilvie, and Cletus McWilliams.

Active pallbearers were Clifton Ladd, Stokes Kennemur, Jack Kennemur, Joe Jones, Ray Stokes Peebles, Ray Stokes Peebles, Jr., John Hendricks, James Hendricks, and Kent Peebles.

In lieu of flowers donations were suggested to be made to First Presbyterian Church.

Franklin Memorial Chapel was in charge of arrangements.

– The Review-Appeal, November 27, 1980

Mrs. Ivy Ellis Holt

A local woman who has made good in the business world is Mrs. Ivy Ellis Holt, who with the exception of 4 years, has operated Holt's Amoco Service on East Main Street since 1932. Twenty-five of these years she operated on her own. For 4 years she served as bookkeeper for Warren Farm Service. Although managing a service station is a man's job Mrs. Holt has been successful in her efforts and has educated her two sons, both of whom are a credit to her. Dr. Spencer Holt, Jr., is head of the Physical Education Department of Henderson State College in Arkadelphia, Arkansas, and James Holt is assistant principal of Palatka High School in Palatka, Florida. She has 6 grandchildren.

Mrs. Holt graduated from Franklin High School in the class of 1923. She attends First Baptist Church and serves as one of the Trustees. She is a former member of the choir and is at present superintendent of the nursery.

Mrs. Holt resides on the Nashville Pike.

As Published In *The Review-Appeal* on June 13, 1968

Ivy Ellis Holt, 88, of Franklin died Wednesday, October 28 at her home in Franklin.

Mrs. Holt was a native of Franklin and a self-employed business woman. She was a member of First Baptist Church, Franklin.

Survivors include her son, James Holt of Florida; three brothers, Raymond Ellis of Nashville, Ural Ellis of Nashville and Leslie Ellis of Nashville; six grandchildren; and 22 great-grandchildren.

Funeral services were 10 a.m. Friday, October 30, at First Baptist Church of Franklin with Rev. Richard D. White officiating. Burial was in Mount Hope Cemetery.

Nephews served as pallbearers.

Williamson Memorial Funeral Home was in charge of visitation.

Ellis Funeral Home in Nashville was in charge of arrangements.

– The Review-Appeal, November 1, 1992

Portrait of An Excellent Citizen

James William Hood

James William Hood lives on Lewisburg Road in the community where he was born and reared. After finishing school he worked for a while at the Standard Farm Store in Franklin, then went to the Williamson County Bank where he has been employed for 12 years and has advanced to assistant vice-president.

Mr. Hood is married to the former Miss Katherine Ladd. He is a member of the New Hope Presbyterian Church where he has served as Sunday school superintendent. He is also an active member of the Civitan Club.

As Published in *The Review-Appeal* on September 22, 1968

A Visit with the Hoods

It was a delight to sit down with James William and Katherine Ladd Hood on a beautiful November afternoon, while they reminisced of a life of service, work and travel.

James William Hood was born in 1933 to Howard L. Hood and Rose Hood Hood (Hood was also Rose's maiden name.) Katherine Ladd was born in 1932 to Joe H. Ladd and Sarah Elizabeth Mangrum. James and Katherine grew up in Williamson County, in the Callie and Clovercroft communities, respectively, and both were educated here – James at Harpeth Elementary and Bethesda High School; Katherine at Trinity Elementary and Franklin High School. According to James, he has never lived more than a mile from where he was born, and he has lived in his present home on Lewisburg Pike for 55 years. In December of 2020, they will celebrate their 65th wedding anniversary.

There were three things James pointed out about the place he grew up on Route 2 in the Callie community. First and foremost, there were over 20 Hood families living there, so relatives were always close at hand. The second is a memory of the old Callie post office. When it was torn down, he ended up with the original board mail slot, which is attached to an outbuilding at his home. The third remembrance is that of a spring on the west side of Lewisburg Pike (Highway 431), the water from which collected in a pipe that ran under the highway and emptied out into a cistern on the opposite side of the road for livestock.

James and Katherine are long-standing members of New Bethel Cumberland Presbyterian Church in Marshall County. James has served as elder for about 40 years. In addition, James has been active in Civitan International for more than 50 years, serving as secretary/treasurer for 30 of those years.

James started his work career at the Standard Farm Store in Franklin. After expressing an interest in working at Williamson County Bank across the street, he was offered a job there in the bookkeeping department. From bookkeeping, his path of ascension went all the way to Sr. Vice President. For all of 35 years, James enjoyed his work and the associations he made in the banking business.

After retiring from the bank in 1991, he enjoyed exploring the county, making photos of old school houses and stores.

Hearing these two talk of their train travels was almost as fun as taking the trip! Every year from 1979 to 1995, James and Katherine boarded a train for a new excursion. James admitted that on their very first train trip, they dismissed the idea of booking a sleeper. Instead, they slept upright in the passenger coach, then quickly added that they never did that again. It didn't take them long to become seasoned rail fans.

Train travel to them was "just riding around," but they were able to go to many cities in the North Central, Southwestern and Western United States, as well as Canada. They traveled to places like Chicago, Portland, the coast of California, Sacramento, Texas, the Grand Canyon, Banff National Park in Alberta, and many more destinations too numerous to mention. Seeing the world-class California State Railroad Museum in Old Sacramento, California, long regarded as North America's premier railroad museum, was a treasured memory.

Like everyone else who has lived in Williamson County for a long time, they are trying to come to terms with the influx of people and the growth that has resulted. Old farms are now residential developments, roads have been expanded and new roads have been created. Old and new routes can be perplexing and the daily battle with traffic is an ongoing challenge. The pace here is faster now, and drivers are a little less patient, but, as they say, "that's progress."

– M.P.F, November 19, 2019

Lewis Morgan Hood

Living at 201 Avondale Drive is Lewis Morgan Hood, Chief of the Franklin Police Department. Born in Williamson County in the Bethesda community, he was educated at Bethesda High School. His wife, the former Miss Willie Blythe Poteete, is a licensed practical nurse. They have a son, Thomas Morgan Hood, a freshman at Columbia State Community College in Columbia, and one daughter, Susan Diane Hood, a sophomore at Franklin High School.

Mr. Hood attends the Primitive Baptist Church on Liberty Pike and is a member of the Tennessee Law Enforcement Association.

As Published in *The Review-Appeal* on November 16, 1967

LEWIS MORGAN HOOD
1925 - 2004

Former Franklin police chief dies at 79
"Hot" Hood was known for
straight-shooting demeanor

FRANKLIN - Lewis Morgan "Hot" Hood, 79, died Sunday at his home.

A veteran of the U.S. Army, Hood spent a lifetime serving his country and the city of Franklin. He fought in the Korean War, and started his civilian career as a fireman. Hood become Franklin's police chief in 1963. He was a city court clerk for 10 years and retired in 1989 after 33 years of service to Franklin.

Will Coffee, 78, who was a police officer when Hood was chief, remembers his old boss as a rather outspoken individual. Friends said Hood got the nickname "Hot" because he had a quick temper.

"He didn't bite his tongue if he had something to tell you, and I liked that about him," Coffee said. "He was good with his men. If you was a little wrong he would correct you on it, but wouldn't put you in front of the firing squad."

Jim Stafford, a Franklin police officer from 1967 to 1979, said Hood was a meticulous individual who liked things his way. Stafford, who became police chief in 1977 and is currently a court security officer, said he remembers Hood was an avid fisherman and woodworker who kept an organized shop.

"If you cast out a fishing line and he didn't like where it was he'd move it," Stafford said. "You could walk into his shop and ask for a certain size screw and he'd put his hand on it within seconds. With Hot Hood, everything had its spot, and if it was off he'd move it."

Hood's daughter, Diane Foster, said her dad treated everyone with respect.

"He had such a big heart and did so much for the city and the police department," she said.

There were fewer than 10 officers when Hood became police chief, according to Stafford. Coffee said there were 13 officers when he joined the force in 1970. Franklin was a smaller town with a population of less than half what it is today.

"There was a lot less crime back then, but there was always the Saturday night drunks and fights," Coffee said.

"We patrolled the nightspots and if people were doing wrong we'd arrest them and take them in." Stafford said there were no detectives or specialized officers when Hood was chief. He said officers worked whatever happened during their shifts.

Stafford called Hood a "great man" who brought an air of professionalism to the city's police department.

"He didn't mind telling you what he thought," Stafford said. "He was very plain-spoken and it didn't make a difference if you were someone working in a field or the president. He'd talk to you the same way."

Hood was a member of the Fraternal Order of Police. He attended the Primitive Baptist Church. He was preceded in death [by parents, Jack and Minnie Veach Hood, and] by three sisters, Rosie Smithson, Margaret Hood and Inez Miller, and a brother, J. T. Hood.

Survivors include: his wife of 58 years, Willie Blythe Poteet Hood of Franklin; his son, Thomas Morgan "Tommy" Hood and wife Debbie of Franklin; his daughter, Diane Foster and husband Barry of Franklin; four nieces, Ruby Lillard, Faye Stafford, Margaret Fann and Louise Miller; two nephews, Ronnie and Jackie Smithson; three grandchildren, Christopher Foster, Lindsay Foster Veach and Hunter Thomas Hood; and three great-grandchildren, Alison and Morgan Foster and Cameron Thomas Hood.

Funeral services, with full police honors, will be held 1 p.m. today at Williamson Memorial Funeral Home, 3009 Columbia Ave., with Bros. Allen Broughton and Pat Denton officiating. Burial will be in Mount Hope Cemetery. Active pallbearers will be Donnie Jackson, Charles Poteete Jr., Terry Poteete, Tony Poteete, Roy Dale Poteete, David Giles, Jimmy Poteete and Eddie Holland. Honorary pallbearers are Maj. Will Coffee (retired), Larry Barnes, Jimmy Stafford, Tim Taylor, Robert "Shotgun" Andrews, Sgt. Charles Fitzgerald (retired), Lt. Bolin Fitzgerald (retired) and Roy Brown. Memorials may be made to Alive Hospice or the American Heart Association.

– The Tennessean, December 14, 2004

Roy D. Hughes

Roy D. Hughes is an outstanding citizen of the Nolensville community where he lives with his wife, the former Miss LaRue McDonald formerly of McKenzie, Tennessee. In his community and throughout Williamson County he is a civic leader and dairyman.

Mr. Hughes was born just over the Williamson County line in Rutherford County and received his public school education in the Eagleville School. He attended the University of Tennessee and Middle Tennessee State University. Just recently he was named on the Board of Directors of the Nashville Milk Producers, Inc.

A member of the Nolensville Methodist Church, Mr. Hughes has been elected to almost every office in the church and at present is serving as chairman of the Board of Stewards. *Continues on next page*

As Published in *The Review-Appeal* on February 29, 1968

He is a member of Hiram Lodge No. 7 Free and Accepted Masons; vice president of the Board of Directors of Columbia Federal Land Bank Association; president of Williamson County Artificial Breeding Association; Committee delegate to A.S.C. County Committee; member of the Board of Supervisors of the Williamson County Soil Conservation Committee.

He is also a member of the Williamson County Farm Bureau and a former member of the Williamson County School Board.

He is the father of three daughters. They are Mrs. Lucien H. Battle who lives at Nolensville, Mrs. Marjorie Claire Chrisman, of Sarasota, Florida, and Mrs. Joe E. Parrish of Homestead, Florida, and six grandchildren.

Roy D. Hughes

Funeral for Roy Demonbreun Hughes, 87, of 2427 Rocky Fork Road, Nolensville, will be at 10:30 a.m. Friday at the Nolensville United Methodist Church, with the Rev. Jimmy Bass, the Rev. Melvin Brooks and Julian Goodpaster officiating.

Burial will be in the Nolensville Cemetery, Waller Funeral Home directing. Mr. Hughes, a farmer and dairyman, died Wednesday.

The family will receive visitors today (Thursday) from 2 to 5 p.m. and from 6 to 9 p.m. at Waller Chapel at 7281 Nolensville Road, Nolensville. A native of Eagleville, he was a former member of the Williamson County school board, a director of Farm Bureau, the Williamson County Farmers Co-op, Dairyman Inc., Middle Tennessee Electric Co-op, chairman of Columbia branch of the Federal Land Bank, chairman of the Williamson County Election Commission, member of the Mill Creek Masonic Lodge and director of the Soil Conservation District.

He served in every office of the Nolensville United Methodist Church, including the laity club, lay speaker and was a charter member of the Seeker's Sunday school class.

Survivors are his wife of 66 years, LaRue McDonald Hughes; three daughters, Carolyn and Lucien Battle of Nolensville, Marjorie Claire and Howard Pitts of College Grove and Evelyn and Dr. Joe Parrish of Carrollton, Georgia; a brother, Clifford H. Hughes of Clanton, Alabama; grandchildren, Hunter Battle, Barbara Battle Draffin, William F. Chrisman III, Karen Chrisman, Wallace, Brent, Bill and Amanda Parrish and Beth Parrish Whitehead and 11 great grandchildren.

Memorials may be made to the Nolensville United Methodist Church.

– The Williamson Leader, July 3, 1997

Harrell T. Hunt

Mr. Hunt is manager of the H. G. Hill Store in Franklin Plaza. He attends the Franklin First Baptist Church.

Mr. Hunt lives at 308 Belair Drive. He is married to the former Miss Mary Rowland, and they have two children, Freeda (Mrs. Wayne Burks) and Eugene, both of Franklin.

As Published in *The Review-Appeal* on September 15, 1966

Hunt, Harrell T., age 94 of Smyrna, Tennessee, and former Manchester area resident, passed away on Monday, October 29, 2012, at the Mayfield Rehabilitation Center in Smyrna. He was a retired Store Manager for the H. G. Hill Food Stores.

Born in Coffee County, Tennessee to his parents, the late Thomas Hunt and Melvina Crosslin Hunt, he was also preceded in death by his wife of 67 years, Mary Rowland Hunt and grandson, Jeffrey Burks.

He is survived by his daughter, Freeda J. Barker of Smyrna, Tennessee; son, Gene Hunt and his wife Evelyn of Antioch, Tennessee; two grandchildren, Dana L. Campbell of Smyrna, Tennessee and Travis Hunt of Fairview, Tennessee; four great-grandchildren, Michael Barker, Jacob, Brandon and Kaleigh Campbell; and one great-great-grandchild, Aubree Barker; and a host of other relatives and friends.

Visitation was on Thursday, November 1, 2012, from 12:00 p.m. until 1:00 p.m., at Central Funeral Home. The Funeral Service followed the visitation at 1:00 p.m. at the Central Chapel with Associate Pastor Scott Whaley officiating. Burial was at the Rose Hill Memorial Gardens. Arrangements with Central Funeral Home of Manchester, Tennessee.

– The Manchester Times, November 7, 2012

Portrait of An Excellent Citizen

Dr. R. H. Hutcheson

Portrait Published in *The Review-Appeal* on June 2, 1966

Dr. R. H. Hutcheson dies, health official 45 years

Dr. Robert Henry Hutcheson, who had served as director of the Williamson County Health Department for more than 20 years, died Wednesday night, March 5, at Williamson County Hospital after an extended illness.

Funeral services were held Friday morning at Franklin Memorial Chapel. The Rev. W. E. Gober officiated and burial was in Williamson Memorial Gardens.

Probably no resident of Williamson County had as interesting a public career as Dr. Hutcheson had.

A native of Henning in Lauderdale County, he was the son of the late James Albert and Rosa Barrier Hutcheson. He attended Webb School in Bell Buckle and was graduated from Columbia Military Academy. He attended Southwestern at Memphis and the University of Virginia before graduating from the University of Tennessee School of Medicine. He served his internship in the Marine Hospital at Norfolk, Virginia.

He was married to Miss Elizabeth Ford 51 years ago. She survives.

He came to Williamson County in July, 1932, from Murfreesboro where he had served as a temporary assistant director. In Williamson County he served as assistant director under Dr. W. Carter Williams.

In 1933 he won a scholarship to Johns Hopkins School of Hygiene where he received his master's degree in Public Health. Upon his return in 1934 he took over as Director of Williamson County Health Department, and in 1935 was called to the State Office of Public Health when Dr. Williams was appointed Commissioner.

Dr. Hutcheson became the State Director of Local Health Service and was given the duty of visiting magistrates and meeting with county courts in an effort to secure appropriations for county health departments. There were only 32 in Tennessee when he took over this service.

In addition to his work with the state he worked under Dr. Leathers and his staff at Vanderbilt University developing a Post-graduate course in Public Health. This work was successful and graduated one class before Dr. Leathers' death when the succeeding dean abolished the course "because of lack of funds."

In 1940 he was appointed Deputy Commissioner and when Dr. Williams resigned to enter service, Governor Prentice Cooper appointed Dr. Hutcheson Commissioner of the Tennessee Department of Public Health.

Dr. Hutcheson served as Commissioner of Public Health and as a member of the Governor's Cabinet under five governors: Prentice Cooper, Jim McCord, Gordon Browning, Frank G. Clement, and Buford Ellington. In 1952 he assumed the duties of director of the Williamson County Health Center in addition to his work as commissioner at a cost of $1 a year to Williamson County. After his retirement he became full-time director of the county health department. In January he told the magistrates he probably would not be able to make the April report and urged them to start looking for his replacement.

From 1943 to 1953 there were more developments in Public Health than anytime in past history. Archaic laws were repealed or amended and services created. Tuberculosis hospitals were built and the Hill-Burton Hospital Construction Program was developed. Because of state and federal laws he organized the state's Medicare and Medicaid programs during the last year of his administration.

Continued on next page

Dr. Hutcheson was a member of the Tennessee Tuberculosis Hospital Commission and later a member of the Board of Trustees of Tuberculosis Hospitals; executive officer of the Licensing Board of Healing Arts; chairman of the Tennessee Hospital Licensing Board; chairman of the Stream Pollution Board; and Diplomat of American Board of Preventive Medicine and Public Health.

Dr. Hutcheson has been the recipient of many awards: the McCormick Award by the State and Territorial Health Officer's Association in 1957; lifetime membership in the P.T.A.; honorary life membership in the Tennessee Dental Society; J. P. Cranz [Krantz] Memorial Award; "Outstanding Physician of the Year" in 1970 by the Tennessee Medical Association; citation by Johnson City Chamber of Commerce for his work toward the establishment of a college of medicine at East Tennessee State University where one of the buildings in the College of Health bears his name; honorary life membership in the Shelby County Medical Association.

At the October session the Williamson County Quarterly Court approved changing the name of the County Health Department to the R. H. Hutcheson Health Center. He was further honored November 19 when a testimonial dinner was held for him and attracted 150 friends from throughout the state in addition to those from Williamson County.

Dr. Hutcheson was a member of the County, State and American Medical Societies and past president of the Tennessee Public Health Association. He was a member of the Southern Branch of American Public Health Association which he helped organize and served as secretary-treasurer and later as president.

In 1949 he was elected president of the State and Territorial Health Officer's Association and during the next several years served on numerous advisory committees to the Surgeon General, two of the most important of which were the Advisory Committee on Industrial Health and the Advisory Committee on Safety.

Shortly after the formation of the Southern Regional Nuclear Board in 1956 Dr. Hutcheson was elected in 1957 by the Board as their Public Health Consultant and resigned in 1972.

Dr. Hutcheson was a regular attendant at the First United Methodist Church, and until its reorganization and change of Sunday School organization he served as superintendent of Adult Sunday School Section.

– *The Review-Appeal, March 13, 1975*

January 1, 1967
MILK
GRADES
Published

In accordance with Section 3 and Section 5 of Ordinance Number 138 of the City of Franklin, Tennessee, the grades of the dairies are published below, so that the public may be informed of the milk sold in Franklin.

Grade "A" Pasteurized
Nashville Pure Milk Co.
Anthony Pure Milk Co.
Purity Dairies, Inc.
Border's Milk Co.
Murfreesboro Pure Milk Co.

Approved:

ASA JEWELL
Mayor

DR. R. H. HUTCHESON
City Health Officer

JERRY MOORE
BOBBY NICHOLS
Sanitation Officers

Portrait of An Excellent Citizen

Harry Perkins Isaacs

Harry Perkins Isaacs was born in Franklin where he was educated and practically grew up in a shoe store. He is co-owner and operator of the new Lunn & Garner Shoe Store on Main Street.

Harry is a member of the Williamson County Chamber of Commerce, the Franklin High School Men's Club, Farm Bureau and the Main Street Improvement Committee.

He is married to the former Miss Lillie Mai (Pill) Cummins [Timmons] of Nashville. He has one son, Harry Leonard of Nashville and one daughter, Martha Ann Galavin of Franklin. Harry attends the Fourth Avenue Church of Christ.

As Published in *The Review-Appeal* on July 20, 1967

Harry Isaacs, Main Street "dean," dies

Harry P. Isaacs, known as the "Dean of Main Street," who had been a businessman on Franklin's Main Street for 51 years, died Sunday night at Parkview Hospital. He had worked Saturday but suffered a heart attack that night and his condition became worse after he was hospitalized.

Funeral services were held Tuesday morning at Franklin Memorial Chapel. Myron Keith officiated and burial was in Williamson Memorial Gardens.

Mr. Isaacs, 67, began working for his uncle, Rainey Lunn, and Bob Garner in Lunn and Garner Shoe Store as a young boy and continued as a salesman in the store after he finished school. Several years ago he and Lonnie Burchett purchased the business and he became the manager.

He is well known for his art work and cartoons and for many years was featured with cartoons at the election parties held by *The Review-Appeal*.

He was an avid sports fan and had kept football records of Franklin High School, BGA, and the old Franklin Training School since 1925. For the past 40 years he had kept the scores of Franklin High and BGA softball and basketball games.

He was a native of Williamson County and was the son of the late Elijah A. and Frances Duncan Lunn Isaacs. He was a member of the Fourth Avenue Church of Christ.

Survivors include his wife, Mrs. Lillie Timmons Isaacs; one daughter, Mrs. William Galavin, both of Franklin; one son, Leonard Isaacs of Nashville; three sisters, Mrs. Percy Jennette and Mrs. James Lawrence of Franklin and Mrs. Paul Stratton of Miami, Florida; three brothers, Eugene Isaacs of Nashville and Fred and Phil Isaacs of Franklin; and four grandchildren.

Active pallbearers were Cortez Isaacs, William Miller, Bill McDonald, Billy and Steve Isaacs, and Jack Lunn.

Serving as honorary were Main Street merchants of Franklin.

Franklin Memorial Chapel was in charge of arrangements.

— *The Review-Appeal, March 23, 1972*

"My Daddy was my best friend, and if any of you would like to be my best friend then all you have to do is be a better friend to me than he was."

— Leonard Isaacs, *Franklin Tennessee... Nestled in the Valley of the Harpeth*, 2014.

Alfred E. Jaqueth

Alfred E. Jaqueth is a resident of College Grove, Tennessee, where he lives with his wife, the former Miss Eula Lee Haley.

Mr. Jaqueth commutes to Franklin each day. He is connected with the Williamson County Board of Education as Coordinator of Federal Promotions. During the summer months he serves as director of the Head Start Program.

He attends the College Grove Methodist Church, is a member of the official board and is just completing a term of service as superintendent of the church school.

Mr. Jaqueth is a member of the College Grove Lions Club of which he has served as president. He is also a member of the Farm Bureau, the Carter House Association and the Williamson County Historical Society.

As Published in *The Review-Appeal* on June 29, 1967

Longtime educator, Jaqueth, dies

Longtime Williamson County educator Alfred Jaqueth died Tuesday, Nov. 11, at his home in College Grove.

Mr. Jaqueth was principal of College Grove School from 1975 until 1985 and prior to that, he was supervisor of secondary education in the central office of the Williamson County Schools system from 1968 until 1975. Mr. Jaqueth was principal at Nolensville Elementary from 1953-55.

He taught at College Grove from 1955 until 1966 and in 1966, he was named the Title 1 coordinator for the school system. "He had a way of making himself a part of your life and he touched so many people," said Frances Greathouse, his secretary at the school for a number of years.

Described as a compassionate and considerate man, Mr. Jaqueth was an active member of the College Grove Senior Citizens Center, the College Grove Lions Club and he had been the music director at the College Grove United Methodist Church. At the request of the family, no services are being held.

– The Review-Appeal, November 12, 1997

After 40 years in education, Alfred Jaqueth says he is enjoying helping his wife Eula Lee farm and doing volunteer community work.

"My wife is the farmer; everybody in the neighborhood knows that, but she doesn't turn down any offer of help," he says.

Jaqueth, a native of New Jersey, laughs that he is still considered a "Yankee" by some people, but says it was love that brought him to Middle Tennessee. He met Mrs. Jaqueth, a native of Williamson County, when she visited relatives in New Jersey. They decided to settle here.

The warm weather in January allowed the Jaqueths to plow their garden and the seeds are just waiting for Spring. And March is calving time for the farm. They will be busy as 60 calves are being born.

Music also occupies Jaqueth. He is the organist for the College Grove United Methodist Church. In addition to gardening and music, Jaqueth is an avid reader. "One of the joys of retirement is reading," he says. "I think I'm just in seventh heaven to sit down and read the newspaper when it comes."

— Cletus Sickler, *"Jaqueth Enjoys retirement after 40 years in Education,"* The Williamson Leader, *February 28,* 1986.

Vergil Roland Jenkins

Vergil Roland Jenkins and his wife, the former Miss Anne Inglehart, live in Forrest Manor Apartments on Fourth Avenue, South.

Mr. Jenkins came to Franklin more than twenty years ago and began business as owner and manager of Jenkins' Ben Franklin Store, and up until earlier this year operated two stores on Main Street. A few months ago [he] began business as owner and manager of location, 338 Main Street.

Carroll and William Jenkins, two boys, are Mr. Jenkins' only children. William is a minister of the Presbyterian Church in Clarksville and Carroll is in Theological school in Richmond, Virginia, preparing for the ministry.

Mr. Jenkins attends the First Presbyterian Church, is an elder and served as chairman of the pulpit nominating committee. He is also a member of the Retail Merchants Committee of the Williamson County Chamber of Commerce.

As Published in *The Review-Appeal* on August 31, 1967

Vergil Roland Jenkins, 85, of St. Petersburg, Florida, and formerly of Franklin, died Friday, April 16, at his residence.

A native of Hopkins County, Kentucky, he moved to St. Petersburg in 1989 from McAllen, Texas. He was former owner and operator of Jenkins' Ben Franklin in Franklin, former elder of Franklin First Presbyterian Church, member of Hiram Masonic Lodge #7 F&AM in Franklin, and Al Menah Shrine Temple in Nashville. He was a member of Woodlawn Presbyterian Church.

Survivors include his wife of 63 years, Anne D. Jenkins; twin sons, W. Roland and V. Carroll Jenkins of St. Petersburg; seven grandchildren; and six great-grandchildren.

Services will be at 12:45 p.m. Sunday, April 25, at Woodlawn Presbyterian Church in St. Petersburg. Anderson-McQueen Funeral Home in St. Petersburg is in charge of arrangements.

– The Review-Appeal, April 18, 1993

BEN FRANKLIN STORES
5c & 10c
LOCALLY OWNED
NATIONALLY KNOWN

"Two Self Serve Stores On Main St. For Your Shopping Convenience"

"Both Mr. and Mrs. Jenkins were born and reared in Madisonville, Kentucky, a town noted far and near for the electrically lighted arched signs over every approach bearing the words, 'The Best Town on Earth,' and under it, 'Heart of the Coal Field, Big Tobacco Market.'... Mr. Jenkins, of Welsh descent, and his wife, formerly Anne Inglehart, is a cross between Dutch and Irish, so he says the twins are a 'Duke's mixture'..."

— Jane Bowman Owen, *Who's Who in Williamson County*, Rick Warwick, ed., originally published in *The Review-Appeal*, April 19, 1945.

Portrait of An Excellent Citizen

Mayor Asa Jewell

Portrait Published in *The Review-Appeal* on April 7, 1966

ASA HICKMAN JEWELL
1910-1989

Asa Jewell

A memorial service for Asa H. Jewell, 78, horse and tobacco marketer and former mayor of Franklin, was Sunday, Feb. 12, at Williamson Memorial Funeral Home.

Mr. Jewell died Thursday, Feb. 9, at his home on Fourth Avenue South.

A native of Lexington, Kentucky, he graduated from MIT where he was a member of Sigma Chi Fraternity.

He moved to Franklin in 1943 to join his father and brothers in the operation of Jewell Tobacco Warehouse.

He also owned Blooded Horse Sales Company of Wilmore, Kentucky.

He was a member of the Franklin Rotary Club.

Jewell served as mayor of Franklin from 1961 to 1969, and earlier had been an alderman.

Survivors include his wife, Margaret Loring Jewell of Franklin, three daughters, Therese W. Jewell of Westford, Massachusetts and Trinidad, California; Margaret L. Gordon of Lexington, Kentucky; and Mary H. J. Lord of Acton, Massachusetts; son, Dr. Asa H. Jewell of Fredericksburg, Texas; brother, Charley Jewell of Columbia; sister, Mrs. John L. Davis of Lexington, Kentucky, and six grandchildren.

– The Williamson Leader, February 17, 1989

The Jewell lineage were English, who came largely from Virginia. They were often wellborn, headed by the second and third sons of wealthy landowners who knew their older brothers would inherit the family land and so wanted their own manors and estates.

Asa Jewell was born 1910, into an old Kentucky family in Lexington. He was the eldest sibling with twin brothers John and Charley, and a baby sister who remained in Lexington. Asa was the bookworm and never athletic, like his brothers. He went to M.I.T. in Cambridge, Massachusetts, and learned in his senior year that he wanted a law degree, and would have been a great lawyer. His father said it was too late to change and would not pay for it.

Like his ancestor, whose horse, Viva America, won The Oaks race at Churchill Downs and came in third at the Kentucky Derby, Asa's other dream was to win the Kentucky Derby, in spite of the fact that his father told him that horses would be his downfall.

About 1934, he saw the beautiful Margaret Loring at the Phi Gamma dance, and knew immediately that she was to be his wife. About 1935, my parents lived in a little apartment in Manhattan and Asa owned the Town and Country Restaurant across the street from the Waldorf Astoria. In this restaurant where the chief cook was from Kentucky, New Yorkers experienced their first taste of Kentucky fried chicken while sitting on deep red velvet upholstered booths.

Asa's and Margaret's evenings were spent dancing on rooftops to the big bands during the depression years. Asa wore a top hat and cape, while Margaret wore Ginger Rogers-style gowns. We think of Fred Astaire, who was one of Asa's idols, but Asa was actually a lot handsomer with his 6'2" frame and black hair and dark eyes.

While in New York and now living in a big old house in Larchmont, Asa and Margaret bore Therese, Asa Jr., and Margaret. This was when he developed tuberculosis thus his doctor advised him to leave New York if he wanted to live. Mary was born after the move to Franklin.

Excellent Citizens and Notable Partings

Upon the invitation of his brothers John and Charley Jewell, we moved to Franklin from NYC and Asa became the third partner to John and Charley Jewell at the Jewell Tobacco Warehouses. I was two years old at the time, and the population of this little farm town was 15,000. He found his niche in doing the accounting work for the warehouses, subsequently taking on the accounting for six other businesses located in the Franklin area.

I remember, as a child, walking from our house on Columbia Avenue (next door to the Carter house) to the Franklin Theatre to watch the Saturday matinee westerns. We had to walk carefully to avoid stepping on the chewing-tobacco spits on the sidewalk. There were lots of farmers lolling in town, especially around the Franklin courthouse.

Asa found he could help by being an alderman to our mayor Frank Gray, who wished to see Asa succeed him when he retired. The election for mayor was a win due, in large part, from John Jewell's help in campaigning for his brother.

As I recall, one of Asa's first primary battles was to take alcohol out of the hands of the bootleggers and make it legal to buy. It was a tough fight because the bootleggers were using their revenue to bribe the preachers to preach against alcohol. We discovered this when my uncle Charley brought the $5,000 to Asa that an honest preacher had received from their local bootlegger.

In 1954, we moved to Winstead Place on South Margin Street. Mother, an artist, was so pleased to be decorating the old dilapidated house. She wanted the house, Asa wanted her to be happy. The role of mayorship was so good for the town that two Senators, Kefauver and Albert Gore, Sr., visited often, hoping to persuade Asa to move to 'big time' politics in Washington. He used the old adage to explain his thoughts on the matter, "I'd rather be a big fish in a small pond, than a small fish in a big pond."

The next real issue that comes to mind is during the time of Martin Luther King's "I Have a Dream" speech in Washington, Asa received warning that there would be riots after this speech. Asa gathered the black (as the African-Americans were called at that time) leaders to our house for a meeting to decide how to create a peaceful transition in Franklin after the speech. Sunday before, our family went to the black church service for a show of support for the black community. It turned out we did the right thing. Nashville burned after; Franklin was quiet. A short time after, our next-door neighbor who owned a gas station on Columbia Avenue, hired the first young black man to serve gas. It was the first job available for one of color that was not a servant job. Other jobs followed to open up income for the blacks. The segregated bathrooms and drinking fountains disappeared at that time.

After that, Asa put a stop to the segregated schools and started the busing of students. I was told a lot of townspeople were up in arms about this last act. It was shortly after, that Asa was no longer mayor of Franklin. Asa seemed quite pleased about retiring as he was feeling the burnout.

Nevertheless, during his time as mayor, Franklin grew phenomenally. Asa had brought the first manufacturing company, Chicago Printed Ribbon & String company, to the outskirts of Franklin. It was toward the end of Asa's mayoral duties that Franklin had grown from a sleepy farm town to what was known as Nashville's bedroom, i.e., commuters who preferred to live in Franklin and work in Nashville.

An aside about my mother, Margaret Loring Jewell was a true blue Yankee. She married Asa on the condition that she could always go back to Maine during every summer. Thus living on the beach next door to our grandparents was a big part of our upbringing. This tradition continues with my cousin, John Jewell, who also married a New England girl who summered on Drakes Island. The challenge of the southern culture weighed heavily on Margaret, and with deliberate planning, she returned north a mere two weeks after Asa Jewell died, in 1987, of esophageal cancer. He died at home, dearly loved by his family, and many others.

– Margaret (Margi) Jewell Gordon, daughter

Portrait of An Excellent Citizen

Dr. C. C. Johnson

Portrait Published in *The Review-Appeal* on April 28, 1966

Dr. C. C. Johnson
Physician, Civic Leader, Succumbs

Dr. Charles C. Johnson, 81, who practiced medicine in Franklin and Williamson County for nearly a half century and was prominent in civic and community affairs here much of that time, died Sunday morning at Williamson County Hospital.

His death was attributed to heart failure although he had been hospitalized since December 7 because of a broken hip. He underwent surgery December 14 to set the break and his condition began to grow worse later in the week.

Funeral services were held at Shorter Chapel A.M.E. Church Wednesday morning with the Rev. G. M. Fleming officiating. Burial was in Toussaint L'Ouverture Cemetery.

Dr. Johnson was a native of Canton, Missouri. He was graduated from the University of Iowa and Meharry Medical College in Nashville in 1917.

He began practice here soon after he completed his medical training. Some 25 years ago he bought a clinic here which he operated until his death. He was a member of the Franklin Housing Authority and had served as co-chairman for several years. When the elementary school on Mt. Hope Street was completed about eight years ago, it was named the Charles C. Johnson School in honor of the man who had worked hard in the interest of his people.

Dr. Johnson was a member of Shorter Chapel A.M.E. Church.

Survivors include his wife, Mrs. Clara E. Johnson, and several nephews.

Stewards and trustees of Shorter Chapel Church served as pallbearers, and Patton Brothers Funeral Home was in charge of arrangements.

– The Review-Appeal, December 22, 1966

City honoring Dr. C. C. Johnson
Black physician started med school with $12

When Charles Claudius Johnson, one of Franklin's first black physicians, came from Missouri to Meharry Medical College in 1906, he had only $12 in his pockets.

He told the president of the college he wanted to be a doctor, but that $12 was all the money he had. He explained he wanted to become a physician so he could find a cure for a disease his father suffered. The school's president allowed him to enroll, and 11 years later Johnson came to Franklin to begin 50 years of medical practice.

Mary Mills, Franklin educator, who was close to Johnson and his wife, Clara, while growing up, going to school and becoming a teacher, recalled some of the highlights from the physician's life as the Franklin board of mayor and aldermen declared Monday Dr. C. C. Johnson Day.

Mrs. Mills, who is principal of the Franklin Middle School, and her husband, Latham Mills, Sr., a nephew of Dr. Johnson, remember much about the generous, good humored man who opened a hospital on Columbia Avenue and worried little about the money patients owed him.

In fact, the former Mary Johnson Knowles (no relation to the physician) knew the doctor and his wife as an elementary school student at the former Franklin Training School on Natchez Street. Dr. Johnson was her grandmother's physician. Both the doctor and his wife had an interest in education, though they had no children, and they frequently visited the all-black Franklin Training School.

A librarian at the school told Dr. Johnson one day that she needed to obtain more books because "little Mary Knowles has read most every volume in the library."

"They became interested in me, and they paid my way through college," recalls Mrs. Mills, who following graduation from Tennessee State, worked for one year as Dr. Johnson's secretary and licensed practical nurse.

Dr. Johnson converted his home into a hospital for blacks when other hospitals in Franklin would not keep mothers of newborn black children overnight.

"He felt they needed a comfortable, sanitary place to stay after their babies were born," recalled Mrs. Mills. "He turned his home into a hospital and built another house next door."

The Johnson Hospital was located on Columbia Avenue, near the site of the present Kentucky Fried Chicken restaurant, and operated from 1948 until 1962 – four years before Dr. Johnson's death.

Johnson would treat blacks or whites and would help people of either race needing money, said Mrs. Mills.

"He'd go on notes for people, knowing they wouldn't have the money to pay him back. He'd pay the notes off for them," she explained.

"When he died, we found bills owed to him for medical care that should have been paid, but people had let them go for years and he never worried about them," she added.

"He was very active in Shorter Chapel AME Church, and he would give things to the church when he really couldn't afford to," Mrs. Mills recalled.

The Church recently honored Johnson at a Black History Month program.

Johnson Elementary School, built in 1958 to serve black students in grades one through eight, was named for Dr. Johnson. In 1971, the school began serving children of all races in grades three and four.

The school will have a special assembly on Monday in observance of Dr. C. C. Johnson Day. The program will include a biography on Johnson, remarks by Mrs. Mills and songs by the Johnson Jubilee Chorus.

"He believed every child should have a good education, and he would tell them," said Mrs. Mills.

Mrs. Johnson was also interested in schools, and trained the chorus at Franklin Training School as a volunteer.

Mrs. Mills, who was a member of the chorus under Mrs. Johnson, recalled, "We always would rank at the top in competition."

Mrs. Johnson also taught piano lessons, and at one time, all of the black churches in Franklin were supplied with pianists who were her students, according to Mrs. Mills.

Though Mrs. Mills doesn't directly credit Dr. Johnson with changing her last name from Knowles to Mills, she admits he had a little to do with it.

Johnson and his wife brought a then sickly Latham Mills from his home in Iowa to Franklin to "nurse him back to health." Mills recovered and went on to serve in the Marine Corps. But it wasn't until several years later that he and Mary Johnson Knowles became sweethearts and were married. "When I knew Latham, he didn't even pay me any attention at all," recalls his wife. "He came to visit at school one day when he was in the Marine Corps and he didn't even notice me."

The Mills' son, Latham Jr., a minister and recreational therapist, is responsible for calling attention to Dr. Johnson's 100th birthday.

"Dr. Johnson and his wife were like grandparents to our children," explains Mrs. Mills. "Latham, at one time, wanted to be a doctor. He wanted to have a special day set aside for Dr. Johnson so people who were not living here at the time he practiced medicine could know about him.

Johnson was born in Canton, Missouri in 1885. Even after he was accepted at Meharry Medical School, he had to drop out to earn money to complete requirements for his degree. He worked as a mason and on a railroad for money to complete his education.

Dr. Johnson was the first chairman of the Franklin Housing Authority. He also was a member of the staff of Williamson County

Hospital, member of the Elks Lodge, member of the American Medical Association, and Member of the W. F. Boyd Medical Association (Tennessee unit).

The physician also liked to fish in his spare time and had a sense of humor.

"He would wash his hands at home and walk around with them in the air waiting for someone to hand him a towel, just as he did in his hospital," recalled Mrs. Mills. "His wife finally told him one day 'If you want your hands dry, you'd better go get a towel for yourself.'"

– The Williamson Leader, February 22, 1985

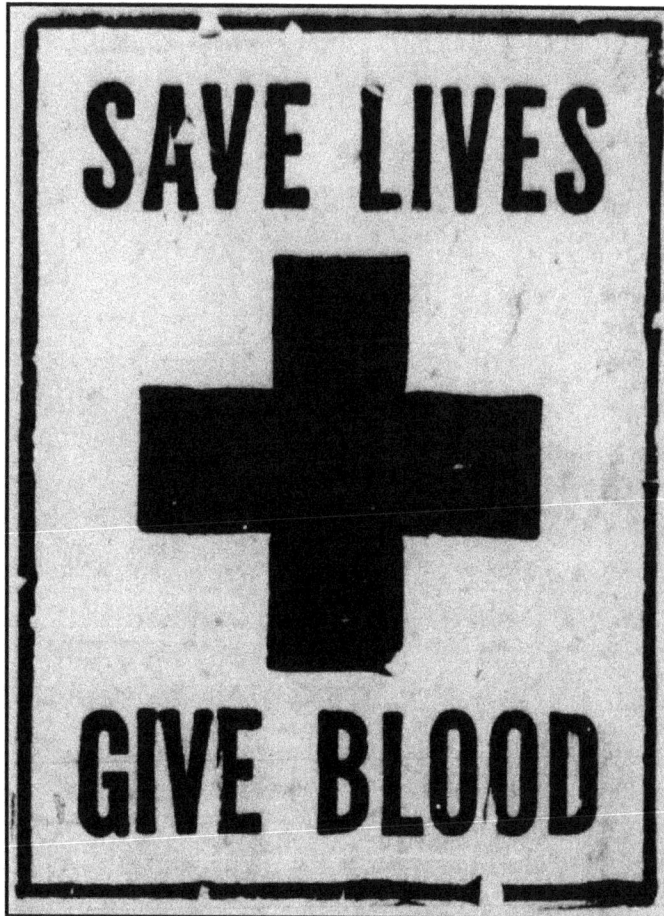

Excellent Citizens and Notable Partings

Portrait of An Excellent Citizen

Howard E. Johnston

Howard E. Johnston, elected last week to the presidency of Breeko Industries, Inc., has seen the concrete masonry business develop from a few simple products to highly diversified production since 1946 when he joined the late Claiborne H. Kinnard in the operation of Franklin Concrete, Inc., which was merged in 1964 with Breeko of Nashville.

Mr. Johnston has worked for the advancement of concrete products in association and organizations at all levels. He has also been closely connected with the Junior Achievement program in Nashville and serves on the Board of Directors. He is on the Board of Trustees for Battle Ground Academy and for a number of years was a member of the Ninth Special School District Board. He is an elder of First Presbyterian Church.

He is married to the former Miss Mary Alice Nolen and they have three children, Howard III, Beverly, and Mary Alice. They live on Murfreesboro Road.

As Published in *The Review-Appeal* on April 4, 1968

Howard Johnston, business, civic, church leader, dies

Howard Earl Johnston, Jr., well-known business, civic, and church leader of Franklin, died unexpectedly at Williamson County Hospital early Thursday morning, November 10, after suffering a heart attack at his home the night before. He was 68.

Graveside services were held Saturday afternoon at Mt. Hope Cemetery. The Rev. Edward K. Beckes officiated.

Mr. Johnston was a native of Hobart, Oklahoma, and was the son of the late Howard Earl and Sue Moss Johnston. He was graduated from Columbia Military Academy in Columbia, Tennessee.

During World War II he served in the 8th Air Force and was a major when he was discharged.

Following the war he joined the late Claiborne H. Kinnard as a partner in Franklin Concrete, Inc., soon after Kinnard founded the firm, which was one of the early manufacturers of concrete block in this area of the state. The company was later sold to Breeko Industries of Nashville and Mr. Johnston became president of Breeko. He retired from Breeko a few years ago.

He was an active member of First Presbyterian Church and served as a trustee and inactive elder.

Mr. Johnston was on the board of directors of First Tennessee Bank.

He served as a member of the Franklin Special School District Board of Education for several years and was a member of the board of trust of Battle Ground Academy.

He was a charter member of the Franklin Rotary Club.

Survivors include his wife, Mrs. Mary Alice Nolen Johnston of Franklin; two daughters, Mrs. Jack (Beverly) Fletcher of Brentwood and Ms. Mary Alice Johnston of Franklin; one son, Howard E. Johnston, III, of Buffalo, Wyoming; and five grandchildren.

The body lay in state at First Presbyterian Church before the services.

Serving as honorary pallbearers were John Charles Wheeler, David Rodenhauser, Harlan Dodson, Felix Weisiger, Gene Mullen, Leonard McKeand, Jr., Warren Taylor, Jack Lee, Bob Hannah, Clem Blackburn, Billy Billington, Stewart Campbell, Horton Early, J. B. Parks, and Dewees Berry.

Active pallbearers were Wilson Herbert, Robert Herbert, Bill Herbert, Joe Herbert, Dr. Herbert Crockett, and Steve Murrey.

The family suggested that memorials might be made to the Middle Tennessee Heart Association, the scholarship fund at First Presbyterian Church, or a charity of the donor's choice.

Franklin Memorial Chapel was in charge of arrangements.

— The Review-Appeal, November 15, 1983

* * *

* * *

Joe Turner Jones

Born in the Triune community of Williamson County, Joe Turner Jones, received his elementary education in the Triune School. He also attended the University of Tennessee, Nashville Branch, and the Dale Carnegie School of Speech. For the past 26 years he has been employed with Southern Bell Telephone Company as installer and repairman. His headquarters are in the practically new building located on Cummins Street.

Mr. Jones lives a short distance from the city limits on the Nashville Highway, with his wife, the former Miss Virginia Stokes and their two children, Teresa and Gary, both students at Lipscomb School.

Mr. Jones is a member of the Franklin First Methodist Church attends the Crusaders Class and sings in the Men's Chorus. He is one of the church's lay leaders and is past president of the Williamson County Layman's Club.

As Published in *The Review-Appeal* on December 14, 1967

Joe Turner Jones, 89, of Franklin, Tennessee, died Oct. 3, 2012. He served his country in the Philippines during World War II and was the recipient of the Purple Heart Award. Retired after 35 years of service from South Central Bell, he was the owner and founder of Franklin Carpet Company.

Mr. Jones was an active member of the First United Methodist Church in Franklin and was a member of the Men's Chorus for 50 years. He enjoyed buying and restoring antique cars. He was a loving husband, father, brother and friend to many.

He was preceded in death by his first wife Virginia Stokes Jones. Mr. Jones is survived by wife, Erma Lee Needham Jones; son, Gary (Annetta "Suzie") Jones; daughter, Teresa (Victor) Blackburn; sister, Martha Waller; grandchildren, Clint and Amanda Hassell and Chasity Jones; several great grandchildren; and nieces and nephews.

Funeral services were conducted Sunday, Oct. 7, 2012 at Williamson Memorial Funeral Home, Rev. Lynn Hill officiating. Interment was in Triune Cemetery.

Active pallbearers were Jack Wheeler, Dan Fuller, George Jones, Barry Sewell, Nickey Jones, Jay Wheeler, Jim Yates, Jack Vaughn and Dr. Lance Needham. Honorary pallbearers were the Horace Edgmon Sunday School Class.

Arrangements are by Williamson Memorial Funeral Home in Franklin.

— The Williamson Herald, October 11, 2012

Portrait of An Excellent Citizen

Myron Keith

Myron Keith is minister of the Fourth Avenue Church of Christ in Franklin. He is married to the former Miss Lois McGill. They have one daughter, Karen, and they reside on Ewingville Drive. Mr. Keith is a member of the Franklin Rotary Club.

As Published in *The Review-Appeal* on October 6, 1966

Mr. C. Myron Keith, age 83, of Franklin, Tennessee. passed away November 13, 2015.

He was a man who loved God and his family and was truly dedicated to his Lord. He began preaching at age 16 until 82 in various congregations predominately in Middle Tennessee.

His last church was Peytonsville Church of Christ and prior to that, 28 years at Fourth Ave. Church of Christ.

He is preceded in death by grandson, Benton Baxter; parents, Charles and Laura Keith; and sisters, Amy Wallace and Barbara Short.

He is survived by his wife of 62 years, Lois Keith; daughter, Karen (Tim) Baxter; grandchildren, Keith and Rusty Baxter; sister, Betty Allamel and much loved nieces and nephews.

Funeral services will be conducted 11 a.m. on Monday, Nov. 16 at Williamson Memorial Funeral Home where we will celebrate his life and his love for God. Interment Williamson Memorial Gardens. Family and friends will serve as pallbearers. Honorary pallbearers will be Peytonsville Church of Christ. Memorials may be made to Churches of Christ Disaster Relief or Graceworks of Franklin.

Visitation will be 3-6 p.m. on Sunday and one hour prior to service at Williamson Memorial Funeral Home, 615 794-2289.

– The Williamson Herald, November 19, 2015

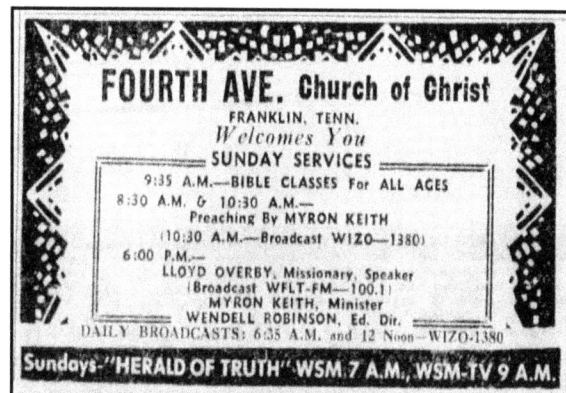

"Fourth Avenue Church of Christ most likely has the distinction of being Franklin and Williamson County's best attended church. ... A total of 850 people average attending both services each Sunday, and Myron Keith, the minister, recalls recent occasions when he has preached to as many as 900. Membership of the church numbers 1,000. The congregation also has the distinction of being one of the oldest in the community, dating its beginning to a little more than 30 years after Franklin became a town. ...

"Keith, who grew up in Birmingham and preached in a number of Middle Tennessee churches, has been minister of the church since December 1963. Wendell Robinson is his associate and the church's educational director.

"'Growth of the church can be attributed to two factors,' says Keith.' 'One is that Middle Tennessee has long been the heartland of the Church of Christ. The second is the number of new families moving into Williamson County as a part of the area's rapid growth.'"

— "Fourth Avenue Church of Christ One of Largest Congregations," *The Williamson Leader*, March 10, 1974.

Portrait of An Excellent Citizen

Brown Campbell Kinnard

Brown Kinnard, a retired farmer, lives on his 900 acre farm on the Carters Creek Pike. He has two children, Mrs. Walter (Carolyn) Ziffer, of Chambon, France and Brown Campbell Kinnard, Jr., of Houston, Texas. He is a member of the First Presbyterian Church and the Franklin Rotary Club and is a director in the Williamson County Farm Bureau. His wife was the former Miss Ida Beasley.

As Published in *The Review-Appeal* on October 20, 1966

BROWN CAMPBELL KINNARD
1898 - 1978

B. C. Kinnard, farm, church leader, dies

Brown Campbell Kinnard, retired farmer of Carter's Creek Pike who was well-known throughout the county and mid-state for his activities in farming, church, and civic affairs, died unexpectedly Tuesday, June 6, at St. Thomas Hospital. He had been admitted as a patient there for tests Monday. He apparently suffered a massive coronary in the late afternoon. He was 80 years old.

Funeral services were held Thursday afternoon at First Presbyterian Church. The Rev. Edward K. Beckes, minister of the church, officiated. Burial was in Mt. Hope Cemetery.

Mr. Kinnard was a member of a family prominent in Williamson County for several generations and was the third generation to own and occupy the family farm, Fairview, on Carter's Creek Pike. The house was built in the mid-19th century by his grandfather, Claiborne Holmes Kinnard, who had acquired the land from Edward Swanson, Williamson County's first settler who came to this part of the country with James Robertson. The farm was a land grant to Swanson, and more than 900 acres were included in the Kinnard operation.

Mr. Kinnard was the son of the late Rebecca Campbell and Claiborne Holmes Kinnard, Jr., who remodeled the farm house in 1898 when bathrooms and the porches were added. He was graduated from Battle Ground Academy.

He was a member of First Presbyterian Church where he had been active in all phases of work. He had served as a deacon for many years and was to be installed as elder in August.

He was an active member of the Williamson County Farm Bureau and the Williamson County Chamber of Commerce and he and his wife served on the Chamber's county beautiful [beautification] division.

He had been a member of the Franklin Rotary Club for many years and was involved in all of its programs. He returned only two weeks before his death from a trip to the Orient with his wife and several friends when they attended the Rotary International convention in Tokyo.

Mr. Kinnard's most recent endeavor was working with the Meals on Wheels program and he had become a driver for the project some two months ago.

Survivors include his wife, Mrs. Sallie A. Kinnard; a daughter, Mrs. Walter (Carolyn) Ziffer of Brussels, Belgium; a son, Brown C. Kinnard, Jr., of Ann Arbor, Michigan; one sister, Mrs. Bolling Warner of Nashville; and nine grandchildren.

Honorary pallbearers were elders, and deacons and members of the Men's Bible Class of First Presbyterian Church, officers and directors of the Franklin Rotary Club and the Farm Bureau, Joe Pinkerton, Fulton Beasley, Tyler Berry, Sr., William W. Ewin, Dr. Thomas Frist, Sr., Fulton Greer, Herbert Kneeland, Sr., Dan Hagerty, Calvin Lehew, William Miller, Paul Redick, John Lloyd Pewitt, Malcolm Wakefield, Robert L. White, Dr. Joe Zanone, and W.C. Yates.

Serving as active pallbearers were Harry Sanders, Eddie Sanders, Claiborne H. Kinnard V., Jon Campbell Kinnard II, Christopher Cabot, John C. Lionberger, Ralph Brown, Henry Bailey, and Brown Cannon.

The family suggested that memorial donations might be made to the Middle Tennessee Heart Fund, the organ fund or the elders' triumphant fund of First Presbyterian Church.

Franklin Memorial Chapel was in charge of arrangements.

— The Review-Appeal, June 15, 1978

Portrait of An Excellent Citizen

Will C. Lanier

Born, reared, and educated in the Allisona community, Will C. Lanier, a retired rural mail carrier, farmer, and trader, will celebrate his 98th birthday in December.

When he married Miss Cornelia Lockridge, they moved to a farm just south of College Grove where he now lives. Mrs. Lanier died in 1958. Their daughter and son-in-law, Mr. and Mrs. Lee Alexander, make their home with him. A son, Robert A. Lanier, lives in Nashville.

As a child Mr. Lanier attended the old Wesley Chapel Methodist Church at Arno which he joined at the age of twelve. He has been a steward in the College Grove Methodist Church since 1905 and continues to be one of its most active and faithful members, both in the Sunday School and in the church activities.

Since 1897 Mr. Lanier has been a loyal member of the Owen Hill Masonic Lodge, holding the offices of junior warden, senior warden, worshipful master, and secretary, which position he held for 40 years.

He has two grandchildren, Mrs. Alfred Elmore of Eagleville and Owen Alexander of Old Hickory, and two great-grandchildren, Keith Elmore of Eagleville, and Lee Ann Alexander of Old Hickory. His one sister, Miss Mary Lanier, lives in Franklin. A brother, George Lanier, died in 1967.

Williamson countians join College Grove residents in being proud of this exceptional excellent citizen.

As Published in *The Review-Appeal* on September 19, 1968

WILLIAM CORLETTE LANIER
1870 - 1968

W. C. Lanier, Prominent CG Resident, Dies

Will C. Lanier, prominent resident of College Grove, died Monday afternoon at a Franklin nursing home.

Funeral services were held Tuesday afternoon at Lawrence Funeral Home in Chapel Hill with the Rev. Chester A. Stephens officiating. Burial was in the College Grove Cemetery.

Mr. Lanier, who would have been 98 years of age on December 10, was a retired rural mail carrier, farmer, and trader. He was born, reared, and educated in the Allisona community and was the son of Mr. and Mrs. Ben Allen Lanier.

After his marriage to Miss Cornelia Lockridge, he moved to the farm on Horton Highway which was his home until his death, Mrs. Lanier died in 1958.

At the age of twelve, Mr. Lanier joined the Wesley Chapel Methodist Church but had his membership at the College Grove United Methodist Church for many years. He had been a steward of that church since 1905 and until he became ill a short time ago attended church regularly and had been one of its most active and faithful members.

Since 1897 he had been a member of the Masonic Lodge in which he had held the offices of junior and senior warden, worshipful master, and secretary, a position he held for 40 years.

He is survived by one daughter, Mrs. L. B. Alexander of College Grove; one son, Robert Allen Lanier of Nashville; one sister, Miss Mary Lanier of Franklin and two great-grandchildren.

Active pallbearers were Page Floyd, James and Billy Ogilvie, Alfred Jaqueth, Earl Culbertson, and James Garrett.

Serving as honorary pallbearers were members of the Men's Bible class of the College Grove United Methodist Church.

– The Review-Appeal, December 5, 1968

LANIER — Monday evening, July 21st, 1958 at 7:30 o'clock in a Franklin nursing home, Mrs. Cornelia Lockridge Lanier, age 84 years. Survived by husband, Will C. Lanier; one daughter, Mrs. L. B. (Louise) Alexander; one son, Robert Allen Lanier, all of College Grove, and two grandchildren.

Remains are at the Lawrence Funeral Home, Chapel Hill. Funeral services will be conducted Wednesday morning at 10:30 o'clock, in the College Grove Methodist Church by Rev. Paul Lanius and Rev. William Tomlin. Pallbearers: John Woods, John Hatcher, Repperd Drumwright, Alison White, James Neely, James Ogilvie, Reed Corlette and J. G. Wade. Interment College Grove Cemetery. Lawrence Funeral Home, Chapel Hill in charge of arrangements.

– Nashville Banner, July 22, 1958

Stephen S. Lawrence

Stephen S. Lawrence of College Grove lives on a farm on Lampkin Bridge Road, with his wife the former Miss Martha West and their two children, Cathy and Stephen A. Lawrence.

Mr. Lawrence is active in state and local historical associations. His interest in historic Franklin began with his serving as chairman of the Williamson County Civil War Centennial committee. He has been an officer on the Carter House Association, APTA *[Association for the Preservation of Tennessee Antiquities]* board and the Franklin Historic Tour Commission. He was the director of Andrew Jackson's "The Hermitage" from 1963 until 1967. Recently he has been appointed as executive secretary of the Tennessee Historical Commission.

Among Mr. Lawrence's many hobbies and sports he likes coon-hunting best. He is engaged in the raising of a registered Angus beef herd.

Mr. and Mrs. Lawrence and their two children make their church home at the First Methodist Church in Franklin.

As Published in *The Review-Appeal* on December 28, 1967

STEPHEN SAMUEL LAWRENCE
1922-2011

Lawrence, Stephen Samuel (Mr. Steve), age 89, died May 14, 2011.

The son of the late Stephen James and Margaret Morel Lawrence, he was also predeceased by son, Stephen Alfred Lawrence; a sister, Marybelle L. Osborn; brother, Francis.

He is survived by his wife of 69 years, Martha West Lawrence; daughter, Catherine Ashley (Richard) Warren; grandchildren, John Richardson (Ginny) Warren of Los Angeles, California, Stephen Fenton (Martha) Warren of San Francisco, California, Rachael Lawrence (Michael) Schiavello of Franklin.

Steve grew up in Davidson County. He was an Eagle Scout and Junior Assistant Scoutmaster of Troop 9. He attended Central High School and in 1939 was honored during "Boys' Week" to serve for one hour as Mayor of Nashville, a program sponsored by the Davidson County Chamber of Commerce. He enjoyed hunting and fishing, and visiting his mother's relatives in Williamson County. He attended the University of Tennessee.

World War II changed his life, as it did many others. In the summer of 1942, he joined the U.S. Navy and served for 28 months in the Pacific Theater as Boatswain Mate 2/C, 88th Naval Construction Battalion.

After the war, Steve enrolled in Vanderbilt University and graduated in 1948 with majors in history and economics. He was Commander of the Sigma Chapter of the Sigma Nu fraternity. Later, he earned a Master's degree in historic preservation from MTSU.

He worked in the sales department of Graybar Electric Company and later, served as Director of The Hermitage and as Executive Secretary of the Tennessee Historical Commission.

Steve took pride in the development of his herd of Angus cattle, and spent his later years in the family farming venture, Lauren Hill. He was also proud of his flowers and especially his roses. In his senior years, he took up golf and enjoyed a winter home in Naples, Florida. He was an avid fly fisherman, using his own handmade flies.

He was active in the field of historic preservation, serving on the boards of the Carter House and of the Carnton Plantation. He was founder and first president of the Williamson County Historical Society, as well as active in the founding of the Heritage Foundation of Franklin and Williamson County, of which he also served as president.

A Memorial service will be held at First United Methodist Church in Franklin on Saturday, May 21st at 2 p.m., with Dr. H. Lynn Hill presiding.

Visitation will be from 5 to 7 p.m. on Friday, May 20th at Williamson Memorial Funeral Home, and one hour prior to the service on Saturday at the church.

In lieu of flowers, memorial gifts may be made to the Carter Center, Atlanta; the Nashville Rescue Mission, Nashville; the First United Methodist Church Building Fund, Franklin; or to the charity of one's choice. WILLIAMSON MEMORIAL FUNERAL HOME, (615) 794-2289.

– The Tennessean, May 17, 2011

Excellent Citizens and Notable Partings

John Marshall Liggett

John Marshall Liggett, better known as "J. M.," is a native of Franklin and has spent most of his adult years in the banking business. He is presently connected with the Harpeth National Bank as Appraiser. He lives with his wife, the former Miss Alice Sexton, on Figuers Drive in School Manor. They have two daughters, Mrs. W. R. (Frances) Selph of Nashville and Mrs. John R. (Mary Ann) Butterfield, of Honolulu, Hawaii. He attends Fourth Avenue Church of Christ. His hobby is fishing.

As Published in *The Review-Appeal* on February 16, 1967

"Jelly" Liggett Dies

John Marshall "Jelly" Liggett, 79, a retired partner and co-founder of Harpeth Insurance Agency, died on Wednesday, February 14 at Williamson County Hospital after an extended illness.

Mr. Liggett was one of the three founders of the well-known local insurance agency and retired branch bank manager of the Harpeth National Bank in Nolensville. He assumed the bank position after retiring from his many years in the insurance business. As a young man he had worked for Williamson County Bank.

He was a native of Wilson County but attended Battle Ground Academy. When he graduated in 1918 from the institution he was named an outstanding athlete and awarded the Athletic Medal by the faculty and his classmates.

He served in the armed forces during World War I. In 1928 Mr. Liggett married the former Miss Alice Sexton. He was a member of the Fourth Avenue Church of Christ and a former member of the Rotary Club.

Mr. Liggett is survived by his wife, Mrs. Alice Sexton Liggett of Franklin; two daughters, Mrs. Mary Ann Butterfield of White Bear Lake, Minnesota and Mrs. Frances Selph of Nashville; five grandchildren and one great-grandchild.

The family suggests that memorial contributions may be made to Battle Ground Academy.

Services were held on Friday at 10a.m. at Franklin Memorial Chapel.

Interment took place in Williamson Memorial Gardens.

— The Review-Appeal, February 20, 1979

Harpeth Insurance Agency, Inc.

J. W. Greer, President

J. M. Liggett, Vice-President

Margherita Meacheam, Secretary

Faye Thompson, Stenographer

❧❧❧❧❧❧❧❧

Portrait of An Excellent Citizen

Davis Milton Lillard

Davis Milton Lillard lives at Hillsboro, in Williamson County, where for the past 11 years he has been principal of Hillsboro High School.

His wife is the former Miss Geneva Baker and they have two children, Paul, 11 years old, is a student at Hillsboro Grammar School and Ruth, 4.

Mr. Lillard is a minister of Primitive Baptist faith and is pastor of the Cool Springs Baptist Church. He is a member of the Hillsboro Civitan Club and is presently serving as president and is vice-president of the Williamson County Education Association.

As Published in *The Review-Appeal* on June 8, 1967

Milton Lillard, minister and educator, dies, services set for Thursday

Minister, educator and public servant Davis Milton Lillard died in his sleep Wednesday, leaving several Primitive Baptist congregations and countless friends in mourning.

Geneva Baker Lillard, his wife of 40 years, said he spent Tuesday delivering fruit baskets to elderly and friends and then passed away quietly at their home at 218 Franklin Road Wednesday morning.

Mr. Lillard was to be buried at Cool Springs Primitive Baptist Church on Christmas Eve. Services were to be held at 3:30 p.m. at the church Thursday, Dec. 24, with Elder John Robbins and Elder Gene Thomas officiating.

"The church was his life," Mrs. Lillard said, yet Mr. Lillard was also deeply involved in the county schools and in the community.

A minister for some 40 years, he preferred to be called "elder" instead of "reverend."

Mr. Lillard was minister of Cool Springs Primitive Baptist Church in Peytonsville and Big Harpeth Primitive Baptist Church on Liberty Pike. He also traveled to several other congregations in other counties to preach.

"We went to a church in McKenzie, Tennessee once a month for the past 34 years, and he preached at Westbrook Towers (a retirement complex) in Murfreesboro on Wednesdays, and he also went to a church in Columbia once a month," Mrs. Lillard said.

Mr. Lillard, age 62, may have died of a heart attack, his wife said.

"He had had this heart condition for the past seven years, but he never complained, and he never quit," she said.

Mr. Lillard was currently serving on the Williamson County School Board, and served an eight-year term as superintendent of schools from 1968-76.

Personnel records at the county school system's central office show that he graduated from Bethesda High School in 1943.

From 1944-46, he served in the U.S. Navy.

He received his bachelor's degree from Peabody University in 1949 and his master's degree, also from Peabody, in 1950.

He taught at Bethesda High School from 1949-51. Then he went to Gadsden, Alabama, and taught for two years, and from 1952-56 he taught in the Montgomery County Schools in Tennessee and became an elementary school principal there. Then he returned to Williamson County as a teacher at Hillsboro School. He was at Hillsboro for 12 years, serving as teacher, basketball coach, and principal. Mr. Lillard was then elected as superintendent.

"Mr. Lillard had to confront a period of the county's most rapid growth. It was probably the biggest challenge he had to face as superintendent," Superintendent Ken Fleming said.

At the conclusion of his second term as superintendent, Mr. Lillard remained at the school system offices as an administrative assistant for a year and a half.

Then his health problems began and he retired from the county schools.

"Mr. Lillard knew everybody, maybe more people than anyone else in the County," Fleming said.

He was serving as vice-chairman of the Williamson County School Board, and chairwoman Carolyn Campbell said his experience was invaluable to the board.

"It's a sad day in the county, and it's a sad day in education," Campbell said.

"He was the sweetest gentleman one could ever meet, and he was the most conscientious person," she said.

One of his closest friends, Dudley Stovall Sr., said it seemed as though people everywhere knew Mr. Lillard and respected him.

"He is certainly going to be missed," Stovall, a fellow minister, said.

He was also a member of the Franklin Civitan Club, American Legion, and on the Board of Directors of the Tennessee Vocational School Board. He was a World War II veteran.

Mr. Lillard is survived by his wife; a daughter, Ruth (Mrs. John) Lawlor of Franklin; a son, Paul Lillard of Nashville: three brothers, Walter Lillard and Marvin Lillard, both of the Cross Keys community, and Leon Lillard of Franklin; and three grandchildren, Paul Claiborne (Clay) Lillard Jr. and Michael and David Forte.

Active pallbearers were deacons of Cool Springs Primitive Baptist Church and honorary pallbearers were ministers and members of the Primitive Baptist Church.

Williamson Memorial Funeral Home is in charge of arrangements.

– The Review-Appeal, December 25, 1987

"For a short time after he finished high school, he worked at the stove plant, then Dortch Stove Works, until he went into the Navy during World War II. He was in a cargo handling group, the only outfit of its kind. The group assembled in Davisville, R. I. and then moved to the West Coast where it was ready to go the Philippines when the war ended. Mr. Lillard helped train recruits at Camp Perry, Virginia, for a short time before he came home. He was discharged after 26 months of service as a yeoman second class."

— Derry Carlisle *Who's Who in Williamson County*, Rick Warwick, ed., originally published in *The Review-Appeal*, October 29, 1959.

Portrait of An Excellent Citizen

BILL DUKE
8/66

W. F. (Jumbo) Little

Portrait Published in *The Review-Appeal* **on August 18, 1966**

Wilburn F. "Jumbo" Little, 82, died Thursday, Dec. 11, 2003, at his residence in Franklin.

Mr. Little was born in Davidson County and served in the U.S. Navy during World War II. He was a retired grocer with Little's Big Star. He was a Williamson County commissioner for 34 years, a 32nd Degree Mason and member of Hiram Masonic Lodge, Franklin Lions Club, 911 Board, J. L. Clay Senior Citizens Center, and various other civic and community boards. Mr. Little also was a member of First United Methodist Church and the Darrell Waltrip Men's Bible Study Group. He was preceded in death by his parents, J. W. and Maggie Roberts Little; two brothers, Sidney and Earl Little; and two sisters; Dorothy Beeler and Mary Frances Little.

Survivors include his wife, Mrs. Edith Smith Little of Franklin; two sons, Tommy (Beverly) Little of Triune and Russell Little of Franklin; a daughter, Brenda (Don) Young of Franklin; two brothers, J. W. Little, Jr. of Franklin and T. Vance Little of Brentwood; a sister, Marie Ehresman of Triune; sister-in-law, Sarah Little of Franklin; brother-in-law, H.Y. Beeler of Brentwood; nine grandchildren, Joshua Little, Matt Reynolds, Ruth Patton, Alex Murphy, Donnie Young and Wesley, Vance, Erica and Krista Little; and five great-grandchildren.

Funeral services will be held at 1 p.m. Saturday, Dec. 13, at First United Methodist Church with Dr. Lynn Hill, Stuart Nunnally and [Rev.] George Jones officiating. Burial will follow in Williamson Memorial Gardens. Active pallbearers will be grandsons. Honorary pallbearers are employees of Little's IGA, Franklin Lions Club, Darrell Waltrip Men's Bible Study Group and the W.C. Yates Bible Class.

Visitation will be from 5-8 p.m. today at Williamson Memorial Funeral Home, with a Masonic service at 6:30, and noon to 1 p.m. tomorrow at the church.

Memorials may be made to First United Methodist Church, Franklin Lions Club Sight Service or J. L. Clay Senior Citizens Center.

– The Review-Appeal, December 12, 2003

Herbert McCall

Herbert McCall is a dairy farmer and lives in the Bethesda community with his wife, the former Miss Mildred Creswell. He has two sons, Dr. Herbert T. McCall of Madison, Tennessee, and Maj. Gen. [sic] Gerald McCall who is stationed in Vietnam.

Mr. McCall is a member of the Bethesda Methodist Church where he serves on the official board, and is magistrate representing the 12th civil district of Williamson County in the County Court.

As Published in *The Review-Appeal* on April 27, 1967

HERBERT LYCURGUS McCALL
1904 - 1984

Funeral for Herbert L. McCall, retired farmer and school teacher and long-time member of the former county court was Wednesday, December 26, at Franklin Memorial Chapel, with the Rev. Stephen Womack officiating. Burial was in the Mt. Hope Cemetery.

Mr. McCall, a resident of the Bethesda community, died December 24 at the Donelson Life Care Center at the age of 80.

A native of Williamson County, he was a retired farmer and school teacher. He served 25 years as a magistrate of the former county court (now the county commission). He also was a member of the Bethesda United Methodist Church and a Boy Scout leader.

Survivors include his wife, Mrs. Mildred C. McCall of Bethesda; two sons, Col. Gerald T. McCall of Fayetteville, Georgia, and Herbert T. McCall of Old Hickory; four grandchildren and one great grandchild.

Officiating at the service was Rev. Stephen Womack and burial followed in Mt. Hope Cemetery. Active pallbearers were William Marlin, Richard King, Billy Giles, Ross Giles, Lester Mosley, Steve Fisher and James King.

– The Williamson Leader, January 4, 1985

Memories of a Granddaughter

My grandfather's middle name was Lycurgus, which is pretty terrible, but Granddaddy seemed to be proud of it. He was the only child of Andrew Lycurgus McCall and Alice Smithson McCall. He attended Battle Ground Academy and what is now MTSU, but I believe back then it was called Middle Tennessee State Teachers College. He had to quit the teachers college when the Great Depression hit and he was needed at home to work the family farm. He worked as a dairy and tobacco farmer and taught at Ash Hill School and Flat Creek School. He married Mildred Creswell and they had two sons, Herbert Travis (my father) and Gerald Thomas. He was an active member of Bethesda United Methodist Church, where he taught Sunday School and led the youth group. He was a boy scout leader and also coached girl's basketball.

In 1961, he was badly injured in a farm accident when all his toes and part of his feet were cut off. In spite of this, he continued to work on the farm and actively serve in his community and on the county commission.

– Susan McCall Fisher, October 2019

"The first McCall found in southeast Williamson County was Lycurgus McCall. He was born December 19, 1814 and died September 23, 1877. Lycurgus was a dedicated citizen, apparently well-liked and well-educated, for he served the county many years as a magistrate. ... Lycurgus' family home was situated on Choctaw Road, where he was a schoolmaster. He gave the land on which the first Choctaw School was built. He married Emmeline Hartley on January 30, 1837.

"Few families have represented the Flat Creek, Choctaw area in County government like the McCalls. From the first McCall to come here, there has been a continuous line of McCalls to be on the County Court. Lycurgus was the first, then Laban Hartley, Will Fay, Andrew Lycurgus, and Herbert McCall."

– Geneva McCall Bolton, *Flat Creek, It's Land and People,* by Ennis C. Wallis, Sr., Jo Ann Petty, Marjorie Redmond, and Martha Ann Hazelwood, 1986.

Thomas McCall

"He enlisted in the Navy and was stationed in Newport, R.I., and Brooklyn Navy Yard. He was finally sent to San Pedro, California with the Pacific fleet. As a sailor aboard the USS Tennessee, he visited many points in South America and the Hawaiian Islands. At the close of his term of enlistment of two years, he called it a day, did not re-enlist, and was discharged at Los Angeles.

On being asked if he belonged to an organization he said, 'No, I'm a Methodist, and a Democrat. That's all."

— Jane Bowman Owen, *Who's Who in Williamson County,* Rick Warwick, ed., originally published in *The Review-Appeal,* June 25, 1936.

Portrait Published in *The Review-Appeal* on August 11, 1966

Thomas McCall,
founder of electric firm, dies

Thomas Luther McCall, well known Franklin businessman, died unexpectedly Saturday, November 17, at his home on Murfreesboro Road. He was 77.

Graveside services were held Sunday afternoon at Mt. Hope Cemetery with the Rev. George Jones officiating.

Mr. McCall was the son of the late Luther Alexander and Maude Wells McCall and was a native of Williamson County.

As a young man he served in the U.S. Navy, and in 1922 he founded McCall Electric Company, one of the oldest businesses that has continued under the founder in Franklin. However, in recent years because of declining health he had given the operation of the business to his son-in-law, Van Montague. He served on the board of directors of Williamson County Bank.

He was a member of the First United Methodist Church.

Mr. McCall was an avid fisherman and made frequent trips to local streams and fishing waters throughout the Southeast.

His wife, the former Miss Rebecca Hardison, died October 27.

He is survived by one daughter, Mrs. Van (Jane) Montague; one sister, Mrs. Earle (Addie Love) DuRard; both of Franklin; two granddaughters, Mrs. Francis (Becky) Eagle of Nashville and Miss Leila Montague of Franklin.

Honorary pallbearers were William E. Knight, Billy Cameron, employees of McCall Electric Company, and the board of directors of Williamson County Bank.

Active pallbearers were Fleming Williams, Robert M. Cook, Frank Stovall, Bob Sewell, Joe Pinkerton, Earle DuRard, William Miller and Dr. Padge Beasley.

Franklin Memorial Chapel was in charge of arrangements.

– The Review-Appeal, November 22, 1979

B. DUKE
8/66

John M. McCord

"He is the middle child of the nine living children of E. D. and Annie Millard McCord, of Duplex, who numbered their children at a round dozen, three of them having died while small.

Soon after Katherine Northcross, an attractive blond, graduated from Franklin High School, she and John, who had been sweethearts since he first came to Franklin, were married, making their home with Katherine's mother on South Fourth Avenue."

— Jane Bowman Owen, *Who's Who in Williamson County,* Rick Warwick, ed., originally published in *The Review-Appeal,* February 17, 1944.

Editorial note: Mrs. McCord's name was originally published as "Kathryn," and corrected to "Katherine."

Portrait Published in *The Review-Appeal* on August 25, 1966

Funeral set today for
former bank president John McCord

Funeral for John Millard McCord, former president of Williamson County Bank (now NationsBank), 75, will be today (Thursday, March 5) at 2 p.m. at Fourth Avenue Church of Christ.

Myron Keith, retired minister of the church, will officiate at the service. Burial will be in Mt. Hope Cemetery.

The body will lie in state at the church one hour prior to time for the service.

Mr. McCord died Tuesday, March 3, at St. Thomas Hospital after a long illness.

A native of Williamson County, he was associated with Williamson County Bank for 37 years and served as president of the bank from 1968 to 1973. As a director of the bank, he also was in charge of a building program that included branch offices on Hillsboro Road and Murfreesboro Road in Franklin and in Brentwood.

Mr. McCord was active in church and civic organizations. He was a member and longtime deacon of Fourth Avenue Church of Christ. He was a member of Hiram Masonic Lodge 7 and was active as an adult volunteer in the Boy Scouts of America. He was a past member of the Williamson County Chamber of Commerce, and Franklin Lions Club.

During World War II, he served in the U.S. Navy.

Survivors include his wife, Mrs. Katherine McCord; three sons, John McCord Jr., James (Bubba) McCord, both of Franklin, and Randall (Kip) McCord of Hendersonville; daughter, Mrs. Steve (Dianne) Johnston of Nashville; three sisters, Mrs. Ellie Marshall Beasley and Mrs. Mary Stem, both of the Bethesda community, and Mrs. Jessie Howes of Nashville, and seven grandchildren.

Active pallbearers will be elders and deacons of Fourth Avenue Church of Christ.

Honorary pallbearers will be past employees and directors of Williamson County Bank.

Williamson Memorial Funeral Home is in charge of arrangements.

– The Williamson Leader, March 5, 1992

This saves me a trip to town when I'm busy!

U.S. MAIL

BANK-BY-MAIL

WILLIAMSON COUNTY BANK

Member Federal Deposit Insurance Corporation

"Where You Can Get 4%

Interest On Savings Deposits"

CLOSED WEDNESDAY — EXTRA HOURS, FRIDAY, 3 to 5:30

Free Southside Parking adjacent to

our Bank

Cletus W. McWilliams

Cletus W. McWilliams is an attorney-at-law and serves as city attorney. He lives at 115 Myles Manor Court with his wife, the former Miss Donna Jean Sanders of Nashville. They have three children, Sandra Louise, 8, Melanie, 5, and John Cletus, 3. The McWilliams attend Fourth Avenue Church of Christ. Mr. McWilliams is a past president of the Rotary Club and is a member of the Williamson County Bar Association and the Tennessee Bar Association.

As Published in *The Review-Appeal* on November 24, 1966

Cletus W. McWilliams, 73, died Monday, Sept. 18, at Williamson Medical Center after a short illness.

Mr. McWilliams was born in Florence, Ala. He served in the U.S. Marine Corps during World War II. He was a retired attorney and executive secretary of the State of Tennessee Supreme Court. Mr. McWilliams was a former speaker pro-tem of the Tennessee House of Representatives. He was a past president of the Franklin Rotary Club, a member of the Williamson County Bar Association and the Tennessee Municipal Attorneys Association. He was also a Paul Harris Fellow. Mr. McWilliams was a member of the Church of Christ.

Survivors include his wife of 47 years, Donna S. McWilliams of Franklin; a son, John McWilliams of Los Angeles; two daughters, Sandra Grooms and her husband Garry of Brentwood and Melanie Wilbourn and her husband Mike of Hampton Cove, Ala.; and six grandchildren, David, Matthew and John Zachary Wilbourn and Kevin, Collin and Kathleen Grooms.

Funeral services will be held on Wednesday, September 20, at 4 p.m., at Williamson Memorial Funeral Home with Myron Keith officiating.

Burial will follow in Mount Hope Cemetery. Active pallbearers will be Jim Crowell, Tom Harlin, Pete Tolley, Jim Martin, Jeff Haley, Jimmy Dunn, Dewees Berry and Jim Oglesby. Honorary pallbearers will be Gerson Schklar, Lillian Schklar, Dr. Arch Smith, Walter Carlisle, Derry Carlisle, Dr. Patrick Murphy, Dr. David Carbonne, Dr. Joe Willoughby, Dr. Shannon Curtis, Jimmy Sanders, Joe Crudo and J. Stanley Rogers.

Visitation with the family will be noon until service time on Wednesday at the funeral home. Memorials may be made to the American Cancer Society or the charity of your choice. Williamson Memorial Funeral Home is in charge of arrangements.

– The Review-Appeal, September 20, 2000

Former state court secretary dies at 73

Cletus W. "Mac" McWilliams is remembered by his colleagues for his hard work and by his friends for his quick wit.

McWilliams and his wife, Donna S. McWilliams, were married 47 years and have three children and six grandchildren. He was born 73 years ago in Florence, Ala.

"The thing I remember about him is his wit. He was one of the funniest men I knew. He had a quick wit and that sort of humor that is hard to describe because you needed to be there," said Bill Ormes, a longtime friend. "He could come up with the appropriate remark at any time that was humorous."

"He was a first-class lawyer and was a good golfer," Ormes added.

Ormes said he and McWilliams enjoyed spending time attending sporting events together.

McWilliams was a retired attorney and executive secretary of the State of Tennessee Supreme Court. He was the former speaker pro-tem of the Tennessee House of Representatives and a past president of the Franklin Rotary Club, Williamson County Bar Association and the Tennessee Municipal Attorneys Association. McWilliams was also the Franklin city attorney for a number of years.

Chief Justice Riley Anderson talked about the difference McWilliams made in his adopted state.

"Mr. McWilliams played an integral role in improving the administration of justice in Tennessee during the 15 years he served as executive secretary for the state court system," Riley said. "It was a period of tremendous caseload growth and added responsibilities for his office. He very capably oversaw many important and positive changes in the judicial system resulting in greater efficiency in the administration of justice. He was a man who was admired and beloved by many and who will be missed by the scores of friends he made and kept within and outside the judicial branch of the government."

Fellow Franklinite Cornelia Clark, administrative director of the court system, praised his contributions.

"Mr. McWilliams' contributions to the judicial system in the state will benefit generations of Tennesseans. He was a dedicated public servant and a devoted family man. His legions of friends will greatly miss his wit and intelligence," Clark said.

Mr. McWilliams continued to stay in touch with the activities of government after he retired.

"Among legislators he served with, he was thought of as a very honest and effective person," said State Rep. Mike Williams, Democratic floor leader from the 63rd District. "I was fortunate to have known him. He was a nice and personable man."

– The Review-Appeal, September 20, 2000

Johnnie Allen Marlin

Johnnie Allen Marlin is a farmer and lives in the Boston Community of Williamson County with his wife, the former Mary Frances Robinson. They have three children, Ellen, who is employed at Franklin Manufacturing Company, Judy, a student at David Lipscomb College and Johnny, a student at Hillsboro High School.

Mr. Marlin is a member of the Williamson County Farm Bureau, and attends the Boston Church of Christ. He serves as one of the Elders, and is also treasurer and song leader.

As Published in *The Review-Appeal* on May 18, 1967

JOHNNIE ALLEN MARLIN
1917-1982

Mr. Marlin dies

Services were conducted Tuesday morning, May 25, for Johnnie Allen Marlin, 65, of the Boston Community.

Marlin died Sunday morning at Williamson County Hospital.

He is survived by his wife, Mrs. Mary Frances Robinson Marlin, Boston Community, and two daughters, Mrs. Mary Ellen Jones, Burwood Community, and Judy Lee Petty, Monmouth, Oregon. His son, Johnnie S. Marlin is from Springfield, Tennessee. His sister, Mrs. Gladys House, Franklin, also survives.

He had seven grandchildren.

Marlin was a farmer and song leader and elder in the Boston Church of Christ.

Pallbearers were Clifton Simmons, Pete Davis, Eugene King, Gary Denton, Mike Jackson, Lynn Simmons, Joey Davis and Buford Davis.

Darrell Trimble and Herbert A. Robinson officiated at the services at the Franklin Memorial Chapel. Burial was in Sparkman Cemetery.

– The Review-Appeal, May 27, 1982

Allen Marlin
By Bill Peach

I was born 4 months after my father died. Uncle Allen was 19 years old and became my "father figure" and role model. He was drafted for World War II. I was 5 years old and clung to him, begging him not to leave. He was in Europe until 1945.

He taught me farming skills—milking, stripping tobacco, hoeing the garden, and grinding sausage. This was his life profession.

For me, his strength was the Boston Church of Christ. When he returned from the War he resumed his role as song leader and building caretaker. That included unlocking the building, checking heaters and window air conditioners for the ideal temperature, and distributing song books, and funeral home fans (summer only).

He was later chosen to be one of three elders He was also the person who hired and fired preachers, and paid them from the Sunday morning contributions.

He was married to Mary Frances (Robinson) and has three children Ellen (Larry) Jones in Burwood, Judy (Jim) Petty in Oregon and Johnny (Retha) Marlin in Springfield.

March 31, 2020

Henry Hunter Mayberry, Jr.

Henry Hunter Mayberry, Jr., is a native of Franklin. He lives on Lewisburg Avenue with his wife, the former Miss Eunetta Clouse of Cookeville. They have one daughter, Eunetta Mayberry Kready, also of Franklin.

Mr. Mayberry is in the real estate and real estate appraisals business with offices on Fourth Avenue, South. For 30 years he was connected with the Phoenix Mutual Life Insurance Co. in Nashville in the mortgage department from which business he retired two years ago. He is a member of the local Real Estate Board and vice president of the Society of Real Estate Appraisals in Nashville.

He is a member of the First Methodist Church.

As Published in *The Review-Appeal* on July 20, 1967

Henry Hunter Mayberry, Jr.
1899 - 1991

Henry Hunter Mayberry Jr., widower of the late Eunetta Clouse Mayberry, 91, died Friday, April 12 at Williamson Medical Center after an extended illness.

Mr. Mayberry is a native of Birmingham, Alabama, member of the First United Methodist Church, and a manager of the mortgage loan division for Phoenix Life Insurance Company in Franklin.

Survived by daughter, Eunetta Kready, of Franklin; and two grandchildren, Winne Whisler Kready and Hunter Parke Kready, both of Franklin

Graveside services were 1 p.m. Saturday at Mount Hope Cemetery with Rev. Ed Crump officiating.

Active pallbearers were William E. Cherry, Judge M. Thomas Taylor Jr., Dan H. Parsons, Richard E. Jordan, Robert Jackson Walker, James Edward Walker, Tommie Layne and Larry M. Cognata.

Honorary pallbearers were Marie Jordan, Mary Jo Vaillancourt, Tia Inman, Men's Coffee Club and the Franklin Lions Club.

Family would like to suggest memorials be made to the Williamson County Rescue Squad, First United Methodist Church or your favorite charity.

Franklin Memorial Chapel was in charge of arrangements.

— The Review-Appeal, April 14, 1991

My father was named Henry Hunter Mayberry, Jr., known as Henry to his friends, Daddy to me and Gandy to his grandchildren. He was a true southern gentleman in every way and even at the age of almost 92, was always immaculately dressed in his classic suit and tie. He was known for his charm, generosity and genteel manners.

As a child, I remember going to the basement to watch him remove 'clinkers' from the furnace and add more coal; a dirty job at best, but even then, he donned a coat and tie.

His roots ran deep in Williamson County and he was proud of that heritage. One of his legendary stories was about his cross-county jaunts upon 'Foxy' from his home called Riverview on Franklin road across the toll road to his aunt who lived in Beechwood Hall on Bear Creek road; a lengthy trip for a young boy and his pony.

One of his hobbies was raising irises, the Tennessee's state flower. He enjoyed every aspect of being in the garden from preparing the soil to planting the rhizomes clad in freshly starched khaki shirt and trousers. What he loved the most was picking the gorgeous blossoms and with a twinkle in his blue eyes shared the fruits of his labor with family and friends across the county. In the springtime our home was filled with sweet fragrances in an array of beautiful colors from his garden.

To this day, my eyes light up when I see one of his irises blooming in a friend's garden and treasure the few that remain in mine. He was my beloved Daddy, an adoring husband, a doting father and grandfather. A patriarch larger than life, at least in my eyes, but those who knew him would agree, he held himself to a very high standard and left very big shoes to fill.

I will always be grateful for his love and kindness. I am, I have been, and I always will be proud to be the daughter of Henry Hunter Mayberry, Jr., a quintessential southern gentleman.

— Eunetta Mayberry Kready, also known as "Little Eunetta" for those who may remember the original, my beautiful mother, Eunetta Clouse Mayberry, with Paula Ligon, January 15, 2020

Excellent Citizens and Notable Partings

Portrait of An Excellent Citizen

Rev. Thomas A. Meadows

The Rev. Thomas A. Meadows has been rector at St. Paul's Episcopal Church since July, 1964, and just recently announced acceptance of a call to serve two Episcopal churches in Louisville, Kentucky.

The Rev. Mr. Meadows is past president of the Board of Directors of the Williamson County Community Action Program and is presently a member of the Board. He was also president of the Franklin Ministerial Association and was one of the organizers of the chaplaincy program for Williamson County Hospital. He is vice-president of the Friends of the Williamson County Library and served on the Citizens Advisory Committee on Housing for the City of Franklin.

As Published in *The Review-Appeal* on January 25, 1968

Rector of St. Paul's Episcopal Dies
By Erin Marie Medick

The Rev. Thomas A. Meadows, 58, rector of St. Paul's Episcopal Church since 1984, died yesterday of cancer.

A memorial service will be held at 11 a.m. next Saturday at St. Paul's, 787 E. Broad St., said his wife, the Rev. Terry Meadows. Mrs. Meadows has assisted at St. Paul's this summer and will continue to serve the 300 members there as priest in charge. She was assigned to St. Mark's Episcopal Church in Upper Arlington.

Mr. Meadows served on several commissions and committees in the Episcopal Diocese of Southern Ohio and was vice president of the Diocesan Council in 1987-88.

He came here from the Indianapolis diocese, and also served in Kentucky and Tennessee. Mr. Meadows received a master of divinity degree in 1958 from Vanderbilt University. He was ordained a deacon in 1963 and a priest in 1964.

— *The Columbus Dispatch (Ohio), September 23, 1989*

The Rev. Thomas Meadows, 58, formerly of Louisville, died Friday in Columbus, Ohio.

He was the rector at St. Paul's Episcopal Church in Columbus and served as vicar of St. John's Episcopal Church in Louisville from 1968-1978.

Survivors: his wife, the former Terry McCormick; a son, Benjamin Meadows of Indianapolis; three daughters, Amy Meadows of Chicago, Hannah Caywood of Salt Lake City and Emily Meadows of Columbus; his mother, Laura Meadows; and a sister Charlotte Jolly of Clarksville, Tennessee.

The body was cremated.

Memorial service: 11 a.m. Saturday, St. Paul's Episcopal Church in Columbus.

Expressions of sympathy: St. John's Episcopal Church in Louisville.

— *The Courier-Journal (Louisville, Kentucky), September 27, 1989*

* * *

The Annual

FISH FRY

at

St. Paul's Episcopal Church

will be held

Saturday July 15

on the Church premises beginning at 5 o'clock

3 Country Hams
will be given away

You do not have to be present to win.

Tickets $1.50

Children under 10 accompanied by an adult will be served free.

Tickets may be obtained from any member of St. Paul's congregation or on the grounds after 3 p.m. on July 15th.

* * *

William Hart Miller

William Hart Miller is a partner in Gray Drug Company with two stores in Franklin, one on Main Street and one on Carters Creek Pike. He and his wife, the former Miss Laura May Tyer, of Nashville, live on Columbia Avenue. Mr. Miller is a member of the First Methodist Church where he serves on the Official Board. He is also a member of the Civitan Club.

As Published in *The Review-Appeal* on October 17, 1966

WILLIAM HART MILLER
1907 - 1990

Popular Main Street businessman William Miller to be buried today
By Bailey Leopard

A piece of Main Street has died.

And pharmacist-businessman William Hart Miller's family and many friends will pay their final respects to him today (Friday, Sept. 14) at 10 a.m. at First United Methodist Church.

Mr. Miller, regarded by the thousands who had come to know him as an owner of Gray Drug Co. as a model Main Street merchant, good citizen and humanitarian, died Tuesday, September 11, at St. Thomas Hospital at the age of 83.

He had been hospitalized earlier with broken bones in his hip and leg caused by a fall, then suffered a massive stroke.

Dr. Edward Crump and the Rev. Arthur Robins, ministers of First United Methodist, where Mr. Miller and his wife attended church, will conduct the final rites. Burial will be in Mt. Hope Cemetery.

Born July 6, 1907 in Nashville, he was the son of Sallie Stockett and William W. Miller. His parents moved from Davidson County to the Ash Grove community (also known as Lick Skillet), off Sneed Road, in Williamson County when he was a baby.

The son of a painter and carpenter, Miller once said he had no idea he would one day be a pharmacist and be an owner of Franklin's oldest retail business.

Like many of his generation, Miller was a self-made businessman. He attended Ash Grove's one-room school and in the seventh grade went to the then two-teacher Grassland School. He also attended Battle Ground Academy for one and one-half years, but completed his schooling at Franklin High School "after money got tight."

After working for his father as a painter's helper and driving an unsuccessful candidate for circuit judge to his campaign stops over a five-county district, Miller went to work on Franklin's Main Street in 1924 as an attendant for a gas station and car rental agency operated by the late N. Y. Walker and Cortez Isaacs.

For 66 years, Miller was a familiar figure on Main Street. In 1926, he was asked to join John Moran Drug Co., which later became Gray Drug Co. He was an owner of the store for 30 years, and remained active as a pharmacist until he was hospitalized earlier this year with health problems. He had sold interest in the drug store earlier to partners Ralph Duke, Bill Garrett and Randy Pennington.

Owners Frank Gray, for whom the drug store is named, and D. C. Kinnard, were so impressed with Miller that they sent him to the Crowe School of Pharmacy in Atlanta, Georgia, in 1938. He recalled in an earlier interview that he completed pharmacy school in nine months.

World War II took Miller out of the drug store for four years as he served as a pharmacist with the Army's 10th Division in Europe.

Miller once recalled that he had already seen penicillin overseas during World War II before it appeared in drug stores in 1946.

Gray's policy of filling prescriptions for people "if they were really sick and needed the medicine but didn't have the money" was continued by Miller and is carried by today's owners.

Miller was noticeably successful as a businessman, and was active in civic, community and church organizations. He served as a director of Sovran Bank of Williamson County and was a member of the Franklin Civitan Club and Hiram Masonic Lodge No. 7. He also was a former director of the Williamson County Chamber of Commerce.

He also guided Gray Drug to take an active role in supporting community endeavors, such as the Franklin Rotary Club Rodeo, the Chamber of Commerce, the annual Christmas Parade, schools, churches and other worthy causes.

Miller has been active in First United Methodist Church. His talents in woodworking and interest in saving historic structures helped preserve the Kennedy House that now serves as offices of the church at the corner of Church Street and Fifth Avenue, South. Several years ago, when a move was afoot to raze the house, Miller organized opposition to tearing away the house and volunteered his labor and money with fellow church member Bob Sewell to restore the building.

At least two organizations recognized Miller for his contributions. He was named the 1979 Franklin Lions Club Businessman of the Year and was the 1981 recipient of the Frank North Helping Hand Award given by the Chamber of Commerce.

Survivors are his wife of more than 50 years, Laura May Tyer Miller, and a brother, Henry North Miller of Brentwood.

Active pallbearers will be William J. Garrett, W. Ralph Duke, Randy Pennington, Joe Pope Jr., William Walton, Dr. Dunklin C. Bowman Jr., L. I. Mills III and Ray Throckmorton.

Honorary pallbearers will be members of the Franklin Civitan Club, officers and directors of Sovran Bank of Williamson County, members of the W.C. Yates Men's Bible Class of First United Methodist Church, employees of Gray Drug Company, Robert Hooper, Paul Satterfield, Jerre Fly Jr., John Jordan, Henry Ross Miller, Nelson Elam, Sammy Lake, Malcom Gibbs, Nathan Sawyer Sr., Bernard Edwards, James Maupin, Marshall Liggett, Fleming Williams, Jesse Short III, William M. Short, Tyler Berry Jr., David Garrett, Charles Grigsby, Dr. Harry Guffee, Dr. A. J. Lee, and Dr. Robert Hollister.

The family requests memorial contributions be made to Franklin First United Methodist Church, Hiram Masonic Lodge No. 7, or a favorite charity.

Williamson Memorial Funeral Home was in charge of arrangements.

– The Williamson Leader, September 14, 1990

Excellent Citizens and Notable Partings

Portrait of An Excellent Citizen

L. I. Mills, Jr.

L. I. (Buddy) Mills, Jr., is principal of Franklin Junior High School. A native of Fayetteville, Tennessee, he was graduated from Morgan Preparatory School in Petersburg and began his college work at Lambuth College in Jackson. After serving with the Army in World War II, he completed his B.S. degree at MTSU in Murfreesboro. He began teaching in Franklin in 1947 and completed his M.A. at Peabody. With a deep interest in sports, he coached the first football team at Franklin Elementary School and has been instrumental in developing the school's full sports program. He serves as an elder of First Presbyterian Church and was recognized last year for 20 years of service as a Boy Scout leader. He is a member of the Rotary Club. Married in 1947 to the former Alma Jean Weatherly of Alabama, he has two sons, L. I. (Buddy) Mills, III, a student at MTSU, and Peter Mills, a senior at Franklin High. The Mills live on Battle Avenue.

As Published in *The Review-Appeal* on January 11, 1968

LILBOURNE IRBY MILLS, JR.
1916 - 1988

Buddie Mills dies

Funeral for Lilbourne Irby (Buddie) Mills Jr., retired Franklin educator who died Tuesday, February 9, of an apparent heart attack, was Thursday at Franklin Memorial Chapel.

The Rev. Steve Jester, James Fiveash and Steve Robinson officiated at the services. Burial was in the Old Orchard cemetery in Petersburg, where members of Mr. Mills' family are buried.

Mr. Mills, a principal and teacher in the Franklin Special School District for 31 years, was scheduled to enter Vanderbilt Hospital Wednesday for open heart surgery. He was seventy-one.

A native of Fayetteville, Mills joined the Franklin Special School District in 1949 as a teacher and became principal of Franklin Junior High School. After suffering heart problems in 1969, he served as a math teacher in the school system until his retirement in 1980.

He studied for his bachelor's degree at Lambuth College in Jackson and Middle Tennessee State University in Murfreesboro, and earned a master's degree from Peabody College in Nashville.

Mills was widely known for his involvement in church and community activities. He was a scoutmaster and a Paul Harris Fellow of the Franklin Rotary Club. He also was active in First Presbyterian Church in Franklin and was treasurer of the Williamson County Knife Club for a number of years.

A veteran of World War II, Mills served in the Pacific theater and retired as a captain in the Army Reserve.

Survivors include his wife, Mrs. Alma Jean Weatherly Mills of Franklin; two sons, Lilbourne l. (Buddy) Mills III of Franklin and Peter James Mills of Mary Hill, North Carolina, and two grandchildren.

Pallbearers were William Moss, Glen Davis, John Moran, Troxler Craig, W.F. Little, Truman Harper, Dr. Ray Gathmann, Earl Davis, Ed Moody, William B. Akin, Frank Akin, John Graham, Pat Fagan and Don Emerson.

Honorary pallbearers were members of the Franklin Rotary Club, the Buddie Mills Bible Class of First Presbyterian Church and the Williamson County Knife Club.

– The Williamson Leader, February 12, 1988

"When asked concerning his ancestry, Mr. Mills replied, 'I believe in the individual not the ancestry, although I am proud of my lineage on both sides. My father's people came to Tennessee from Virginia ... The McKinneys of Scots origin, also came to this country from the British Isles. But, do you know, I am glad they decided to come to America for I had rather be called an American than by any other nationality.'"

— Jane Bowman Owen, *Who's Who in Williamson County*, Rick Warwick, ed., originally published in *The Review-Appeal*, December 2, 1948.

Portrait of An Excellent Citizen

Van B. Montague

Van B. Montague has been a resident of Franklin since 1958 when he became associated with McCall Electric Company. He is a native of Ripley, Tennessee, and was graduated from Battle Ground Academy here where he participated in a number of sports. He attended the University of Tennessee in Knoxville.

Before moving to Franklin, Mr. Montague was a buyer for Goldsmith's, one of the largest department stores in Memphis.

He is a member of St. Paul's Episcopal Church and has served on the vestry. He is also a member of the Franklin Rotary Club which he served as treasurer.

Mr. Montague is an avid tennis player and helped revive local interest in the sport a few years ago. He encourages young people now to become interested in the game.

He and Mrs. Montague, the former Miss Jane McCall of Franklin, and their two daughters, Becky, 16, and Leila, 9, live on Hillsboro Road.

As Published in *The Review-Appeal* on August 1, 1968

VAN BETTIS MONTAGUE
1922 - 2016

Van Bettis Montague died on December 17 at the age of 93 following a brief illness. He was the son of the late William Larimore Montague and Leila Bettis. He was preceded in death by a son, Thomas Larimore Montague, sisters Elise Clark, Ruth Wadsworth, brother, William Larimore Montague, and son-in-law, Francis Eagle. Van is survived by his wife of 70 years, Jane, daughters Rebecca Eagle and Leila Eaton (Andrew), grandson Justin Eagle (Samantha) and three great-grandsons.

Born in Bells, Tennessee, and raised in Ripley, Van graduated from Battle Ground Academy where he excelled in athletics, especially football. He was later inducted into the BGA Athletic Hall of Fame. After high school he joined the Navy and served two years in the Seabees. He returned from service and attended the University of Tennessee. In 1946, Van married Jane McCall and they moved to Memphis where he pursued a career in sales. Ten years later the family returned to Franklin where he joined the family business, McCall Electric Company. Van was a lifelong member of St. Paul's Episcopal Church, Franklin, a past member of the vestry, and a member of the Rotary Club.

Services will be held on Friday Dec. 23rd at 2 p.m. at St. Paul's Episcopal Church with The Rev. William Barton officiating. Visitation will be one hour prior to service in Otey Hall. In lieu of flowers, contributions may be made to St. Paul's Episcopal Church, Franklin, Battle Ground Academy or St. Jude Children's Hospital, Memphis.

WILLIAMSON MEMORIAL FUNERAL HOME, 615-794-2289.

— The Williamson Herald, December 22, 2016

"Upstairs over the [Corner] Drug Store, was a big room where Mrs. Daly Thompson taught ballroom dancing. That's where Van Bettis Montague, a great football player, met and married Jane McCall. She was a black-haired beauty, and one of the smartest people I have ever known."

– Leonard Isaacs
Franklin, Tennessee … the Jewel of the Harpeth

Excellent Citizens and Notable Partings

Tom C. Moody

Tom C. Moody is co-owner and manager of Quality Recappers, with offices on Main Street and Columbia Ave. He and his wife, the former Isabelle Wiggs, reside on Hillsboro Road. Their two children Tom C. II and Sandra, are both married and live in New York City. He is a member of Franklin First Methodist Church where he serves as superintendent of Sunday School, and the Franklin Lions Club.

As Published in *The Review-Appeal* on November 3, 1966

Tom Moody, business and civic leader, dies

Thomas Calvin (Tom) Moody, prominent Franklin business and civic leader, died early Thursday morning, Jan. 9, at Williamson County Hospital. He had been in declining health for the past year because of cancer.

Funeral services were held Friday afternoon at Franklin Memorial Chapel and burial was in Williamson Memorial Gardens. The Rev. Stuart Nunnally, the Rev. W. E. Gober, and the Rev. Virgil Peters officiated.

Mr. Moody was a native of Bethpage in Sumner County and was the son of the late Denville Moody, Sr., and Connie Neal Carr Moody. He was educated in the public schools of that area and early in his career became associated with the Goodyear Tire and Rubber Company. He was located in several Middle Tennessee towns and was in Murfreesboro just prior to moving to Franklin April 1, 1944, when he went into business for himself and opened Quality Recappers in a building on Main Street.

After World War II he was joined in the business by his brother, D. E. Moody, Jr., and they formed the partnership, Moody Brothers Quality Recappers. The business was moved a few years ago from Main Street to Columbia Avenue.

Mr. Moody was a charter member of the Franklin Lions Club and was a member of the Williamson County Chamber of Commerce, for which he was a member of the Board of Directors for several terms. He was serving on the Selective Service Board for Williamson County and had been a member for many years. He had also been a member of the Franklin Planning Commission for a number of years.

He was a charter member of the Franklin High Men's Club and had been one of the staunchest supporters of the school even after his children were graduating. He campaigned actively for funds to build the stadiums at both the Columbia Avenue locations and on Hillsboro Road. He worked with the Boy Scouts and was a Scoutmaster.

A member of First Methodist Church, he served as Sunday School superintendent, chairman of the Commission on Education, and other church offices. In his earlier years in Franklin he had also worked with the Sunday School Department of First Baptist Church in many capacities.

On April 3, 1937, he was married to Miss Isabelle Wiggs of Murfreesboro who survives. They resided on Hillsboro Road. He was 60 years old at the time of his death.

In addition to his wife, he is survived by one daughter, Mrs. Sandra M. McGhee of Franklin; one son, Tom Moody II of Houston, Texas; four brothers, Ed Moody, Jr., of Franklin, Charles and James Moody of Nashville, and Jack Moody of Ashland City; two sisters, Mrs. W. J. Newsome and Mrs. Frank Mayo of Nashville; and five grandchildren, Jennifer and Lisa McGhee of Franklin, and Tommy III, John, and David Moody of Houston.

Honorary pallbearers were employees of Quality Recappers, members of the men's Bible Class of First United Methodist Church and the Franklin Lions Club, and A. M. Blankenship.

Serving as active pallbearers were Paul Pigg, Bob Sewell, Bob White, Ivie Haralson, J. C. Anderson, Herbert Bowen, W. F. Little, Loy Hardcastle, Judge James Short, Ralph Duke, Haywood Cole, Fred Cowart, and R. W. Ritter.

Franklin Memorial Chapel was in charge of arrangements.

— The Review-Appeal, January 16, 1975

Portrait of An Excellent Citizen

BILLDUKE

Robert Nathaniel Moore

Robert Nathaniel Moore is owner and operator of R. N. Moore Feed and Seed Company. He lives on Margin Street with his wife the former Miss Catherine Morrow of Mt. Pleasant. They have one son, Robert N. Moore, Jr., who operates a governmental counseling firm with offices in Atlanta, Washington, and Nashville. Mr. Moore is a member of the Fourth Avenue Church of Christ and the Lions Club, and serves as alderman of the Town of Franklin. He is also a member of the Zoning Board.

As Published in *The Review-Appeal* on March 2, 1967

Moore dies following accident

Funeral services were held Thursday for Robert Nathaniel Moore Sr. a prominent retired Franklin businessman who served on the city's Board of Mayor and Aldermen for 42 years.

Moore, 92, broke his hip Dec. 2 at his home on 424 South Margin Street. He died from complications surrounding the break on Jan. 3 at Williamson Medical Center.

Originally from Maury County, Moore started the Peoples Coal Co. in Franklin in 1929, the year after he married the former Catherine Morrow, now deceased. He opened the R. N. Moore Feed and Seed Co. in the 1940s and closed both businesses when he retired in 1979.

Moore was elected alderman in 1936 and served 21 two-year terms. He was named *The Review-Appeal* Man of the Year in 1974.

"It was my privilege to serve with (Moore) for 19 years," said Ed Woodward [Woodard], former mayor of Franklin. "This is a great loss to our community. He was one of the most dedicated men that I've ever been around. The city will be indebted to him for quite a long time for his services as alderman.

Services officiated by the Rev. Myron Keith were held at Williamson Memorial Funeral Home. Burial was at Williamson Memorial Gardens.

Survivors include: son, Robert N. Moore, Jr., a Franklin real estate developer and a former Sixth District Congressional candidate; and sister, Mary Moore Harris, of Columbia.

Pallbearers included Virgil H. Moore Jr.; J. B. Erwin, Eugene Erwin, Frank Harris, Monroe Lovell, and Charles Craig Morrow.

Memorial gifts can be sent to the Fourth Avenue Church of Christ and the American Heart Association.

Williamson Memorial Funeral Home was in charge of the arrangements.

– The Review-Appeal, January 6, 1989

Editor's Note: Other sources, such as the Social Security Death Index, census records and WWII draft card, indicate 1898 as Mr. Moore's birth year. We used the year 1896, which is recorded on his grave marker.

Frank A. North

Franklin Anderson North has lived in Williamson County his entire life. He was graduated from Battle Ground Academy and attended Vanderbilt University.

Since 1947 he has been connected with Cherokee Insurance Company in Nashville and holds the position of assistant secretary.

He is a member of the First Presbyterian Church which he serves as elder. He has held office in the Nashville Presbytery and is on the Board of Directors and Executive Committee of Monroe Harding Children's Home. He is a member of the Franklin Rotary Club and has served as secretary and treasurer in past years.

The son of Mrs. Carrick North and the late Mr. North, Mr. North is married to the former Miss Elouise Cole of Gallatin and they have three children. Mrs. Michael Whitaker, Frank, Jr., and Mary. The Norths live on Battle Avenue.

As Published in *The Review-Appeal* on July 25, 1968

Frank A. North dies; rites today at 10 a.m.

Frank Anderson North, well known Franklin insurance executive and church and civic leader, died Sunday morning at Williamson County Hospital. He had suffered a heart attack May 15 while playing tennis but was thought to be sufficiently recovered to return to his home. He was dressing to leave the hospital when the fatal attack occurred. He was 60 years old.

Funeral services will be held this (Tuesday) morning, June 3, at First Presbyterian Church. The Rev. Edward Beckes, minister of the church, will officiate. Burial will be in Mt. Hope Cemetery.

Mr. North was a native of Williamson County and was a descendant of pioneer families of the county. He was the son of the late Carrick H. and Mary Thomas Anderson North. He was graduated from Battle Ground Academy and attended Vanderbilt University.

With experience in the insurance business throughout his business career, he was a partner and president of Harpeth Insurance Agency, Inc., which has offices on East Main Street.

He was one of the most devoted members of First Presbyterian Church which he served as elder and treasurer.

Mr. North was an active member of the Franklin Rotary Club which he had served in many capacities and had been awarded the Paul Harris Fellow, the highest award given by Rotary International.

He was an active member and past president of the Williamson County Chamber of Commerce.

An avid tennis player, he was a charter member of the Carnton Club and served on the committee which designed and built the courts there.

He was married to the former Miss Elouise Cole of Gallatin, who survives. He is also survived by two daughters, Mrs. Michael (Sharon) Whitaker of Summerville, Tennessee, and Mrs. Gary (Mary) Hawks of Cadiz, Kentucky; one son, Frank Anderson North, Jr., of Nashville; and three grandchildren, Aubrey and Cole Whitaker and Brandt Hawks.

Serving as honorary pallbearers will be the officers of First Presbyterian Church and members of the Men's Bible Class, officers of Harpeth Insurance Agency, members of the Franklin Rotary Club, and the men's tennis team of the Carnton Club.

Active pallbearers will be Fred Dismukes, Ed Reynolds, Ed Wilson, Jack Pratt, A.D. Denny, Shearer Irvin, John Bragg, and Phillip Fulcher.

In lieu of flowers the family suggested that memorials might be made to the Middle Tennessee Heart Association.

Franklin Memorial Chapel is in charge of arrangements.

– The Review-Appeal, June 3, 1980

Portrait of An Excellent Citizen

Paul Ogilvie

Portrait Published in *The Review-Appeal* on July 16, 1966

PAUL BARRY OGILVIE
1921 - 1994

Paul Barry Ogilvie, 73, died Friday, Aug. 5, 1994.

Mr. Ogilvie was a Nashville native. He lived in Franklin and was the founder and president of the First Franklin Federal Savings and Loan. He was a member of the Historic Franklin Presbyterian Church and a veteran of World War II.

Mr. Ogilvie was a Battle Ground Academy and Vanderbilt University graduate. He began his business career with the Colonial Milling Co. This was followed by posts in the mortgage loan and appraisal divisions of Guarantee Mortgage, Mutual Life of New York and the Veterans Administration. In 1956 he became one of the founders of First Franklin Federal Savings and Loan, where he also served as director and president. He also served as a director and past president of the Tennessee Savings and Loan League.

Mr. Ogilvie served his community as a commissioner and past chairman of the Franklin Housing Authority, he was a founding member and past president of the Heritage Foundation, he was a member of the Rotary Club, past president of the Williamson County Chamber of Commerce, vice president of the Williamson County Historical Society and founding member and board member of the Historic Carnton Plantation.

Mr. Ogilvie is survived by his brother, Guilford Lee Ogilvie, San Diego, California;

two nieces, Carolyn Ogilvie Savage, Franklin, and Linda Ogilvie, Nashville; two nephews, David G. Ogilvie, Franklin, and Charles Hudson Ogilvie, Stewartstown, Pennsylvania.; three great-nieces, Melissa S. Lau, Claire Savage and Morgan Ogilvie; and one great-nephew, C. Edward Savage.

Services will be held 10 a. m. Monday, August 8, at the Historic Franklin Presbyterian Church with the Rev. Sara Hughes, Rev. William Berger and Rev. Robert Cowperthwaite officiating.

Burial will be in the Woodlawn Cemetery.

Visitation will be held today from 4 p.m. to 6 p.m. at Franklin Memorial chapel.

Memorials may be made to the Historic Franklin Presbyterian Church, Battle Ground Academy or the Carnton Association.

Active pallbearers will be: C. D. Berry III, W. W. Billington, William N. Dearborn, Charlie Fox III, Thomas C. Harlin, Thomas Holman, Oliver Kittrell and Livingfield More.

Honorary pallbearers will be: William Keyes, Robert Sewell, Shearer Irvin, Dr. Joseph Willoughby, Leonard McKeand Jr., C. K. McLemore, John Gaultney, Walter Carlisle, John Charles Wheeler, S. McPheeters Glasgow, James Houston Akin, William Ormes, William Lauderdale, Ronald S. Ligon, James Leesom, Stewart Campbell, Sr. and Richard Jordan.

– The Review-Appeal, August 7, 1994

Walter W. Ogilvie

Walter W. Ogilvie is a well-known horse breeder and trainer and livestock farmer of the Allisona community. Affectionately called "the mayor of Allisona," he has lived in the same house his entire life. He was graduated from Branham and Hughes Academy in Spring Hill and attended the University of Tennessee. After World War II he taught in the GI On-the-Farm Training Program. He helped organize and was a charter member of the Tennessee Walking Horse Breeders Association. He was an elder of the College Grove Presbyterian Church for 54 years and, when that church dissolved recently, moved his membership to First Presbyterian Church in Franklin. He is a 32nd degree Mason and a Shriner.

Mr. Ogilvie is married to the former Miss Kathleen Smith of Murfreesboro and they have one daughter, Mrs. Stanley D. Musgrave of Stillwater, Oklahoma, three sons, Billy Ogilvie of College Grove, Walter Ogilvie, Jr., of Indianapolis, Indiana, and James Frank Ogilvie of Atlanta, and eleven grandchildren.

As Published in *The Review-Appeal* on October 19, 1967

Walter Ogilvie, 92, Allisona farmer, dies

Walter William Ogilvie, a well-known resident of the Allisona community near College Grove, died Thursday afternoon, July 7, at his home, Maple Crest Farm. Even though he was 92 years of age, he had not been ill and death was unexpected.

He had lived on the same farm his entire life and until a few years ago when he and his wife built a small house next to the family home he had lived in the same house. He was the son of the late William Harris and Annie Lou Ogilvie. He was graduated from Branham and Hughes Military Academy in Spring Hill and had enjoyed the alumni reunion in recent years. He also attended the University of Tennessee. He was affectionately known as the "Mayor of Allisona."

Mr. Ogilvie was a horse breeder, trainer, and livestock farmer. After World War II he taught in the GI On-the-Farm Training Program. He helped organize and was a charter member of the Tennessee Walking Horse Breeders Association and helped state [start] the first walking horse show in this area many years ago.

He was a member of the Presbyterian Church. He served as an elder of the College Grove Presbyterian Church for 54 years, and, when that church was closed, he moved his membership to First Presbyterian Church in Franklin where he was elected elder emeritus. He was a 32nd degree Mason and a Shriner and had been a member of Owen Hill Masonic Lodge No. 172 for 50 years.

He was married to Miss Kathleen Smith who survives.

Also surviving are one daughter, Mrs. Katherine Musgrave of Arno [Orono], Maine; three sons, Bill Ogilvie of Maple Crest Farm, Jim Ogilvie of Franklin, and Walter W. Ogilvie Jr. of Indianapolis, Indiana; twelve grandchildren; and one great-grandchild.

Funeral services were held at the College Grove United Methodist Church Saturday, July 9. The Rev. Edward K. Beckes, minister of First Presbyterian Church, officiated. Burial was in the Ogilvie family cemetery.

Pallbearers were Roscoe Smith, Richard Johns, Robert Wilson, George Jackson, Jr., Sam Rucker, Paul, Jason, and Powell Ogilvie.

Lawrence Funeral Home was in charge of arrangements.

– The Review-Appeal, July 14, 1977

William H. Ogilvie House is 100 Years Old This Christmas

The William Harris Ogilvie House on Route 2, College Grove, Tennessee, will be celebrating its 100th year at Christmas time.

William and Annie Lou Ogilvie were married in 1884. Their first child, Walter W. Ogilvie was born there on June 15, 1885. William H. was the son of Jason Wilson Ogilvie and a grandson of Richard and Cynthia Ogilvie.

Bill Ogilvie, son of Walter and Katherine Smith Ogilvie, and his wife Jackie, reside in the old home.

— Craig Ogilvie, *Ogilvie Kith and Kin*, vol.3, no.2, p.8., Dec. 1984.

Glen Overbey

From an interview with T. F. Overbey —

"My sons Glen and Beasley and I operate our three farms of 1100 acres, and Beasley trades on the side. We have eight families on our places and have never had any trouble keeping help. We raise wheat, oats, barley, rye, corn, tobacco and cover crops. ... We use tractors and mules for cultivation. I prefer the 11 mules and my mare, but the boys think tractors are better."

— Jane Bowman Owen, *Who's Who in Williamson County,* Rick Warwick, ed., originally published in *The Review-Appeal,* January 11, 1945.

Portrait Published in *The Review-Appeal* on May 5, 1966

ALBERT GLEN OVERBEY
1896 - 1972

Joint Services For A. G. Overbey, Sister

Joint funeral services for Albert Glen Overbey, one of Williamson County's best known and most philanthropic residents, and his sister, Miss Annie P. Overbey, of Nashville, were held Monday afternoon at Franklin Memorial Chapel.

Mr. Overbey, 76-year-old merchant and civic leader, died Saturday afternoon at Williamson County Hospital where he had been in critical condition since he suffered a heart attack at church the Sunday before, Miss Overbey, 73, died three hours later at Vanderbilt Hospital after an extended illness.

They were natives of Hickman County but they had lived in Williamson County on the Carter's Creek Pike for many years. Their parents were the late Mr. and Mrs. Frank Overbey.

Mr. Overbey was a member of the Board of Directors of Harpeth National Bank and of the Board of Trust of the Williamson County Hospital, Battle Ground Academy, and the War Memorial Public Library. He was one of the founders of the Library and for a number of years was chairman of the Board.

He was a charter member of the Franklin Rotary Club and had not missed a meeting of the club in 25 years. In 1971, the Franklin Civitan Club honored him with a plaque for his outstanding Citizenship and service to the community.

Mr. Overbey was a veteran of World War I and was a member of American Legion Post 22. He was a member of the Berea Church of Christ.

He was a large landowner and he operated a country general store on Carter's Creek Pike at the Bear Creek Road intersection, thought to be the last of its kind in this area.

Miss Overbey retired several years ago after working for both the federal and state governments.

They are survived by four sisters, Mrs. Emma Jane Hunter of Lexington, Tennessee, Miss Eunice Overbey of San Bernardino, California, Mrs. Mary Landrum of Marion, Arkansas, and Miss Dorothy Overbey of Auburn, Alabama; and one brother, Beasley Overbey of Franklin.

Herbert A. Robinson and Ned Elliott officiated at the final rites and interment was in Mt. Hope Cemetery.

Honorary pallbearers included the members of the Board of Directors of Harpeth National Bank, of Williamson County Hospital, of Battle Ground Academy, and the Public Library, officers of the Berea Church of Christ, Dr. Harry Guffee, Dr. Robert Hollister, and members of the Rotary Club.

Active pallbearers were Frank Notgrass, Vernon Beard, Brown Cannon, Brown Kinnard, Harry Sanders, Park Huff, and Everett Bizwell.

Franklin Memorial Chapel was in charge of arrangements.

— The Review-Appeal, February 3, 1972

Franklin High School

Franklin, Tennessee
1968 Summer School

REGISTRATION DATE JUNE 7th, 8 P. M.
SCHOOL BEGINS JUNE 10th

Franklin High School will offer a county wide summer
school program available to every boy and girl in Williamson County and surrounding counties who are interested in make-up work or taking additional subjects.
Make-up work will be offered to 7th and 8th grade students on recommendation by the school in order to be
promoted.

As approved by the State Board of Education the maximum of only 1½ credits of new work can be offered, 2
credits of review work and 1 new and 1 review credit.
Registration fees due first day of school or those desir-
ing to do so may pay ½ June 10th and ½ July 1st. (No
weekly payments acceptable).

Subjects Offered:

All Social Studies
All Math–Arithmetic (7th & 8th grade)
            Arithmetic (9th grade)
            Algebra 1 and 2
            Plane Geometry
English – 1, 2, 3, and 4
Science – General Science, Biology and
            Chemistry
Typing 1–
Driver Training
Mechanical Drawing
Other subjects if enough enrolled & desired

Tuition Is As Follows:

1½ New Credits $75.00
1   New and 1 Review 75.00
2   Review Credits 75.00
1   New Credit 50.00
1   Review Credit 50.00
½   New Credit 40.00
½   Review Credit 40.00

Staff:

The Franklin High School offers, as a part of its carefully developed educational program, a superior and
highly-trained staff. The teaching staff in the Franklin
High School summer school is composed, for the most
part, of the regular faculty members.

Signed,

CARL OWEN, Principal

W. C. YATES, Superintendent

Carl Newell Owen

Carl Newell Owen, although a native of Davidson County, has been coaching and teaching in Williamson County for a number of years. He has served as coach and teacher at Bethesda High School, principal at Thompson Station School, principal of Fairview Elementary School and is now principal of Franklin High School where he has been since the resignation of Barry Sutton.

In addition to all the clubs and associations pertaining to the Williamson County Schools Prof. Owen is also a member of the National Secondary School Principals Association. He is a Rotarian.

Prof. Owen is married to the former Miss Sara Jane Keller and they have three children. Tim is a second grade student at Fairview Elementary School and Pam and Phil haven't reached school age. The Owens still reside at Fairview where they attend the Liberty-Lincoln Church of Christ.

As Published in *The Review-Appeal* on February 8, 1968

J. H. T. Paine

Joseph Hamilton Thompson Paine is a prominent farmer and cattleman of West Harpeth Road. In addition to a large farming operation he serves as president of the Tennessee Valley Beef Producers Association and has directed semi-annual feeder calf sales for the association for several years. He is a member of the Farm Bureau.

For the past 17 years Mr. Paine has been Packmaster for Pack 135 of several lively Cub Scout dens. He is an elder for First Presbyterian Church and has been active in committee work for the local church, Presbytery, and Synod. He also serves on a committee for long-range plans for Monroe Harding Children's Home.

Mr. Paine is married to the former Miss Jean Rathborne of Decatur, Georgia, and they have three children, John, Emmy, and Rene.

As Published in *The Review-Appeal* on April 11, 1968

JOSEPH HAMILTON THOMAS PAINE
1906 - 1970

Ham Paine, Leader in Church, Welfare, Dies

Joseph Hamilton Thompson Paine, known by most of Williamson County as "Ham" Paine, died Wednesday morning, Dec. 23, at Vanderbilt Hospital.

Private funeral services for members of the family were held Thursday afternoon at Franklin Memorial Chapel and burial was in Williamson Memorial Gardens.

Memorial services were held Sunday afternoon at First Presbyterian Church, Dr. James A. Cogswell, minister of the church, officiated at both services.

Mr. Paine 64, was a prominent farmer and cattleman, a leader in church activities at local and state levels and a worker in welfare and inter-racial programs. For the past several years he had a feature in *The Review-Appeal* "Quotable Quotes by Ham Paine."

Born and reared in Baltimore, Maryland, he was the son of the late Gordon Paxton and Emma Thompson Paine. He was the grandson of Joseph Hamilton Thompson, who was a pioneer in Nashville banking and who was one of the founders and an officer of the old Nashville Trust Company.

Mr. Paine was educated in private schools in Baltimore where he was graduated from the Gilman Preparatory School in 1924. He was employed with the Ford Motor Company in Paris, France, the Banker's Trust Company in New York, and the old King-Dobbs wholesale grocery in Atlanta before entering the army in 1941 during World War II.

He was stationed in Hawaii and was discharged with the rank of captain after the war.

He was married in 1943 to the former Miss Jean Rathborne of Decatur, Georgia, who survives.

After the war Mr. Paine bought a large farm on West Harpeth Road and moved his family here. He stocked his land with Aberdeen Angus cattle and became active in livestock organizations. He served as president of the Tennessee Valley Beef Producers Association and had a major role in several agricultural testing programs with the University of Tennessee.

Mr. Paine was a member of the First Presbyterian Church which he served as elder. He was active in visitation for the church, particularly newcomers, a project he termed "friendship evangelism." He was intensely interested in World Missions and was active in men's work, attending each annual Men's Conference for 19 years.

He taught a Sunday School class here for a number of years and for ten years he conducted a Sunday School class at New Hope Presbyterian Church where he also preached at times when the church was without the services of a pastor.

His service reached a wider range at the Presbytery and Synod levels and he helped start new churches.

He served as counselor at a number of camps and conferences for young people and was a member of the Board of Monroe Harding Children's Home.

Cubmaster of Pack 135 for 17 years, Mr. Paine was given the Silver Beaver Award in 1963, the highest award in Scouting at the Council level.

He was a member of the first Williamson County Welfare Advisory Committee and helped organize the first inter-racial fellowship here known as the Laymen for the Betterment of Williamson County.

Disturbed over teenage boys expelled from school, he developed a tutoring program to enable them to keep up with their class.

Surviving in addition to his wife are one son, John H. E. Paine of Atlanta; twin daughters; Misses Emmy and Rene Paine; and a brother, Gordon Paxton Paine of Devon, Pennsylvania.

He became ill last May and underwent treatment for several weeks at Vanderbilt Hospital for a brain tumor. He returned to the hospital two months ago and subsequently had brain surgery.

In lieu of flowers friends were asked to make contributions to the Gift for the Christ Child for World Missions at the First Presbyterian Church or their favorite charity.

— The Review-Appeal, December 31, 1970

Portrait of An Excellent Citizen

Clyde Pewitt

Clyde Pewitt is co-owner with his brother, Elbert Pewitt, of Pewitt Bros. Tune and Tire Service on Columbia Avenue.

Born and reared in Williamson County he received his education at Franklin High School. He served two years with the United States Navy during World War II in the Pacific area and was discharged on his 21st birthday. He is married to the former Miss Judith Church and they have 4 children. Linda is a junior at Franklin High School, Suzanne attends Lipscomb School and the two boys, Johnnie and Jere are students at Battle Ground Academy. Clyde was a member of the Junior Chamber of Commerce for several years but is now a Rotarian, and serves on the Board of Directors of the Chamber of Commerce. He is a member of the County Court and is a candidate for re-election in the November election. He has also served as foreman of the Grand Jury.

The Pewitts live on the Nashville Highway and attend the Fourth Avenue Church of Christ.

As Published in *The Review-Appeal* on October 24, 1968

Mr. Clyde Pewitt, age 88 of Franklin, passed away Aug. 26, 2016.

He was a veteran of the U.S. Navy, owner and operator with Elbert "Duck" Pewitt of Pewitt Brothers Tune & Tire Service and a member of Grassland Heights Baptist Church. He served as Williamson County Commissioner for many years. Member of the Mason Hiram Lodge #7 and Williamson County Jaycees.

Preceded in death by parents, Johnnie Moore and Sarah Frances Sullivan Pewitt; wife, Hazel Bradley Pewitt; mother of his children, Judith Church Pewitt; siblings, Elmer, Albert and Elbert Pewitt, Ann Ashlee Dugan, Lucille Moran and Virginia Meacham. Survived by wife, Virginia Fisher Pewitt; sons, Johnnie Clyde (Nancy) Pewitt and Jere D. (Linda) Pewitt; daughters, Linda Pewitt and Suzanne (Bobby) Bratcher; grandchildren, Bryan (Erin) Pewitt, Jennifer Pewitt, Holly (Nathan) Koogler, Jeremy (Mica) Pewitt, Sharon (William) Crabtree, John (LeMai) Taylor, Amber (Dave) Huegel, Josh (Carolyn) Bratcher and Abbey Bratcher and ten great-grandchildren.

Funeral service will be held 11 a.m. Tuesday, Aug. 30, 2016 at Williamson Memorial Funeral Home, Jim Taylor officiating. Burial will follow in Williamson Memorial Gardens. Johnnie Pewitt, Jeremy Pewitt, Bryan Pewitt, Bobby Bratcher, Josh Bratcher, Nathan Koogler, William Crabtree and Jere Pewitt will serve as pallbearers. Honorary pallbearers: Dr. John Dixon, Dr. Jeff Bethurum, Billy Knight, Paul Pearre, Jimmy Sullivan, Fleming Williams, Louise Lynch and Jena Crawford.

Memorials may be made to the Dementia Society of America, P.O. Box 600, Doylestown, PA 18901. Visitation will be 5-7 p.m. Monday and one hour prior to the service at Williamson Memorial Funeral Home & Cremation Services, 615-794-2289. www.williamsonmemorial.com

– The Williamson Herald, August 28, 2016

Portrait of An Excellent Citizen

Joe Pinkerton

"He is the only child of Mrs. Elizabeth Hyde Pinkerton and the late Joe Pinkerton [Sr.] and was born out on the Murfreesboro Road ... In 1933 Joe married Estelle McCombs of Nashville. She was born in Boston, Massachusetts. ... In his endeavor to forge ahead and make his life a worth-while undertaking, he has ever kept in mind the old adage, 'Be content with what you have; never with what you are.'"

— Jane Bowman Owen, *"Who's Who in Williamson County,"* Rick Warwick, ed., originally published in *The Review-Appeal,* August 26, 1940.

"Joe Pinkerton was a born banker. He was financially shrewd, honest, wise, accurately analytical, pleasant, gracious, and 'people' inclined. He was more than a handler of money and banking procedures. He was a church man and a community builder. ... Joe Pinkerton's mark has been drilled deeply into the foundation of Franklin and Williamson County."

— W.C. Yates, *Tales of a Tennessee Yeoman, 1991.*

Portrait Published in *The Review-Appeal* on February 17, 1966

JOSEPH ANDERSON PINKERTON, JR.
1910-1987

Veteran banker Joe Pinkerton dies at 76

Funeral for Joe Anderson Pinkerton, a figure in Franklin banking circles for more than 50 years, was Wednesday at First Presbyterian Church, with Dr. Tom Walker officiating. Interment was in Mt. Hope Cemetery.

Mr. Pinkerton who rose from a bank teller to chairman of the board of directors of Williamson County Bank, died Sunday, Aug. 30, at his home in Franklin of an apparent heart attack. He was 76.

A native of Franklin, he attended Franklin Elementary School and Battle Ground Academy, graduating in 1929. He also attended Andrew Jackson Business College in Nashville.

His professional career began in 1930 at the former Harpeth National Bank in Franklin. He served as a teller for 10 years before advancing to assistant cashier and finally cashier.

He joined Williamson County Bank in 1947 as executive vice president and director. He was named president in 1950 and chairman of the board in 1968. He became senior chairman in 1976 and honorary chairman earlier this year.

Mr. Pinkerton loved his community, and many organizations have been the beneficiaries of his concern and dedication. He was involved in the founding and funding of many charitable organizations.

In 1941, he was one of the organizers of the Middle Tennessee Council of the Boy Scouts of America, and he was twice honored for his significant contributions. He was presented the Silver Beaver Award in 1950 and the Long Rifle Award in 1970.

Pinkerton was also involved in the establishment of the old County Center, the forerunner of Jim Warren Park. He was a charter member and one of the organizers of the Franklin Lions Club in 1946. He was an organizer of the United Givers Fund in 1963, and was the recipient of its outstanding community service award in 1970.

He was also an organizer of the Franklin Industrial Corporation to encourage industrial development in Williamson County.

Other organizations that benefitted from his support include the Mt. Hope Perpetual Care Association, Carnton Association, Carter House and Franklin Rotary Club.

Mr. Pinkerton was a member of the First Presbyterian Church and served in many capacities over the years, including deacon, elder, treasurer and chairman of the board of trustees.

He was also a strong supporter of Battle Ground Academy, serving as a member of the board of trustees for many years.

He is survived by his wife, Estelle; two sons, Dr. Joe Pinkerton Jr. [III], a surgeon in Kansas City, Missouri; Dr. Frank Pinkerton, a professor at Carson-Newman College in Jefferson City; one daughter, Mrs. Betty Sue Sherwood of Atlanta, and eight grandchildren.

Pallbearers were Tommy Butts, George Bivins, Sam Fleming, Tom Ridley, Bob Sewell, Stewart Campbell, Nelson Elam, Malcolm Gibbs, Marshall Liggett, William Miller, James Vaughn and Albert Ragsdale.

Honorary pallbearers were officers and directors of Williamson County Bank; elders and deacons of First Presbyterian Church; board of directors of Battle Ground Academy; board of directors and officers of Carnton Association; Claude Yates, Emmett Strickland, Dan Parsons, J. B. Parks, Wayne Glasgow, Warren Gray, Dr. Thomas Frist Sr., Calvin Lehew, Dr. Calvin Stewart and Millard Jefferson.

Memorial contributions may be made to the Middle Tennessee Heart Association., the Carnton Association, and Mt. Hope Cemetery Perpetual Care Association or your favorite charity.

Franklin Memorial Chapel was in charge of arrangements.

— The Williamson Leader, September 4, 1987

Excellent Citizens and Notable Partings

John D. Pinkerton

"Mr. Pinkerton was reared in Murfreesboro. His parents, Mr. and Mrs. Jose Pinkerton, live at Christiana now. His family is part of the Pinkerton clan that settled originally in Franklin after coming across the mountains from North Carolina, but his branched off and went to Murfreesboro. He has six brothers, Jim, Whit, and Nat Pinkerton, who live in Nashville, Herbert Pinkerton of Detroit, Michigan, Clay Pinkerton of Christiana, and two sisters, Mrs. Ruth Neal, who teaches at Unionville in Bedford County, and Miss Willie Mae Pinkerton of Nashville."

— Derry Carlisle, *Who's Who in Williamson County,* Rick Warwick, ed., originally published in *The Review-Appeal,* March 23, 1961.

Portrait Published in *The Review-Appeal* on July 7, 1966

JOHN DAVISON PINKERTON
1913 - 1999

John D. Pinkerton, 86, died yesterday at NHC Healthcare of Franklin. Mr. Pinkerton was born in Rutherford County and was a longtime resident of Williamson County.

He was a retired area manager with Middle Tennessee Electric Membership Corp. with 42 years of service. He joined the Franklin Noon Rotary Club in 1959, which he served as a treasurer, secretary and as a member of the Rodeo Committee. He was named a Paul Harris Fellow by the club in 1985, the highest honor bestowed by Rotary in recognition of community service.

"I've always respected and admired Mr. Pinkerton for what he accomplished in expanding park facilities and recognition of youth activities. I've known him through Fourth Avenue Church of Christ and we always stayed in touch after he left the board of aldermen," said Clyde Barnhill, a Franklin city alderman.

Mr. Pinkerton was the first inductee into the Williamson County Business Hall of Fame. A quote from that induction: "His passion for the good of Franklin and Williamson County has always been at the forefront of his heart, soul and mind. He truly loves this community."

Mr. Pinkerton was also a charter member of the Franklin Park Board and Pinkerton Park on Murfreesboro Road is named in his honor. He served as a Franklin city alderman, a member of the Industrial Committee of the Chamber for many years (the forerunner of Economic Development), served the Chamber as its president in 1963 and again in 1968, and was a member of the Fourth Avenue Church of Christ for more than 40 years.

"His passion for the good of Franklin and Williamson County was always at the forefront of his heart, soul and mind," said Nancy Conway, president/CEO of the Williamson County-Franklin Chamber of Commerce. "He truly loved this community."

Survivors include his wife, Mrs. Frankie Nance Pinkerton of Franklin; a son, John Pinkerton and his wife Melba of the Versailles Community; three daughters, Mrs. Sylvia Morton and her husband James of Murfreesboro, Mrs. Jane Bray and her husband Norman of Amelia Island, Florida, and Mrs. Judy Reynolds and her husband John of Brentwood; two sisters, Mrs. Ruth Neal of the Longview Community and Miss Willie Mae Pinkerton of the Link Community; 11 grandchildren; 15 great-grandchildren; and three great-great-grandchildren.

Graveside services will be conducted Saturday at Whitworth Cemetery in the Link Community of Rutherford County with Myron Keith officiating. Active pallbearers will be his grandsons. Honorary pallbearers will be employees and past employees of MTEMC and members of the Franklin Noon Rotary Club. Visitation will be from 4-8 p.m. Friday at Williamson Memorial Funeral Home.

Memorials may be made to the Franklin Noon Rotary Club Scholarship Fund, Fourth Avenue Church of Christ or the church of your choice.

Williamson Memorial Funeral Home is in charge of arrangements.

– The Review-Appeal, October 22, 1999

William Ross Price

Born and reared in Williamson County, Ross Price now resides on the Murfreesboro Road. He is a retired farmer, and is employed with Noble & Oden, contractors. His wife, before her marriage, was Miss Ella Lane and they have two daughters, Mrs. Coy Smith who now resides in Florida and Mrs. Betty Ann Bennett of Franklin, and two grandchildren.

Mr. Price was an elder in the Thompson Station Church of Christ for 20 years but is now a member of the Fourth Avenue Church of Christ. He is also a member of the Civitan Club.

As Published in *The Review-Appeal* on September 26, 1968

WILLIAM ROSS PRICE
1905 - 1987

William Ross Price, 82, died Wednesday at his home.

A native of Williamson County, Mr. Price was a retired painter and a member of Fourth Avenue Church of Christ in Franklin.

Survivors include his wife, Mrs. Dorothy Walker Price of Franklin; two daughters, Mrs. James (Betty) Demumbran of Franklin and Mrs. Coy (Jessie) Smith of Sandford [Sanford], Florida; four sisters, Mrs. Josie Johnson of Thompson Station, Mrs. Ruth Pewitt, Mrs. Liza Mai Lane and Mrs. Anna Laura Pewitt, all of Franklin;

two grandchildren and three great-grandchildren.

Funeral services will be at 1:30 p.m. today at Williamson Memorial Funeral Home with Myron Keith and Jim Taylor officiating. Burial will be in Williamson Memorial Gardens.

The Senior Citizens and the Franklin Civitan Club will serve as honorary pallbearers.

Elders and deacons of Fourth Avenue Church of Christ will serve as pallbearers.

— The Review-Appeal, March 20, 1987

"Both Mr. and Mrs. Price are natives of Williamson County. Ross Price is the son of Rachel Brown Waller and Jasper Ben Price. His father was a peace officer and farmer from the Eighth District for many years. Mrs. Price, the former Miss Ellie Mae Lane, was the daughter of Mr. and Mrs. J. J. Lane of Franklin. ...the Prices are the ultimate in what hard work, understanding, cooperation and faith will bring to a family. They sum it up this way: our home, two fine daughters, two splendid sons-in-law, the work we both enjoy most, our church, and being citizens of the greatest nation in the world with some of the most wonderful neighbors anyone ever had just add up to a good life."

— Nat Osborne, Jr., *Who's Who in Williamson County,* originally published in *The Review-Appeal,* March 17, 1955.

"Their antique business is, as Mrs. Price says, 'something to keep two old people busy and to prevent us from taking an aspirin and going to bed.'"

— "Antiques Both Hobby, Business for Prices," by Jan Slusher, *The Williamson Leader, August 17, 1975.*

Editor's note: Ella Mae Lane Price died November 8, 1976 at the age of 64.

Excellent Citizens and Notable Partings

Portrait of An Excellent Citizen

Dr. Walter Pyle

Dr. Walter Pyle will return to his office in the Medical Arts Building Monday after two months of service in Vietnamese civilian hospitals. A few years ago he participated in a similar volunteer program at the Albert Schweitzer Hospital in Haiti.

A native of Texas and graduate of Vanderbilt University School of Medicine, Dr. Pyle has practiced in Franklin for 31 years. He is married to the former Miss Cara Sneed of Calvert, Texas, and they have two children, Walter Pyle, Jr., of Calvert, Texas, and Mrs. Wendell Brittain of Asheville, North Carolina, and five grandchildren.

As Published in *The Review-Appeal* on December 7, 1967

WILLIAM WALTER PYLE
1908 - 1977

Dr. Walter Pyle dies after 40 years of practice here

Dr. William Walter Pyle, dean of practicing physicians in Williamson County, died early Tuesday morning, March 15, at Williamson County Hospital. He had been in declining health since last fall when he had lung surgery.

Funeral services will be held this (Thursday) morning at 10 a.m. at Franklin Memorial Chapel. Dr. William Greathouse, the Rev. Charles Murphy, and Myron Keith will officiate.

The body will be taken to Texas where interment will be held at the Beal family cemetery at Cameron, Texas.

Survivors include his wife, Mrs. Cara Sneed Pyle; one daughter, Mrs. Susan Sneed Pyle Hart of Odessa, Texas; one son, William Walter Pyle, Jr., of Cameron, Texas; a sister, Mrs. Martha Pyle Pettie of California; two brothers, Robert Lee Pyle, Jr., of Kansas City, Missouri; and John Herschel Pyle of Carefree, Arizona; and five grandchildren.

Dr. Pyle, 68 at the time of his death, was a native of Higgensville, Missouri, and was the son of the late Robert Lee and Mattie Lou Ellis Pyle. He was reared in Texas and was graduated from Southwestern University in Georgetown, Texas. He came to Nashville in 1931 to attend Vanderbilt Medical School. He received his M.D. degree in 1935 and in that year was married to Miss Cara Sneed of Calvert, Texas.

His internship was served at the U.S. Marine Hospital and Charity Hospital in New Orleans, Louisiana. He spent three months in special work in New York before moving to Franklin in December, 1936. He was connected with the Public Health Service until February 7, 1937, when he began the private practice of medicine and surgery.

Dr. Pyle established the Pyle Clinic which served medical and surgical patients until the Williamson County Hospital was established in 1958. He was chief of staff at the county facility in 1960 and again in 1969.

The hospital's board of trustees voted in February to dedicate one of the new wings to Dr. Pyle.

In the early '60s Dr. Pyle built the Medical Arts Building on West Main Street across from the hospital where several local physicians and dentists have or have had offices.

Because of Dr. Pyle, both Dr. Joseph Willoughby and Dr. Robert Hollister chose to practice medicine in Franklin. Dr. Pyle met Dr. Hollister during a working trip to Haiti, where he performed surgery in the Albert Schweitzer Hospital.

In 1966 Dr. Pyle served for two months in Vietnam where he worked in the Mekong Delta area in Vietnamese hospitals to teach new techniques to the native medical staffs. The program was sponsored by the American Medical Association

For the past few years, Dr. and Mrs. Pyle lived on Parker Branch Road where they had built a new house.

Dr. Pyle was a member of St. Bartholomew Episcopal Church in Nashville.

On February 1 of this year Dr. Pyle was honored by the Williamson County Hospital Board of Trustees and the medical staff for his outstanding devotion to the medical field and his undying loyalty to the Franklin community during his 40 years of service here. He was presented a brass plaque inscribed with the resolution adopted by the board and staff in a ceremony at the hospital. Darrell Chisholm, hospital administrator, and Hubert Hill, chairman of the board of trustees, made the presentation.

The resolution was signed by Dr. A. J. Lee, chief of staff, as well as Hill and Chisholm.

Serving as active pallbearers will be Darrell Chisholm, Dr. Joe Willoughby, Dr. Harry Guffee, Dr. Joseph Toh, Paul Buchanan, Joseph Ross, Herbert Stuart, and the Rev. Donald Foster.

Honorary pallbearers include Dr. Robert McCrackin, Dr. Robert Roy, Dr. Burton Grant, Dr. Eugene Regen, Sr., Dr. Eugene Regen, Jr., William Bowen, Keith Crawford and Dr. David Alexander.

In lieu of flowers the family requested that donations may be made to the Dr. Walter Pyle Memorial Fund at Williamson County Hospital, c/o Darrell Chisholm, Franklin, Tennessee.

Franklin Memorial Chapel is in charge of arrangements.

— The Review-Appeal, March 17, 1977

Excellent Citizens and Notable Partings

Mrs. J. E. Ragan

A Franklin woman, interested in many civic activities, but especially interested in the Williamson County Heart Council, is Mrs. J. E. Ragan, the former Miss Edna Harper, of Spring Hill. Mrs. Ragan was born in Marshall County but spent most of her girlhood days in Maury County, graduating from Spring Hill High School. Since her marriage to Mr. Ragan they have made Franklin their home. They now live on the corner of Columbia Avenue and Battle Avenue. They have three children, Mrs. Dennis Ford, who lives in Meadowgreen, Wayne, who lives in Hillsboro Acres and Mike a freshman in Middle Tennessee State University, and three grandchildren.

Mrs. Ragan is a member of the Franklin Business and Professional Woman's Club, in which she has held many offices, and was named "Woman of Achievement" by the club. She has served as chairman of the Williamson County Heart Council and chairman of Heart Sunday. She is on the Board of Senior Citizens and is a member of the Order of Eastern Star 234 in Spring Hill. Mrs. Ragan is employed in the offices of Dr. Harry Guffee and Dr. Joel Lee and attends the Fourth Avenue Church of Christ.

As Published in *The Review-Appeal* on October 3, 1968

EDNA HARPER RAGAN
1916-1994

Edna Harper Ragan, 78, died Saturday, April 30, at Claiborne and Hughes Convalescent Center in Franklin.

Mrs. Ragan was a native of Marshall County and a resident of Franklin. She was a secretary and nurse for Dr. A. J. Lee and a member of U.D.C. *[United Daughters of the Confederacy]*, Business and Professional Women's Club, Spring Hill O.E.S. *[Order of the Eastern Star]*, past member and past chairman of the board of J. L. Clay Senior Citizens, helped organize Jim Warren Park, and was a member of Fourth Avenue Church of Christ.

Survivors include one daughter, Bettye Ford of Franklin; two sons, Wayne Ragan of Alpharetta, Georgia, and Mike Ragan of Birmingham, Alabama.; two brothers, Hyde S. Harper Jr. of Brentwood and Brownie W. Harper of Franklin; two sisters, Ruth Troope of Franklin and Lois Neelley of Clinton, Mississippi; and five grandchildren.

Active pallbearers were Hugh Williams Sr., Glen Davis, Hal Crowell, Hyde Harper Jr., Hyde Harper III, John Neelley Sr., Bill Troope, Brownie W. Harper, Tandy Rice and Dr. A. J. Lee.

Funeral services were conducted on Monday, May 2, at Williamson Memorial Funeral Home with Myron Keith and Jim Taylor officiating. Burial was in Williamson Memorial Gardens.

– The Review-Appeal, May 4, 1994

"She was Edna Harper of Spring Hill before her marriage. Her parents are Mr. and Mrs. Hyde S. Harper, who are still residents of that Maury County town.

"Mrs. Ragan did not work away from home until eleven years ago when she became receptionist at the old Dan German Hospital. Then seven years ago when the Williamson County Hospital was opened and the small private hospitals here were closed she took her present position with Dr. Rice.

"Her very busy life extends greatly beyond her home and work, and because of her many accomplishments she has been chosen 'Woman of the Year' by the Franklin Business and Professional Women's Club of which she is a member.

"Indeed, Edna Ragan combines in generous proportions all the characteristics for a woman to be successful in both homemaking and professional service."

— Derry Carlisle, *Who's Who in Williamson County*, Rick Warwick, ed., originally published in *The Review-Appeal*, May 20, 1965.

James Albert Ragsdale

James Albert Ragsdale is a native of Williamson County and lives on Battle Avenue with his wife, the former Miss Elizabeth Lewis. He owns and operates S. E. Farnsworth & Co. on Columbia Ave.

Mr. Ragsdale is a member of the First Methodist Church where he serves on the Official Board. He is a Mason, a member of the Board of Directors of the Williamson County Bank and is one of the directors of the Williamson County Chamber of Commerce.

As Published in *The Review-Appeal* on April 6, 1967

JAMES ALBERT RAGSDALE
1910 - 1989

James Albert Ragsdale, 79, of Franklin died Nov. 2 at his home. A native of Williamson County, Mr. Ragsdale was a retired general contractor for S. E. Farnsworth & Co. A past master of Hiram Lodge No. 7, he was a former owner of S. E. Farnsworth Co. He was a member of the board of directors of Sovran Bank and a member of First United Methodist Church.

Survivors include his wife, Mrs. Elizabeth Lewis Ragsdale of Franklin; six nephews, Irvin B. Dean of Corpus Christi, Texas, Ted Nitschke of Kingsport, Tennessee, David Nitschke of Scottsbluff, Nebraska, Edward Albert Dean of San Antonio, J. B. Simmons of Spring Hill and Milton Clark of Burwood and three nieces, Deborah Deen Ball of Franklin, Katherine Alley of Franklin and Mrs. Ruby Dodd of Burwood.

Funeral services will be 2 p.m. today at Williamson Memorial Funeral Home with Edward Crump and Art Robins officiating. Burial will be in Mt. Hope Cemetery.

Pallbearers will include William Miller, Mike Duncan, Gene Turns, Marshall Liggett, Edward Woodard, Billy Reynolds, Charlie Sawyer Jr., Richard Marlin and Robert Sewell.

Williamson Memorial Funeral Home is in charge of arrangements.

– The Review-Appeal, November 5, 1989

S. E. Farnsworth & Co.

"The Quality Builders"

Contractors
Builders' Supplies

S. E. Farnsworth **Albert Ragsdale**

Phone 8

Paul Redick

"Success, to me, is making the world a little better place to live during your lifetime."

— Paul Redick, "A sense of humor... A sense of commitment," by Ken Russell, *Williamson Scene,* April 2, 1986.

Portrait Published in *The Review-Appeal* on April 21, 1966

WILLIAM PAUL REDICK
1911 - 2002

Former BGA headmaster dies at 91

Paul Redick, 91, of Franklin died Monday, May 20, 2002. A native of Camden, a son of Phillip Redick and Mabel Maiden, Mr. Redick served in the U.S. Navy during World War II and attended the University of Tennessee at Martin and Cumberland University in Lebanon. He played football and other sports and was elected to the Sports Hall of Fame at both universities. Mr. Redick received his master's degree in education at Peabody College. He was a teacher, coach and administrator at Castle Heights Military Academy in Lebanon (1936-50), headmaster at Battle Ground Academy (1950-68) and served as director of Camp Hy-Lake for Boys (1935-60). His life touched thousands of boys throughout his career.

After leaving BGA, Mr. Redick served as director of special schools for the State of Tennessee. From 1974-76 he served as vice president of public relations at Harpeth National Bank. Mr. Redick served as president, secretary, treasurer and program director of the Franklin Rotary Club where he received the Paul Harris Fellow Award for his work. Mr. Redick was the author of the "Americana Series" on WENO Radio and wrote several patriotic articles for local newspapers, also authoring two books, *It Happened at Hy-Lake* and *They Preached Me A Sermon*. He served on the administrative board of First United Methodist Church and as teacher of the Hal [Peoples] Bible Class.

Cumberland University awarded the Phoenix Award to Mr. Redick for "outstanding contribution in the field of education" and he received the "Outstanding Citizen" recognition from *The Review-Appeal*.

He was preceded in death by a brother, Herbert Redick, and a sister, Reba Wilson.

Survivors include his loving wife of 66 years, Betsy; a son, Bill Redick; a daughter, Becky (Owen) Waldrop; two sisters, Adelaide Hollis and Ruth Elkins; two grandsons, Al (Laura) Waldrop and Harp (Peggy) Waldrop; a granddaughter, Paige (Craig) Mills; eight great-grandsons, Graham, Jack, Charlie, Ford, Hays and Duke Waldrop and Ben and Russell Mills; and one great-granddaughter, Eliza Mills.

Graveside services will be held at 11 a.m. today, May 22, at Williamson Memorial Gardens with the Rev. Stuart Nunnally officiating. Active pallbearers will be grandsons and nephews, Al and Hays Waldrop, Craig Mills, Jim and John Hays, Phil Hollis and Jim Elkins. Honorary pallbearers are the Franklin Noon Rotary Club and the Hal [Peoples] Bible Class of First United Methodist Church. Visitation with the family will be one hour prior to the graveside services at Williamson Memorial Funeral Home.

In lieu of flowers, contributions to honor Mr. Redick's life may be made to the William Paul Redick Faculty Endowment Fund c/o Battle Ground Academy Development Office, First United Methodist Church or the charity of your choice. Williamson Memorial Funeral Home is in charge of arrangements.

– The Review-Appeal, May 22, 2002

Excellent Citizens and Notable Partings

Portrait of An Excellent Citizen

Clair D. Regen

Clair D. Regen, son of the late Mr. and Mrs. M. T. Regen, was born and reared in Franklin. He was educated at Battle Ground Academy, Massey's Military Academy in Pulaski, and Davidson College in Davidson, N. C. and during his college days participated in football and basketball. He is president of C. D. Regen Co., Inc. located on N. Fifth Avenue (Hillsboro Road).

Mr. Regen is married to the former Miss Elizabeth Faw and they live on the Nashville Highway. They have two daughters, Mrs. Betty Regen Collins of Nashville, and Mrs. George H. Hodges, Jr., of Jacksonville, Florida.

A member of the First Presbyterian Church since young manhood, he has served as an elder for 23 years.

Mr. Regen is also a member and past president of the Lions Club and now serves as Tail Twister. He is a Mason, member of the Blue Lodge, the Chapter and the Commandery. He is past master of the Blue Lodge and past commander of the Commandery.

As Published in *The Review-Appeal* on November 9, 1967

Clair D. Regen, 90, of Franklin died at his home Thursday, Sept. 24.

Mr. Regen was a native of Lynnville and was a self-employed contractor and member of the First Presbyterian Church. He was a member of Hiram Lodge No. 7, Knights Templar, Franklin Lions Club and an elder at his church.

He is survived by his two daughters, Betty Cathey, Spring Hill, and Kernan Hodges Jr., Jacksonville, Florida; two grandchildren and two great-grandchildren.

Services were Saturday at the First Presbyterian Church with the Rev. Thomas D. Walker and the Rev. Fairfax Fair officiating. Burial was in the Mount Hope Cemetery.

Active pallbearers were: Dr. Eugene Regen Jr., Dr. David Regen, Barney Regen, John Bell Regen Jr., C. J. Brumit, Frank Akin, Jimmy Akin, and Robert Walker.

Honorary pallbearers were: Malcom Gibbs, William Custer, Jack Custer, Bob White, Emmett Strickland, Dr. L. Rowe Driver, Dr. Davis C. Hill, Dr. Joseph Willoughby, Dr. Bryant Savage Jr., and the Men's Coffee Club of the First Presbyterian Church.

Memorials may be made to the First Presbyterian Church, Hiram Lodge No. 7, Franklin Lions Club or the charity of your choice.

Franklin Memorial Funeral Home handled the arrangements.

— The Review-Appeal, September 27, 1992

Clair D. Regen   Wm. Thomas Lewis

Clair D. Regen Co.

Since 1931

AIR CONDITIONING

PLUMBING   HEATING

SHEET METAL CONTRACTING

*"We Don't Do All The Work,
We Do The Best"*

Telephone 794-3645

CLAIR D. REGEN CO.
SINCE 1931
"WE DONT DO ALL THE WORK, WE DO THE BEST"

Home Of
CLAIR D. REGEN CO.
Air Conditioning—Heating—Plumbing—Sheet Metal

"In March 1938, Clair formed a plumbing partnership with S. E. Farnsworth on Columbia Avenue under the trade name of Farnsworth and Regen, and this business was active until January 1, 1942, when the younger member of the firm bought out his partner. ... In 1947, Clair built a concrete block building on South Fifth Avenue near the edge of town ... The business now operates under the name of Clair D. Regen Company, Plumbing, Heating & Sheet-metal Contractors."

— Jane Bowman Owen, *Who's Who in Williamson County*, Rick Warwick, ed., originally published in *The Review-Appeal*, November 11, 1948.

Portrait of An Excellent Citizen

Mrs. M. T. Regen

Mrs. M. T. Regen, a native of Texas, has lived in Franklin since her marriage to the late Mr. Regen fifty years ago. She has been active in a number of organizations. As a member of the First Presbyterian Church, she has participated in all phases of its work and has held office and positions of leadership in its various groups. For her service she was presented a few years ago a Life Membership pin in the Women of the Church. She has promoted the work of the Daughters of the American Revolution and has been regent of Old Glory Chapter here for a number of years. The Magazine Club has also been one of her prime interests.

Mrs. Regen has four sons, Dr. Eugene Marshall Regen of Nashville, Clair D. Regen of Franklin, William Marvin Regen of Lebanon, and John Bell Regen of Kingsport; nine grandchildren; and eleven great-grandchildren.

As Published in *The Review-Appeal* on August 10, 1967

CAROLINE LOUISE HILL REGEN
1883 - 1967

Mrs. Regen, Leader Here 50 Years, Dies

Mrs. Marvin T. Regen, who had been a leader in many activities in Franklin during the more than half century she lived here, died Monday night at Williamson County Hospital, where she had been confined for the past several weeks.

Funeral services were conducted Wednesday morning at First Presbyterian Church. Dr. James A. Cogswell and Dr. T. B. Cowan officiated and burial was in Mt. Hope Cemetery.

Mrs. Regen, the former Miss Caroline Louise Hill, was born in Trenton, Tennessee, January 3, 1883, and was the daughter of Dr. John Edgar Hill and Fannie Carothers Hill. Because of Dr. Hill's health the family moved to Texas in 1885. They lived in Bandera for two years and then moved to Manor, which was Mrs. Regen's home until 1908 when she moved to Austin until the time of her marriage to Mr. Regen in 1916.

She was a graduate of Baylor College for Women, now known as Mary Hardin Baylor College in Belton, Texas, and attended the University of Texas in Austin. Her only venture in the business world was in filling an unexpired term of tax assessor for Travis County, Texas

She had a number of relatives in Franklin and Williamson County and met Mr. Regen during a visit here. He was a widower with five sons whom she reared as her own and with such care and affection that they regarded her as their mother. Mr. Regen, who owned and operated a funeral home here many years, died in 1954.

For a number of years Mrs. Regen was chairman of the Red Cross Roll Call for Williamson County and she also was in charge of many of the sewing projects of the Red Cross.

She had served Old Glory Chapter of the Daughters of the American Revolution in a number of offices and was regent for several terms. She was a leader of the Magazine Club.

One of the most active members of First Presbyterian Church, she was recognized for her service a few years ago with a Life Membership in the Women of the Church. Only when she entered Williamson County Hospital did she relinquish her duties.

Survivors include four sons, Dr. Eugene Marshall Regen of Nashville, William Marvin Regen of Lebanon, John Bell Regen of Kingsport, and Clair D. Regen of Franklin; one brother, Claude E. Hill of Austin, Texas, eleven grandchildren, and eleven great-grandchildren. One son, Dr. Kelsey Regen of Richmond, Virginia, died in 1965.

Serving as honorary pallbearers were the elders and deacons of First Presbyterian Church.

Active pallbearers were Dr. Eugene Regen, Jr., Dr. David Regen, Barney Regen, Jon Watson Regen, John Bell Regen, Jr., George Hodges, Jr., J. D. Moore, Dr. Davis Hill, and Glenn Eddington, Jr., of Greeneville, Tennessee.

In lieu of flowers the family requested donations to the scholarship fund of First Presbyterian Church or to the cancer fund.

Franklin Memorial Chapel was in charge.

— The Review-Appeal, August 24, 1967

Joseph Lee Ridley

Joseph Lee (Hokey) Ridley is deputy commissioner in the Department of Conservation for the State of Tennessee. Prominent in the political realm of the state for many years, he was appointed to this position by Gov. Buford Ellington when he was elected for a second term. Mr. Ridley had held this same position during the earlier administration of Gov. Ellington. He served a number of years in the General Assembly, both in the House of Representatives and in the Senate.

Mr. Ridley is a native of Williamson County and has been prominent as a farmer and in the real estate business. He has been one of the strongest supporters of the Farm Bureau and has held office in the Williamson County organization. He is an active member of the Thompson's Station Methodist Church, the American Legion, Elks, Shriners, Masons, and the Williamson County Chamber of Commerce. He and his wife, the former Miss Virginia Terrell, live at 706 Hillsboro Road. They have one son, John of Nashville, and twin granddaughters.

As Published in *The Review-Appeal* on June 6, 1968

JOSEPH LEE RIDLEY
1896 - 1983

Rites conducted for leader J. L. Ridley

Funeral for Joseph Lee (Hokey) Ridley, retired Williamson County farmer and political leader, was Tuesday at Franklin Memorial Chapel.

He served as deputy commissioner of agriculture during both of Gov. Buford Ellington's terms. He also served in both houses of the state legislature and chaired several committees.

He was the first person to realize Tennessee had a water problem and established a water purity commission on which he served with ex-governor Jim McCord and Governor Ellington.

Mr. Ridley, who served on the staff of two governors and as a member of the General Assembly, died Sunday at Williamson County Hospital after an extended illness. He was 86 years old.

The Williamson County native farmed for many years, but also sold real estate, specializing in farm sales.

Ridley was a former member of the Williamson County Hospital board of trustees and served as chairman at one time.

He was the driving force behind efforts to have the hospital built. He obtained federal and state money under the Hill-Burton program.

He was also a member of the American Legion, Elks Club, Shriners, Williamson County Chamber of Commerce, a director for the Tennessee Burley Association, a director for Tennessee Farm Bureau and the Williamson County Farm Bureau.

The Jaycees cited Ridley in 1950 as an Outstanding Citizen. This was the first such honor the Jaycees gave and only a few others have been given in the past 30 years.

Ridley was married to the late Virginia Morton Terrell in 1920. She died in November 1981.

Mr. Ridley was a long-time member of the Thompson's Station United Methodist Church.

Survivors include one son, John D. Ridley; two grandchildren, Nancy R. Slater of Florida and Virginia Marciano of New York, and seven great grandchildren.

— The Williamson Leader, January 6, 1983

"Joseph Lee Ridley, better known as 'Hokey' by his hundreds of friends, entered the service in August 1918, at the age of 22, and was sent to The University of Tennessee, Knoxville, where he received three months of intensive training with the Motor Transport Corps, consisting of mechanical work on all kinds of motors from motorcycles to airplanes. He was working with Will Bass in an automobile shop when he was called to service and his training followed along the line of what he already knew. He became an expert with engines and after completing the course was sent to Camp Johnson at Jacksonville, Florida, to follow up the same work and advanced training was received in Philadelphia, Pennsylvania. It was here he was stationed when the Armistice was signed and he received his discharge."

— Jane Bowman Owen, *Who's Who in Williamson County*, Rick Warwick, ed., originally published in *The Review-Appeal*, November 8, 1945.

Portrait of An Excellent Citizen

Charles A. Rigsby

Charles Rigsby is a young business man of the College Grove Community and up until this week has been operator of Rigsby's Market, but sold the business this week. However this does not put him out of the business world for he operates a photography shop in his home and in the building formerly occupied by the Bank of College Grove.

Mr. Rigsby is past president of the College Grove Lions Club, a member of the Owen Hill Masonic Lodge and is on the Williamson County Welfare Advisory Board. He attends the College Grove Baptist Church and has served as secretary, treasurer and superintendent of the Sunday School.

He makes his home with his parents, Mr. and Mrs. George Rigsby.

As Published in *The Review-Appeal* on October 31, 1968

Charles A. Rigsby, 69 of Chapel Hill and formerly of College Grove, Tennessee, died Feb. 11, 2010 in Franklin, Tennessee.

Mr. Rigsby was born in Davidson County.

He was a graduate of College Grove High School, Class of 1959, a charter member of First Baptist Church, College Grove, and was presently a member of Harpeth Lick Cumberland Presbyterian Church in Allisona. Mr. Rigsby was a former customer representative for Williamson Medical Center in Franklin and was also the former owner of Charles Rigsby Photography and co-owner of College Grove Drugs, both in College Grove, Tennessee. He organized and was the first Scout Master of the College Grove Boy Scout Troop. He was a member and past president of the College Grove Lions Club and was a former member of GraceWorks Advisory Board of Williamson County. Mr. Rigsby was a 33-year member of the College Grove Fire Department, which he served as Chief of the Department for 30 years. He was a member of the Tennessee Fire Chiefs Association and was a charter member of the Williamson County Fire Chiefs Association. Mr. Rigsby helped form the first responder program now in place in Williamson County.

He was preceded in death by his parents George D. and Pauline Bellenfant Rigsby; sister Evelyn Rigsby. Mr. Rigsby is survived by a sister Marjorie (Aubrey) Ghee, Holts Corner Community, Tennessee; brother James E. (Hazel) Rigsby, Eagleville, Tennessee; two nieces; two nephews; three great nieces; four great nephews; one great-great niece.

Funeral services were conducted Feb. 15, 2010, from the chapel of Lawrence Funeral Home; Rev. John Hyden and Rev. Earl Pitts officiating. Burial followed in Cothran Cemetery in Bedford County.

In lieu of flowers, memorial donations may be made to Harpeth Lick Cumberland Presbyterian Church, the American Cancer Society or the American Heart Association.

— The Williamson Herald, February 18, 2010

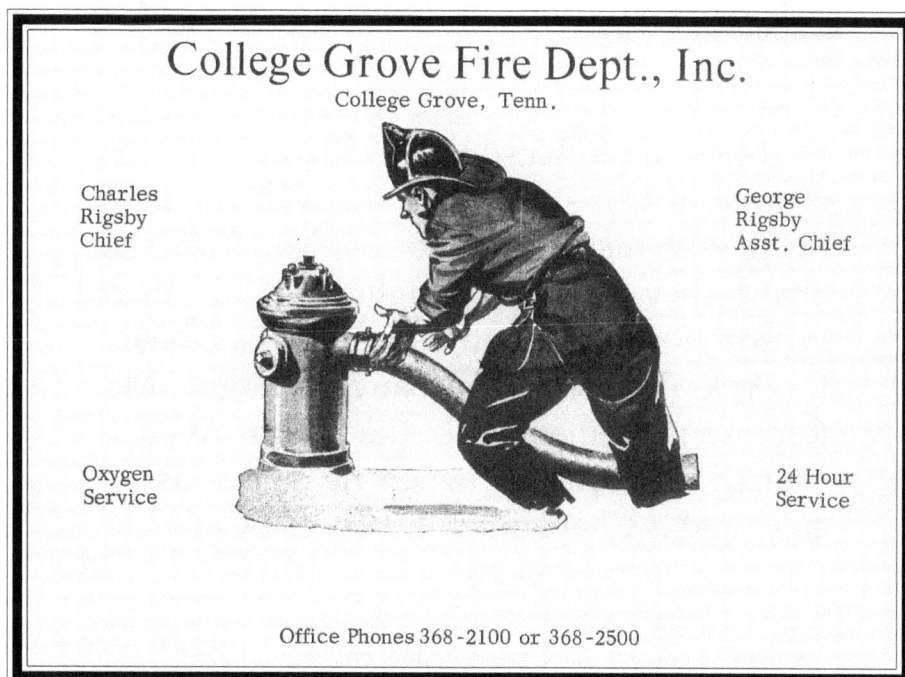

College Grove Fire Dept., Inc.
College Grove, Tenn.

Charles Rigsby Chief

George Rigsby Asst. Chief

Oxygen Service

24 Hour Service

Office Phones 368-2100 or 368-2500

Herbert A. Robinson

Herbert A. Robinson, a minister of the Church of Christ, lives on the Murfreesboro Road, with his wife, the former Miss Eva Mai Shaw. They have two daughters, Mrs. Albert Wilson (Ruth) of Nashville and Mrs. Donald L. Peck (Louise) of Albany, Georgia. Mr. Robinson is a member of the Fourth Avenue Church of Christ of which he serves as an elder and is Chaplain of the Civitan Club.

As Published in *The Review-Appeal* on January 5, 1967

Herbert A. Robinson, 86, a well-known Church of Christ minister and partner in Franklin Memorial Chapel Funeral Home, died Sunday at Williamson County Hospital.

Services were Tuesday at Franklin Memorial Chapel with Myron Keith, Jim Taylor and Mack Wayne Craig officiating.

Mr. Robinson was a native of the county and served as a minister in the Churches of Christ for over 50 years and was instrumental in the forming of several area Churches of Christ.

Active at his home congregation of Fourth Avenue Church of Christ, Mr. Robinson had been an elder of the congregation since 1958.

A former partner with the Bethurum, Henry and Robinson Funeral Home in Franklin, Mr. Robinson was a partner and president of Franklin Memorial Chapel, Inc., at the time of his death. He had held that post since 1957.

Mr. Robinson was a former member and past chaplain of the Franklin Civitan Club.

"Franklin has lost one of its finest citizens and the Fourth Avenue Church of Christ has lost one of her great leaders." Myron Keith, Fourth Avenue Church of Christ minister, said.

Survivors include his wife, Mrs. Eva Shaw Robinson, Franklin; daughters, Mrs. Albert (Ruth) Wilson, Nashville, Mrs. Donald L. (Louise) Peck, Boulder, Colorado; granddaughters, Mrs. Edwin (Judy) Hart, Sunnyvale, California, Mrs. Ladon (Anita) Baltimore, Nashville, Mrs. Janet Fowlke, Santa Ana, California, Mrs. Lloyd (Christy) Sewell; grandsons, Robert L. Wilson, both [sic] of Marietta, Georgia, Randy Wilson, Nashville, Kenneth Peck, Denver, Colorado, Larry Robinson, Los Angeles, California; eight great-grandchildren and one great, great-grandchild.

Honorary pallbearers were elders and deacons of Fourth Avenue Church of Christ. Franklin Memorial Chapel personnel and Middle Tennessee area funeral directors.

Active pallbearers were Robert L. Wilson, Randy Wilson, Kenneth Peck, Larry Robinson, John Harper, Dale Pewitt and William Puckett.

Burial was in the Sparkman Cemetery.

— The Review-Appeal, May 2, 1985

Portrait of An Excellent Citizen

Mrs. Floyd Sandlin

Mrs. Floyd Sandlin is one of Franklin's Main Street merchants being a partner in the Sandlin Drug Company. Mrs. Sandlin's husband operated the drug store prior to his death and since then she has continued its operation. She was before her marriage Miss Lucinda Kimmins of Shelbyville.

Mrs. Sandlin is active in the Business and Professional Woman's Club and has held several offices since she has been a member. Her main interest is in the Williamson County Heart Unit and has served as chairman of the Unit. During the time of her chairmanship two important Heart Forums were held here. She is also chairman of Memorial Gifts of the Middle Tennessee Heart Association. She was delegate to the Tennessee Heart Association convention this year and has been named to attend in June of next year, when the convention is held in Nashville. She is also a member of the Carter House Association and the American Legion Auxiliary.

Mrs. Sandlin attends the First Christian Church in Nashville.

As Published in *The Review-Appeal* on September 12, 1968

LUCINDA KIMMINS SANDLIN
1910-2001

Franklin civic leader, drugstore owner, Lucinda K. Sandlin, dies

Franklin – Lucinda K. Sandlin was a business leader at a time when women were expected to stay at home and raise a family. An energetic woman, she was able to do both well.

Sandlin, 90, the former owner of, and bookkeeper for, Sandlin Drug Co., died Monday at her Franklin home.

Born in Bedford County, Sandlin and her husband, Floyd, moved to Franklin in 1950. Four years later, they bought Gill Drug Store.

Floyd died in 1963 and Sandlin, along with partners, operated Sandlin Drug's locations on Main Street and on Carter's Creek Pike until 1974, when the Main Street store was closed. At that time she sold all her interest but continued to work in the store until it was sold in 1995.

"Sandlin has been a civic leader for many years, participating in anything that would enhance the city of Franklin," said Franklin/Williamson County Chamber Chairman Ralph Walker in 1999 as he presented her with a Living Legend Award.

"Lucinda is known as a mentor to the many young people she has influenced and can be credited with always encouraging others to strive for their full potential," he said.

She had been a member of the Business and Professional Women's Club since 1956, volunteered many hours to the Middle Tennessee Heart Association, and in 1973 earned the coveted Helen B. Fariss Memorial Award.

Through it all, Sandlin gave back to the community because, as she said, she loved Franklin.

"Franklin has given so much to me over the years, and I hope that I have given back to the community," she wrote the chamber during her award ceremony.

Survivors include her daughter, Thelma D. Pewitt, Franklin; sister, Mary Kimmins Cross, Shelbyville, Tennessee; grandchildren Dale and Amy Pewitt and Valerie Suggs; five great-grandchildren; nephews Kim and Paul Cross; and cousins John Kimmins and Edward Slayton.

Funeral services will be at 11 a.m. Thursday in Williamson Memorial Funeral Home, 3009 Columbia Ave., with Jim Barton officiating.

Burial will follow in Lynchburg Cemetery with James Cotton, Bill Cook, Paul Johnson, Martin Brown, John Barton and Roy Wilhoite serving as active pallbearers.

Honorary pallbearers will be Dr. Jeff Bethurum, Dr. Richard Lane, Dr. David Nierste, Dr. Jennifer Peppers, Cliff Frensley, Joe Jones, Dave Buchanan, Julia Barton, Amy Pewitt, Virginia White, Ellis and Gary Sandlin, Evelyn and Bama Ray, Jack Custer, Elbert Heithcock, Josie Singleton and the Women's Sunday School First Presbyterian Church.

Visitation will be from 1-4 p.m. and 6-8 p.m. today in the funeral home. Memorial contributions may be made to Berea College or Willowbrook Hospice.

– The Tennessean, January 31, 2001

W. P. Scales

W. P. Scales is in his 58th year in the business of education in Tennessee, 56 of those years in the Williamson County System. Mr. Scales was county superintendent of schools in this county for 20 years and upon his retirement eight years ago was made an honorary member of the Tennessee Education Association. He has continued with the schools as manager of custodial and maintenance materials.

Mr. Scales is a native of Williamson County. He completed his preparatory training at the prep school department of Peabody College in 1911 and began teaching after his graduation. He taught at New Providence in Montgomery County for one year and at Brownsville in Haywood County for a year. He returned to Williamson County and was principal at Harpeth School for 22 years. He was math instructor at Bethesda High School for 3 ½ years and was at Trinity School for two years.

From the time he started teaching he began working on his B.S. degree on Saturdays and during vacations and was graduated from Peabody College in 1949 during the time he was superintendent.

He was married in 1918 to Miss Susie May Baugh who died in 1954. He married again in 1959 to the former Miss Mary Katherine Scales of College Grove and their home is at 347 East Main Street in Murfreesboro. Mr. Scales owns a farm at Harpeth and spends some of his time there.

He is member of Cowles Chapel Methodist Church where he served as superintendent of the Sunday School for 30 years. He is also a member of the Masonic Lodge at Bethesda and served as secretary for 35 years.

As Published in *The Review-Appeal* on September 5, 1968

WILLIAM PRESTON SCALES
1893 - 1983

William Preston Scales, Williamson County educator, dies

William Preston Scales, age 89, formerly of Franklin and a resident of Murfreesboro, died on Thursday, March 24, at Middle Tennessee Medical Center in Murfreesboro. A native of Williamson County, Mr. Scales was a well-known Tennessee educator. He was the son of the late John Scales and Elizabeth Seyers Scales.

Mr. Scales was active in the field of education in Tennessee for 59 years and 57 of these years were in the Williamson County school system. He was superintendent of schools in Williamson County for twenty years and upon his retirement in 1970 was made an honorary member of the Tennessee Education Association.

On November 20, 1977 there was a dedication service for the purpose of naming a newly constructed school the W. P. Scales Elementary School.

Mr. Scales was a graduate of Peabody College. He taught math and geography at Bethesda High School for three and one-half years.

He was principal of New Providence in Montgomery County for one year, principal of Holly Grove High School in Haywood County for one year, principal of Trinity High School for two years, and principal of Harpeth High School for twenty-two years.

He was a member of Cowles Chapel Methodist Church in Franklin where he served as superintendent of the Sunday school for thirty years.

He was a fifty year Mason. He became a member of the Bethesda Lodge 201 in 1921 and served as secretary for 35 years. He transferred to the Mt. Moriah Lodge 18 after moving to Murfreesboro.

Funeral services were held at Franklin Memorial Chapel on Saturday, March 26, with the Reverend Fenton Warren and Milton Lillard officiating. Burial was in the Mt. Hope Cemetery. Family visitation was held on Friday evening, March 25, at the funeral home.

Honorary pallbearers were: members and past members of the Board of Education, members and past members of the Williamson County Court, Administrative Board of Cowles Chapel Church, members of Bethesda Lodge, members of Mt. Moriah Lodge, Murfreesboro, W. H. McCord, Jr., J. C. Anderson, C. C. Brown, Wilson Herbert, Jerry Fly, Jr., Joe D. Wilson, Gilbert Allen, Claude Yates, Fleming Marlin, George Northern, Henry Woodside, Robert Mosley, Paul Butts, Dr. Harry Guffee, B. H. Paschall, Joe Billingsley, Ed Mosley, H. C. Meacham, John Beasley, Sam Ogilvie, T. S. Nelms, Jr., Hollis Qualls, Tom Brown, Newt McCord, Millard Mitchum, Billy Martin, Kirk McGee, Thomas Herbert, Billy McCord, Joe Herbert, Jim Stevenson, Maurice Hood, Mitchell Wright, Tom Stoddard, H. C. Coat, J. B. Buchanan, John Horn, John Stevenson, Gerald Hood, Allen Brown Marlin, Reedy Childress, Fuller Arnold.

Active pallbearers: Taylor Wright, Wayne Wright, James Wright, Randall Wright, Steven Wright, David Wright and Alfred Goldthwaite.

Survivors are: his wife, Nina Adams Scales, Murfreesboro; nephew, Oden Flippen, Franklin; niece, Sara Bechick, Washington, D.C.; three stepdaughters; eleven step-grandchildren; two step-great-grandchildren.

Dr. John T. Netterville, superintendent of the Williamson County schools, stated, "W. P. Scales was a scholar and a gentleman. He set standards in his personal and professional life that brought honor to himself, his schools, and his community."

Netterville said, "We pause at the passing of Mr. Scales, reflecting on our present blessings, and expressing our thanks for him for the leadership he provided for this community."

"W. P. Scales Elementary School will continue this expression of our feeling for him, for our children, and our children's children, to appreciate for years to come."

The Scales family has requested that contributions be made to the W. P. Scales Elementary School or to favorite charities.

– The Review-Appeal, March 29, 1983

BILL DUKE
7/66

Bob Sewell

"Ewell is the kind of person who believes in 'look before you leap.' Before he married Ruth Alexander, daughter of Mr. and Mrs. Alvin Alexander of Bethesda, on October 5, 1940, he had bought a lot, erected a five-room house of field stone, the plan being his and Ruth's brain work, and even had the furniture in place. Everything was in order when he brought his bride home and ready to set up housekeeping in a big way."

— Jane Bowman Owen, *Who's Who in Williamson County*, Rick Warwick, ed., originally published in *The Review-Appeal*, February 7, 1946.

Portrait Published in *The Review-Appeal* on July 21, 1966

ROBERT EWELL SEWELL
1915 - 1999

Robert Ewell Sewell, 84, died Friday, November 5, at Baptist Hospital. Mr. Sewell was a native of Williamson County, born in the Shoals Branch Community and the son of the late R. Ernest Sewell and the late Daisy Beasley Sewell. He founded Sewell Electric Company, worked at the former Harpeth National Bank, the former McCall Electric Company and with the late Frank Beasley at the former Franklin Supply Company before going into business for himself in 1945. He founded two radio stations, the former WFLT in 1961 and the former WIZO in 1968. In 1963, he was named a Melvin Jones Fellow, a top award from Franklin Lions Club in which he was an active member. In 1997, he was named as an original member of the Williamson County—Franklin Chamber of Commerce Business Hall of Fame. He was an active member of Franklin First United Methodist Church.

Survivors include his wife, Mrs. Ruth Alexander Sewell of Franklin; a son, Dr. Robert A. Sewell and his wife Cynthia of Nashville; a daughter, Mrs. Barbara Jones and her husband Dr. David S.; a sister, Mrs. Hester Hill, all of Nashville; and four grandchildren, Dr. Nathan A. Sewell of Richmond, Virginia, Malcolm L. Sewell of Knoxville, Martin S. Jones of Nashville and Eleanor Jones of San Francisco.

Funeral services will be conducted at 2 p.m. today at First United Methodist Church with the Revs. Bob Lewis and Bob Cowperthwaite officiating. Burial will follow in Mount Hope Cemetery. Active pallbearers will be Charles E. Morton, Billy Alexander, Millard Jefferson, Ed Moody, John Bragg, Tom Harlin, Tom Yarborough, Walter Carlisle, Bill DePriest, William E. Cherry, Jim Hayes, Frank Walker, W.B. Holt, Van Montague, Dr. Keith Hagan, Dr. James Sullivan and W.F. Little. Honorary pallbearers will be members of the Men's Bible Class at F.U.M.C. and Franklin Lions Club and past and present employees of Sewell Electric Co. Visitation will be one hour prior to service at the church.

Williamson Funeral Home is in charge of arrangements.

– The Review-Appeal, November 7, 1999

Portrait of An Excellent Citizen

Jesse E. Short, Jr.

Jesse E. Short, Jr., is one of Williamson County's best known farmers. He owns and farms a large acreage in the Fifth District and is also office manager and bookkeeper for Jewell Brothers Tobacco Warehouses. Mr. Short held a position with Williamson County Bank from June 1, 1927, until March 15, 1943, and serves now as a member of the Board of Directors and honorary vice-president. He has been a member of the bank's finance committee since the early 1940s. He is the oldest member of the committee and of the bank's personnel in length of service.

Mr. Short has been a member of the Fourth Avenue Church of Christ since early in life. He is also a member of the Williamson County Farm Bureau and the NFO *[National Farmers Organization]*. He served as a magistrate for the Fifth District from 1948 until 1954.

He and Mrs. Short, who was formerly Miss Alma Bennett, live on New Highway 96. They have four children, Mrs. James E. Warren of Nashville, Jesse E. Short, III, who is associated with his father in the farming operation, Walter B. Short, who is now with Williamson County Bank, and William Miller (Bilbo) Short, a student at Southwestern College in Memphis, and four grandchildren.

Mr. Short was graduated from the Baylor School in Chattanooga and attended Vanderbilt University.

As Published in *The Review-Appeal* on June 20, 1968

JESSE EDELIN SHORT, JR.
1908 - 1979

Jesse Edelin Short, Jr., 71, well-known retired farmer and former bank employee, died Tuesday morning at Williamson County Hospital. He had suffered a stroke of paralysis Sunday night.

Funeral services were held Wednesday afternoon at 2:30 at Franklin Memorial Chapel. Myron Keith officiated, and burial was in Mt. Hope Cemetery.

A native of Williamson County, Mr. Short was the son of the late Jesse E. and Lucille Cotton Short. He was educated at Battle Ground Academy but was graduated from the Baylor School in Chattanooga. He attended Vanderbilt University.

During his school years he began working part-time at the Williamson County Bank but became a full-time employee in 1927. At that time he was one of three employees in the bank. He was advanced to the officer status and continued in the banking business until 1943 when he resigned to take over full time operation of large family farmlands on Boyd Mill Pike.

He continued his interest in the bank and was named a director in 1944 and retained the office of vice-president. He was active on the board of directors until his death and had been a member of the executive directors committee and was a member of the audit committee this year.

His interest in livestock and agriculture began while he was in the bank and he pioneered in many aspects of farming. He made numerous trips outside the state to find top livestock to bring back to Williamson County to improve stock here. He began a dairy on his farm and has one of the top herds in this area. He was an organizer of the Tennessee Farmers Artificial Breeders Association. Mr. Short was one of the county's leading tobacco growers and frequently experimented for the best variety to grow in this area. For a number of years during the burley sale season he worked at Jewell Brothers Tobacco Warehouses. During World War II he served on the selective service board. He was a magistrate on the old County Court from 1948-1954. He was a former director of the Williamson Farmers Co-Op and the Dairy Council of Nashville. He was a member of the Farm Bureau.

He was a member of the Fourth Avenue Church of Christ.

Mr. Short was married to the former Miss Alma Bennett who survives. Also surviving are one daughter, Mrs. James E. (Mary Anne) Warren of Nashville; three sons, Jesse Short, III, and Walter Short of Franklin, and William (Bilbo) Short of Memphis; one sister, Mrs. Lucille Short Bennett of Columbia; one brother, Judge James C. Short of Franklin; and seven grandchildren.

Active pallbearers were directors of Williamson County Bank, Hiram Beasley, Harry Roberts, Stewart Campbell, and Carter Conway.

Franklin Memorial Chapel was in charge of arrangements.

Joe Pinkerton, senior chairman of the board of Williamson County Bank, made the following statement:

"Jesse Short was a Director of Williamson County Bank for nearly thirty-five years. Until his death, he remained very active in the bank's affairs and was relied on by all of us for his financial counsel and his wise advice.

"He touched the lives of great numbers of people in different endeavors as an outstanding farmer and a pioneer in this area in tobacco, dairy farming and cattle raising.

"We at WCB have lost a close personal friend, a wise, business associate, and a confidante whose good humor and consistent optimism influenced all those around him."

— The Review-Appeal, June 7, 1979

Portrait of An Excellent Citizen

B. Wayne Sims

Wayne Sims is manager of the local National Stores on Main Street. He lives on Highland Avenue with his wife, the former Miss Martha Roberts of Columbia and their two small children, Beth and Chris.

Mr. Sims is an active member of the Retail Merchants Committee of the Williamson County Chamber of Commerce. He is a member of the First Methodist Church, serves on the Official Board and is president of the Crusaders' Class of the Church School.

A member of the Franklin Rotary Club, he is interested in all civic activities of the town and country.

As Published in *The Review-Appeal* on July 13, 1967

Wayne Sims

We became friends from our being merchants on opposite corners at 4th and Main. He was manager at National Stores for years, before becoming a traveling operations manager for their 26 stores. When the Sullivan/National stores closed, I called him to offer him a temporary job until he found a permanent position. He did not want another traveling job. I made him an offer and he accepted. He was 49 years old and I was 51. We closed Pigg & Peach in 2003 after our 16 years together.

He had many skills. He could repair or build anything. He made beautiful bird houses, and children's toys. He continues volunteering at the Williamson County Hospital.

He was very active in and devoted to the Methodist Church and Lions Club. He is married to Martha, with 2 children, Beth and Chris.

– Bill Peach, March 31, 2020

National Stores Corp.
Savings for the Entire Family
Franklin, Tenn.

Store chain names new president

National Stores, a wholly-owned subsidiary of Washington Industries which operates a department store in Franklin, has named W. D. Mattingly to the presidency of the chain.

Wayne Sims is manager of the Franklin National Store, located on Main Street.

National operates 40 department stores in Tennessee and Kentucky and is the owner of three Sullivan's Department Stores in the Nashville area and four other cities in the two states.

– Williamson Leader, January 12, 1975. Excerpt.

John Sloan

Squire Sloan for more than 20 years has been a prominent member of the Williamson County Court. His stately home, in a beautiful setting on Maplewood Farm, on Concord Road in the 15th District, is the scene of an annual barbecue of which he is host for the members of the County Court at the July session.

Mr. Sloan has long been closely identified with the old English sport of fox hunting. He rides with the Hillsboro Hounds and for the past ten years has been Master of the Hounds. His horse, Bank Robber, in 1944 won the Iroquois Steeplechase.

Mr. Sloan brought Guernsey cattle to Middle Tennessee and was the first president of the Tennessee Guernsey Breeders Association.

He is married to the former Miss Margaret Howe and they have four sons, John, Jr., who lives on Murray Lane in Brentwood and is very active in many affairs in Williamson County; George, who lives on Old Hickory Boulevard and recently bought two farms on Carl Road; Thomas Howe, who has returned to Nashville to live after being in Georgia several years; and Paul, who taught at MBA last year and will teach at Lansing College in England next year.

Mr. Sloan, is a communicant of St. Paul's Episcopal Church in Franklin and has served on the Vestry.

John Sloan is not only an excellent citizen of Williamson County but he is also one of the most successful and highly-respected citizens in Tennessee. He is president of Cain-Sloan Company, of which his father, the late Paul L. Sloan, was one of the founders in 1903.

As Published in *The Review-Appeal* on August 8, 1968

Sloan, former commissioner, dies

Funeral services for Brentwood resident John Elliott Sloan Sr., 82, who died of an apparent heart attack at his home Tuesday, will be at 10 a.m. today at Christ Episcopal Church.

Mr. Sloan was a former president of Cain-Sloan department store, a Williamson County commissioner for 37 years, and a founder of the Iroquois Steeplechase.

He was the son of Paul Sloan, a founder and president of Cain-Sloan Co., and Anne Joy Sloan of Nashville.

While serving on the Williamson County Commission, Mr. Sloan was instrumental in incorporating the city of Brentwood in 1969.

"He instituted the idea of incorporating the city so that we could have control over our own destiny at a time when there was a lot of development going on around us," said Brentwood city commissioner Joe Sweeney.

Because of his interest in protecting the community character of Brentwood, Mr. Sloan also helped establish the Brentwood Homeowners Association in 1980, and he served on its board of directors for three terms until 1986.

Mr. Sloan was a 1925 graduate of Vanderbilt University. He became vice-president of Cain-Sloan Co. in 1933 when his father died.

He served as president of the department store from 1937 until 1970.

A founder of the Hillsboro Hounds Fox Hunt in 1932, Mr. Sloan served as Master of the Foxhounds from 1957 to 1974.

Foxhunt events scheduled at Panorama Farm in Franklin today have been cancelled due to Mr. Sloan's death, but tomorrow's races at the farm will be held. A formal Hunt Ball in Mr. Sloan's honor will be held as scheduled at Belle Meade Country Club tomorrow night.

Mr. Sloan continued foxhunting into his 70s, and concentrated on bird hunting after he was injured during a hunt. He also continued to travel, having recently returned from a trip to Australia. He was planning a second trip to Colombia, South America, at the time of his death.

The family home, Maple Grove on Concord Road, was built by Mr. Sloan in the mid-1930s. The family lived [there] for more than 50 years.

Mr. Sloan was a member of the Vanderbilt University Board of Trust, a member of the Vanderbilt Athletic Board and a past president of the Vanderbilt Alumni Association. He served on the Montgomery Bell Academy Board of Trust and the Senior Board of Directors of First American Bank.

He is survived by his wife, Mrs. Margaret H. Sloan; four sons, John Elliott Sloan Jr. of Franklin, George Arthur Sloan II of Brentwood, Thomas Howe Sloan and Paul Lowe Sloan III, both of Nashville; a brother, Paul Lowe Sloan Jr. of Nashville; two sisters, Elizabeth Sloan Bainum of Houston and Katherine Sloan Thomas of Nashville; and nine grandchildren.

The Rev. Samuel G. Miller Jr. will officiate at today's funeral. Burial will be in Mount Olivet Cemetery. In lieu of flowers, memorials may be made to the Boys Club or Montgomery Bell Academy.

– The Review-Appeal, March 18, 1988

CS

CAIN-SLOAN Co.

the greatest store of the Central South

DOWNTOWN AND GREEN HILLS VILLAGE

Model RP656

John L. Smith

John L. Smith, a native of Williamson County, has been connected with the Franklin Fire Department for 35 years and has served as fire chief for the past 22 years. He has also been with the street and sewer department of the City of Franklin for 21 years and holds the position of superintendent. He is a communicant of St. Philip's Catholic Church and is one of the church trustees. He is a member of the Knights of Columbus, the Benevolent and Protective Order of Elks, and the Moose Club. He served in the U.S. Navy during World War II and was assigned to the aircraft carrier [USS] Lake Champlain. He is a member of the American Legion and is commander of the VFW of Franklin.

Chief Smith is married to the former Miss Elizabeth Heithcock and they have one daughter, Brenda, a student at Aquinas Junior College in Nashville.

As Published in *The Review-Appeal* on January 18, 1968

JOHN LEWIS SMITH
1907 - 1975

Franklin's fire chief Johnny Smith, 68, dies

Funeral services for John Lewis (Johnny) Smith, Franklin's fire chief, were held at St. Philip Catholic Church Saturday at noon. Burial was in Mt. Hope Cemetery. The Rev. John C. Henrich conducted the Mass of Christian Burial.

Smith, 68, died Friday, Dec. 26, at Baptist Hospital in Nashville where he had been a patient for a few weeks following a stroke of paralysis. He resided at 311 Meadowlawn Drive.

He was a native of Williamson County and was a veteran of World War II.

Smith had been connected with the city of Franklin for 42 years and had seen the Franklin Fire Department grow from a volunteer organization to a well-organized municipal department. He retired in the fall of last year from the position of superintendent of the city's water and sewer departments, which he had held since 1947. The new water quality control plant's office building, dedicated in September, was named the John L. Smith Building.

He was a member of the National Association of Fire Chiefs, the Tennessee Fireman's Association, the Knights of Columbus, the Elks Lodge, the Veterans of Foreign Wars, and local Moose Lodge.

He was a communicant of St. Philip Church and had been one of its most devoted members all of his adult life.

He is survived by his wife, Mrs. Elizabeth Heithcock Smith of Franklin; one daughter, Mrs. Tom Mitcham of Nashville; and granddaughter, Laura Kate Mitcham of Nashville.

Honorary pallbearers were Mayor Ed Woodard, J. W. Little, Marshall Liggett, Bob King, Police Chief Morgan Hood, Ted Cook, Morton Fisher, James Culberson, and fire chiefs from throughout Tennessee. Members of the Franklin Fire Department were active pallbearers.

The funeral cortege Saturday included a Franklin fire engine draped in black and a number of fire chiefs in official cars from throughout the state.

Franklin Memorial Chapel was in charge of the arrangements.

– The Review-Appeal, January 1, 1976

POLICE · FIRE

794-2513   794-3411

Mrs. Paul Smith

Mrs. Inge Meyring Smith was born in Dresden, Germany, and came to New York with her parents in 1938. She completed her preparatory education in New York and attended the City College of New York. She completed work for her B.S. degree in Elementary Education at George Peabody College in 1965 and received her M.A. degree in Early Childhood Education in June, 1966. She is now working toward the degree of Education Specialist.

During World War II she was married to Paul Smith of Franklin. They live on Battle Avenue with their three children, Stefan, Mont, and Ingelein. Mrs. Smith's father, Walter Meyring, also makes his home with them.

Mrs. Smith has operated a kindergarten in Franklin since 1952. She is also a consultant for the Head Start Program throughout the southeastern region. She travels throughout the area during the summer months to assist in the pre-school program and during the school year conducts Saturday workshops for the year-around Head Start programs.

She also has done volunteer work with the Williamson County Community Action Program with young children and mothers in a co-operative nursery school and kindergarten situation.

As Published in *The Review-Appeal* on August 15, 1968

She is a member of a number of professional organizations and was the first president of the Middle Tennessee Association for Children Under Six. She conducts workshops frequently for MTACUS. She was also elected to membership in Kappa Delta Pi, an honorary fraternity in education.

She is a member of the First Presbyterian Church where she teaches an adult Sunday School class. For a number of years she directed the church's Junior Church program. She is also a charter member of Xi Alpha Sigma Chapter of Beta Sigma Phi Sorority.

'One of the Miracles' Tells Harrowing Uplifting Story
By Kerri Bartlett, Assistant Editor

As Inge Smith, 89, renowned Franklin educator, waited for an assembly April 5 at Battle Ground Academy Lower School, she got the feeling that something was amiss.

"I just thought I was here to talk to the babies," she said. Not expecting friends, press and special attention, her vibrant smile curved into a suspicious grin aimed at Clay Stafford, creator of the recent documentary, "One of the Miracles: The Inge Meyring Smith Story," premiering April 18 at the Franklin Theatre. "What are you doing to me, Clay?" she asked.

"'Are you ready?' said the fox to the hen," Stafford responded. "It's a surprise."

Stafford played the fox, who planned the surprise assembly celebrating Smith's life and the 90-day countdown to her 90th birthday on the auspicious date of July 4. As he led her down the winding corridor of the school that she founded, she calmly went with flow of uncertainty with charm and grace, just as she approaches all endeavors in her life until she finally met the smiling crowd of students, faculty and friends in the gymnasium ready to hear her life stories and sing "Happy Birthday."

Surprises and challenges have surfaced time and again in Smith's life, and she faced each one head on with vigor, confidence and empowerment - the qualities of a heroine, one might say.

She never expected to be the star of a documentary or the subject of a book, *Born for America: The Inge Smith Meyring Story,* or one of the most beloved figures in the Franklin community. "I am not the heroine at all," Smith said. Some might disagree.

Born Jewish in Dresden, Germany, Smith narrowly escaped the concentration camps of the Holocaust by fleeing to America in 1938 with her mother and father. There were no survivors in her extended family in Germany. As a young girl, she experienced prejudice, injustice and oppression that she was helpless to fight against.

The threat from Hitler and his growing army ostracized her family further and further from the lives they had made for themselves. The school that Smith loved banned her from attending, and the government seized her father's small silk wholesale business leaving the family with little hope for a future. Thus, her parents decided that in order to survive, they must escape to America.

Cameron Gracey, 13, BGA seventh grader, described Inge Smith as a loving teacher at the surprise assembly.

"The only thing that my father was able to take from the store were the scissors in his pocket," Smith said. "And without education, you have nothing; no future. Education was foremost in my family." Smith and her parents embarked for the United States in 1938. When the immigration worker saw that Smith's birth certificate showed her birthday to be July 4, he said, "You were born for America," and stamped the paperwork with no questions asked. The family soon arrived in New York Harbor on Thanksgiving Day.

Smith's forward-thinking teaching methods would eventually propel her to the forefront of the field of education, not only in Franklin, where she and her husband had made their home, but nationally. Smith would open two schools in Franklin — Smith Preschool and Harpeth Academy, which later became Battle Ground Academy Lower School. Also, Smith was handpicked by the Kennedy-Johnson administration to create and implement the curriculum for the Head Start program for low income families, which helped shape U.S. government policy in education.

"There is no one like Inge," said Diane Parker, an art teacher at BGA Lower School, who worked with Smith for decades. "She was an incredible teacher. She was right about teaching from day one - you teach to the child. She was ahead of her time."

"If you love what you are doing and have a passion for it, everyone else will feel the same way," said Smith.

Stafford, a best-selling author whose filmmaking, writing, producing and directing skills carried him to Universal Studios and PBS, discovered that Smith had an important story to tell when he enrolled his children at Smith Preschool.

"I didn't know all of Smith's story, but I knew that it needed to be told and that we needed to make a film," he said. "I think that Inge's experiences are what make her so special."

Stafford said he believes that Smith's drive to make a difference with her life by bringing love and understanding to the world was born in her childhood in Germany as well as the challenges she overcame in the United States.

Inge Smith arrived in America on Thanksgiving Day in 1938 with her mother and father. "Here, we are right off the boat," Smith said.

"Her whole approach to education encompasses accepting all races, religions, beliefs and genders," Stafford said. "She is a woman, a Jew and a German, all difficult things for the Caucasian establishment to accept. She went from yellow and non-yellow benches to black-and-white entrances. She realized that if this is allowed, [the Holocaust] is what happens."

Now partially retired, Smith swims twice a week and participates in "the fun stuff" at Smith Preschool. She has three children, seven grandchildren and six great grandchildren. She said that she has been lucky.

"Life's been so good to me. This community has nurtured me and loved me and have done everything to make me believe that I belong here," she said.

One of the Miracles: The Inge Meyring Smith Story will premiere to a sold out Franklin Theatre April 18, with an encore showing April 27 at 7 p.m. For more information, please visit www.oneofthemiracles.com. The book *Born for America: The Life of Inge Meyring Smith,* by Inge Smith, with Pam Horne, is expected to be released at the end of April.

— The Williamson Herald, April 11, 2013

"The purchase of 175 Franklin Road, the future home of Harpeth Academy, took place in 1969.

"The turn-of-the-century Victorian brick home of Reams and Leah Rae Osborne was a beautiful piece of architecture near the downtown entrance of Franklin. It was situated beautifully on a large piece of land that bordered the Harpeth River's northern bank. Structurally it was everything we wanted. Mr. Ligon and Dr. Willoughby envisioned a small, intimate learning environment where children would be academically stimulated. We were not interested in an austere institutional setting that would stifle or intimidate our students. The Osborne home ... was ideal."

— Inge Smith, *Born for America*, by Inge Meyring Smith with Pam Horne, O'More Publishing, 2012.

Excellent Citizens and Notable Partings

Richard Hanes Sparkman

Mr. Sparkman is owner of Sparkman Jewelers. He is married to the former Miss Christine O'Bryan and they have three children, Patricia Ann, Judith Sue and Richard Hanes, Jr. They live on Buckworth Avenue and attend Fourth Avenue Church of Christ. Mr. Sparkman is a member of the Rotary Club.

As Published in *The Review-Appeal* on September 22, 1966

RICHARD HANES SPARKMAN, SR.
1916 - 1997

Funeral for Richard Hanes Sparkman Sr. of Beech Grove Road, Columbia, was at 2 p.m. Wednesday at Williamson Memorial Funeral Home, with Myron Keith and Bill Miller officiating. Burial was in Alexander Cemetery in Spring Hill.

Mr. Sparkman died Sunday at the age of 80 in Hillview Nursing Home in Columbia. He was the owner of Sparkman Jewelers at 324 Main St. and had owned the store for 32 years. His son, Hanes, has been running the store for the past five years, though Sparkman would lend his expertise and visit with customers until he was placed in the nursing home six months ago.

He formerly operated a successful dry cleaning business, now Fashion Cleaners, in Franklin. To start in the jewelry business, he bought two stores in Franklin, the former Franklin Jewelers and the former Blackburn Jewelers, and combined them.

Sparkman, who until 25 years ago lived on Franklin's Buckworth Avenue, bought the place where he was born and raised from his brother, Tom. He moved back to Beech Grove Road.

Once he was back at his home, he won a "couple of bushels of ribbons" on various Tennessee Walking Horses. He would enter all the Tennessee shows including the National Celebration at Shelbyville plus shows in Orlando, Florida; Baton Rouge, Louisiana; Montgomery, Alabama; Jackson, Mississippi; and Little Rock, Arkansas.

More than 25 years ago, when open heart surgery was new, he was the 15th person to undergo the operation at St. Thomas Hospital.

Born in Maury County, he was a veteran of the U.S. Army during World War II. He was a former city alderman and longtime member of the Franklin Rotary Club. He was a member of the Tennessee Walking Horse Breeders' and Exhibition [Exhibitors'] Association, Tennessee Retail Jewelry Association and a member of the Fourth Avenue Church of Christ.

Survivors include his wife, Mrs. Christine O'Bryan Sparkman of Columbia; son, Hanes, and his wife, Jan, of Franklin; two daughters, Mrs. Bobby (Patsy) Morel of Brentwood and Mrs. Chet (Judy) Travirca of Gautier, Mississippi; brother, Tom of Columbia; two sisters, Mrs. Eula Dale of Franklin and Mrs. Dot Coley of Lafayette, and six grandchildren, Brittan, Meg and Hayden Morel, Tripp Sparkman, Keller and Meredith Medlin.

Memorials may be made to the American Heart Association.

— The Williamson Leader, February 20, 1997

Portrait of An Excellent Citizen

Prof. C. B. Spencer

Portrait Published in *The Review-Appeal* on March 10, 1966

Spencer, Charles B. – Departed this life February 19, 1985 at Williamson County Hospital.

Survivors include a dear wife, Mrs. Anne Wilson Spencer; a devoted daughter and son-in-law, Patricia Diane and Sherman Williams; three loving grandchildren, DeShawn, Charles (Chucky), Nicole (Nikki) Williams; sisters, Mae Frances Spencer, Atlanta, Georgia, Willie Lee Whittle, Gulfport, Mississippi, Claudia Moffet, Taylorsville, Mississippi; brothers, James and Jessie Spencer, Collins, Mississippi; foster mother, Mrs. W.A. (Mattie) Flowers; sisters-in-law, Carrie F. Wilson and Ada Wilson; brother-in-law Albert Wilson; a host of nieces, nephews, cousins, other relatives and friends.

Mr. Spencer will lie in state Friday, February 22, from 3:00 p.m. until 7:00 p.m. at which time family visitation hour will begin and last until 8:00 p.m., Shorter Chapel Church, Natchez and Fowlkes Street, Franklin, Tennessee.

Funeral service Saturday, February 23, 1985, 1:00 p.m. at the above church, Rev. Barry Cox officiating assisted by Rev. Samuel Henderson, Elder William F. Scruggs and Bishop H. C. Nesbit.

Honorary Pallbearers: TSU Extension Services, Nashville Sportsman's Club, Stewards and Trustees of Shorter Chapel Church and Kappa Alpha Psi Fraternity. Active Pallbearers and Floral Bearers selected from friends.

Interment National Cemetery, Madison, Tennessee, Monday February 25, 1985, 2:00 p.m. Service entrusted to Patton Brothers Funeral Directors, 1306 South Street, 256-3608.

– The Tennessean, February 22, 1985

Mr. Charles B. Spencer, the second son of the Rev. William and Mrs. Addie Spencer, was born September 10, 1915, in Collins, Mississippi. He departed this life February 19, 1985.

He professed a hope in Christ at an early age. He later transferred his membership to the Shorter Chapel A. M. E. church where he was faithful until the time of his passing.

He was educated in the public schools in Mississippi. He received his B. S. degree from Alcorn State University and a masters degree from Tuskegee Institute, Tuskegee, Alabama. He did further study at Tennessee State University and the University of Tennessee.

He was a member of the Sportsman Kennel Club, Rucker's Recreation park, and Kappa Alpha Psi Fraternity. He served three years in the United States Army.

Thirty-seven years ago, Mr. Spencer was united in Holy Matrimony to the former Anne V. Wilson, who survives. This union was blessed with one lovely daughter, Patricia Diane.

He leaves to cherish his memory and to mourn his passing, wife, Mrs. Anne W. Spencer; daughter, Mrs. Patricia Diane Williams; son-in-law, Sherman Williams; grandchildren, DeShawn, Charles and Nichole Williams; sisters, Ms. Mae Frances Spencer, Atlanta, Georgia, Mrs. Willie Lee Whittle, Gulfport, Mississippi, and Mrs. Claudia Moffet, Taylorsville, Mississippi; brothers, James and Jesse Spencer, Collins Mississippi; one brother-in-law; four sisters-in-law; a devoted sister-in-law, Miss Carrie F. Wilson; foster mother, Mrs. W. A. (Mattye C.) Flowers; a host of other relatives and many friends.

– Funeral Program, Shorter Chapel Church, Saturday, February 23, 1985, Franklin, Tenn.

Chester A. Stephens

Chester A. Stephens lives at College Grove in Williamson County where he serves as pastor of the College Grove Methodist Church. His wife was the former Miss Ina Owens and they have three children, Mrs. Joe Stone of Lynchburg, Mrs. Randall Davis of McMinnville, and Charles E. (Buddy) Stephens, a student at Martin College in Pulaski. Rev. Stephens is a member of the College Grove Lions Club and Woodman of the World Lodge. He is president of the Tennessee Conference Brotherhood, and a member of the Conference Board on Hospitals and Homes, and Conference Social Concern. He is also a member of the State Alcoholic Study Commission and District Director of TRAFCO *[Television, Radio and Film Commision of the Methodist Church]*.

As Published in *The Review-Appeal* on February 23, 1967

Stephens, Rev. Chester, Fayetteville, Tennessee — Age 86 of 209 Hillcrest Circle, Fayetteville, died Wednesday, August 20, 2003 at home.

Funeral services will be conducted Saturday, August 23, 2003 at 11 a.m., at the First United Methodist Church in Fayetteville, with Rev. Allen Black, Rev. Tom Smith and Rev. Maurice Moore officiating.

Burial will be on Saturday afternoon, at 4 p.m., at the Wilson County Memorial Park Cemetery, in Lebanon, Tennessee.

He was a native of Fentress County, son of the late George W. and Sarah Winningham Stephens. He was a Methodist Minister and a member of the Fayetteville First United Methodist Church.

Survivors include a daughter, Naomi Davis of McMinnville; son, Buddy Stephens of Lebanon; five grandchildren and eight great-grandchildren.

He was preceded in death by a daughter, Kathaleen Stone; son, Jimmy A. Stephens; granddaughter, Alicia Stephens; sister, Trannie Key and four brothers, Eddie, Elis [Ealis], Ellis and Elbert Stephens.

Rev. Stephens will lie in state at the church on Saturday, from 10 a.m. until time of services. Visitation with the family will be Friday evening, 5 - 9 p.m., at Higgins Funeral Home.

In lieu of flowers, Memorials may be made to the Alicia Stephens Memorial Scholarship Fund. Higgins Funeral Home, 931-433-2544.

— The Tennessean, August 22, 2003

In April of 1968, The Methodist Church and the Evangelical United Brethren Church merged and become the United Methodist Church. The constituting ceremony took place at the 1968 General Conference of the Methodist Church, in Dallas, Texas. The hymnal pictured here commemorated the first General Conference of the newly formed United Methodist Church held in Atlanta, Georgia in 1972.

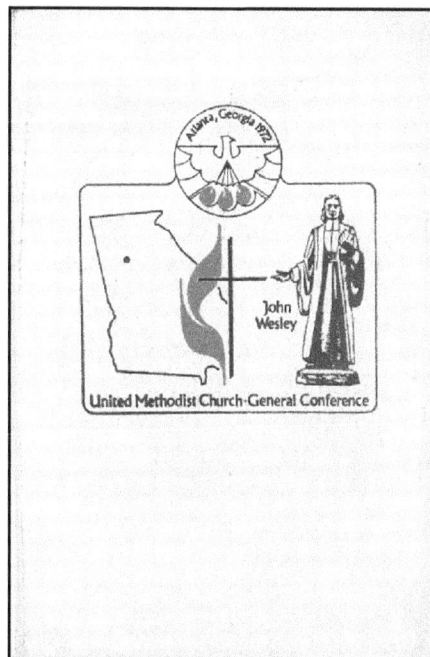

United Methodist Church-General Conference

Emmett T. Strickland

"Memories of My Father"

My father was born on October 30, 1910, in Hartford, Alabama. He went to high school in Hartford and played all sports, with a particular love for football. He had a beautiful tenor voice and was in all the high school plays and musicals.

After graduating from high school, he came to Tennessee Tech (Tennessee Polytechnic Institute). He had a part-time job at Draper and Darwin which allowed him to play ball at Tech. Many times, he became discouraged and wanted to go home. Coach Putty Overall was a great influence and refused to give up on Emmett. "Strick" was student body president his senior year and also Athlete of the Year. Tech was where he met his wife, Martha Belle Hamblen, so he remained at Tennessee Tech and graduated. Later on, he received his master's degree from Peabody College, now Vanderbilt University.

His first coaching assignment was in Oneida, Tennessee. This was followed by coaching assignments at Donelson High School and West High School. At West, he coached Red Foley's daughter, Shirley, later Pat Boone's wife. When she wrote her book "One Woman's Liberation," she

---

Portrait Published in *The Review-Appeal* on June 16, 1966

devoted a chapter to Emmett, as he had had such an influence on her life. He also won 3 state championships in 1944, 1946 and 1948, and in other years, a second-place, and two third-place finishes.

Many such occurrences happened over the years. His "boys" at West honored him each year, telling of the advice he gave them and how it influenced their lives. Billy Lawrence, a Prisoner of War in Vietnam, told of how Emmett Strickland's teachings helped him to survive those hard years as a prisoner.

After being a principal at Waverly Belmont Junior High, he was asked to be Superintendent of Schools in Franklin, Tennessee, for the 9th Special School District. He and Martha Belle remained in Franklin for the remainder of their lives. This was home to the family, which included their two children, Linda Sue and John, adopted in 1946 and 1950. He integrated schools in Franklin in 1966, starting with kindergarten and added a new grade each year as they moved up. His plan was later approved by the courts to take precedence over the Federal Government's plan for desegregation. He loved the students and always did what he felt best for the children.

I could not have been blessed with better parents. We always came first. They lived the lessons they taught. They never asked us to do something that they did not do. If I had been asked to pick out parents, I could not have done better. John and I were so fortunate.

My father was honest, fair and caring. He loved education and as superintendent, he visited all the classrooms and was very supportive of the teachers, staff and students. My family went to First United Methodist Church every Sunday. My dad's love of church, family and education was steadfast throughout his life. I am so blessed to have had him in my life.

by Linda Sue Strickland Conrad, February 2020

Mr. Emmett T. Strickland Nashville/Franklin, Tennessee, Age 91, Tuesday, January 29, 2002.

Retired Superintendent of Franklin Ninth Special School District. Former coach at West High School where he successfully led his teams to six state basketball championships. Selected as an outstanding administrator in the United States by the National Association of Secondary School Administrators, National Amateur Sports Hall of Fame, Tennessee Tech Sports Hall of Fame and the Tennessee Sports Hall of Fame. Active community leader by starting Senior Citizens, past president of Franklin Noon Rotary Club, Past Chairman of American Red Cross. Member of Franklin First United Methodist Church.

Survived by wife of 65 years, Mrs. Martha Belle Strickland, Nashville, Tennessee; son, John Strickland; daughter, Linda Sue Strickland Franklin both of Franklin, Tennessee; sister, Mrs. Martha Tanksley, Davenport, Florida; grandchildren, Stephen Daves, Skyler Skelley and Laura Strickland.

Funeral services will be conducted 2:30 p.m. Thursday, January 31, 2002 at Williamson Memorial Funeral Home, Rev. Robert H. Lewis and Rev. Stewart J. Nunnally officiating.

Interment Spring Hill Cemetery, Nashville, Tennessee. Active Pallbearers, Stephen Daves, Skyler Skelley, Tom Conrad, John Grayson, Ralph Brown, Jimmy French, Billy Smith and Charlie Adwell. Honorary Pallbearers, Coach Strickland's West High School Athletes and Franklin Noon Rotarians.

Memorials may be made to Franklin First United Methodist Church or the American Heart Association.

Visitation will be 2-4 p.m. and 6-8 p.m. Wednesday and one hour prior to service at Williamson Memorial Funeral Home, (615) 794-2289.

— The Tennessean, January 30, 2002

Prof. Barry Sutton

"A capable, well-trained educator, the friendly young principal is one of the better known athletes in Middle Tennessee. As a Golden Gloves champion and later a professional boxer, he has built for himself a splendid reputation as a keen competitor as well as a gentleman."

— Nat Osborne, Jr., *Who's Who in Williamson County,* Rick Warwick, ed., originally published in *The Review-Appeal,* August 18, 1955.

Portrait Published in *The Review-Appeal* on March 31, 1966

Barry Dale Sutton, Lebanon, Tennessee — Age 88, Monday, April 19, 2004. Preceded in death by parents, Edgar H. and Dana Copas Sutton; wife, Anne West Sutton; son-in-law, Henry C. Blackburn. Survived by wife, Katherine Sutton; daughter, Nancy Sutton Blackburn; two grandchildren, Susanne Blackburn Nelms and Michael David Blackburn; three great grandchildren, McKensie and Will Nelms and Emma Blackburn; son-in-law, Tony Nelms all of Knoxville, Tennessee; step daughter, Peggy (Bobby) Blackburn; step grandchildren, Ken Blackburn, Angela Bates and Jennifer Lloyd all of Brush Creek, Tennessee.

Mr. Sutton was a Veteran of the U.S. Navy. He spent most of his professional life as an educator and public education administrator. He was a graduate of Cumberland University and Peabody College. He served as Principal of Franklin High School from 1955-1967 and served as Principal of Lebanon High School from 1967 to his retirement in 1980. He was inducted into the Golden Gloves Hall of Fame in March of 2001.

He was a Member of the Lebanon Rotary Club where he was a Paul Harris Fellow. He was a past Member of the TSSAA Board of Control. He was a Member of the Retired Teachers Association. He was a Member of the College Hills Church of Christ where he was a Deacon.

Visitation will be held on Tuesday, April 20, 2004 from 3:00 til 7:30 p.m. at the Partlow Funeral Chapel. Funeral to follow with Dr. Larry Locke officiating.

Burial will be held 10 a.m., Wednesday, April 21, 2004 at Williams Cemetery in Difficult, Tennessee. Pallbearers: David Blackburn, Ken Blackburn, Herb McKay, Campbell Brandon, Jack Cato and Ernest Cotton.

Honorary Pallbearers: Bobby Blackburn, Jere Young, Jack Kittrell, Tom A. Sanders, Bill Arnold, Dudley Turner, Dr. Robert Carver Bone, Rick Stewart and the College Hill Prime Timers.

In lieu of flowers, you may make contributions to the College Hills Building Fund.

PARTLOW FUNERAL CHAPEL, (615) 444-7007.

— The Tennessean, April 20, 2004

SUTTON — Mrs. Anne West —
Age 61, Monday, August 25, 1980.

Survived by husband, Mr. Barry Sutton; one daughter, Mrs. Nancy Sutton Blackburn, Louden, Tennessee; two grandchildren, David and Susanne Blackburn, Louden, Tennessee; one sister, Mrs. Effie Johnson, Anderson, Indiana; one brother, Mack West, Summertown, Tennessee.

Remains are at Nave Funeral Home, where services will be held 2 p.m. Wednesday, August 27, 1980, conducted by Brother Larry Locke.

Pallbearers: Campbell Brandon, Doyle Jarman, Pete Andrews, Ralph Denney, Mark J. Smith, Bruce Plummer, Mitchell Wright and Billy Rankin.

Interment Williams Cemetery, Difficult, Tennessee.

In lieu of flowers you may donate books to the Lebanon High School Library.

NAVE FUNERAL HOME, Lebanon, Tennessee.

— The Tennessean, August 27, 1980

Prof. Daly Thompson

"To one who is always kind and fair

And has a helping hand to share;

His patience never gets on end

For he is all the students' friend."

"Dedication" to Principal, Daly Thompson,
Franklin High School Yearbook, 1949

Portrait Published in *The Review-Appeal* on May 26, 1966

DALY THOMPSON
1889 - 1967

Daly Thompson Dies, Educator Many Years

Prof. Daly Thompson, an educator in Williamson County since 1929 and one of the county's most beloved citizens, died Tuesday afternoon at Baptist Hospital after an illness of several weeks.

Funeral services will be held this (Thursday) morning at 10:30 at First Methodist Church. Officiating will be the Rev. Stuart J. Nunnally, Dr. John L. Dickson, the Rev. Fenton Warren, and Myron Keith. Burial will be in Williamson Memorial Gardens.

Mr. Thompson, 77, a native of Randolph County, Arkansas, was the son of the late Mr. and Mrs. Gideon Thompson. He attended Sloan-Hendricks Academy in Arkansas before completing his preparatory work at Battle Ground Academy in Franklin. He was graduated from Vanderbilt University where he received his B.A. degree and received his master's degree at George Peabody College.

He taught in Shelby County, Tennessee, and in Pocahontas, Arkansas, before coming here as principal of Franklin High School in 1929. Upon his retirement after 26 years in that position, he was honored by students and faculty associates, both those under him at that time and in years past, at "Daly Thompson Day," the only man in Williamson County who has been so honored.

Since his retirement he served on the faculty of BGA as teacher of Bible and Latin. Just last week The Review–Appeal published a tribute to Mr. Thompson written by one of his students last year, who said that "through the help of such a man as Daly Thompson, I learned what it was really like to be a working Christian."

He was a very active member of the First United Methodist Church and was chairman of the official Board of Stewards for almost 25 years. He taught a ladies' Bible class for about that same length of time. In earlier years he sang with the choir and Men's Chorus.

He was a charter member of the Franklin Lions Club and served the organization in many official capacities.

For 35 Years Mr. Thompson was an active member of both the local and state tuberculosis associations and in May of this year was given the J. P. Krantz Memorial Award – for his outstanding service in the field of tuberculosis control. The award, presented at a state meeting in Chattanooga, is the highest honor given in the field. Mr. Thomson served as president of the Williamson County Tuberculosis Association on two occasions for a total of 12 to 14 years and as state president for two years. At the time of his death, he was a director of both the local and state associations.

During his tenure in the county school system he was prominent in the state teachers' organization. He was also in the Knights Templar Commandery.

Mr. Thompson was married to the former Miss Ouida Blankenship who survives.

Also surviving are one daughter, Mrs. Dan Finch [Sara Evelyn] of Nashville; a son, the Rev. Daly Thompson, Jr., of Memphis; a brother, Roy Thompson of Nashville; and four grandchildren, Mike and Pat Finch of Nashville, and Ruth and Daly Thompson, III of Memphis.

Honorary pallbearers are the members of the Board of Trustees and the faculty of Battle Ground Academy and the official Board of the First Methodist Church.

Serving as active pallbearers will be T. F. Lance, J. R. Lanier, Harold Meacham, W. P. Scales, Earl Beasley, J.L. Ridley, Ralph Brown, and Paul Redick.

In lieu of flowers, donations may be made to the building funds of either Battle Ground or First Methodist Church.

Until time for the services the body is at Franklin Memorial Chapel, which is in charge of arrangements.

– The Review-Appeal, September 28, 1967

Excellent Citizens and Notable Partings

Martin Tohrner

Martin is operator of the Martin Tohrner Produce Company on Bridge Street. He lives with his wife, the former Miss Peggy Shatz, on the Nashville Highway. He is a member of the Lions Club of which he is past president, and is a director of the Chamber of Commerce. He is also chairman of the Senior Citizens of Franklin and serves on the Advisory Committee. He attends church at The Temple on West End in Nashville.

As Published in *The Review-Appeal* on December 8, 1966

Businessman Martin Tohrner dies

Funeral for Martin Tohrner, retired Franklin businessman, longtime civic leader, was Wednesday at Franklin Memorial Chapel, with Rabbi Randall Falk officiating. Burial was in Temple Cemetery in Nashville.

Mr. Tohrner died Monday in a Nashville hospital following an extended illness. He was 85.

A businessman in Williamson County for many years, Mr. Tohrner founded the American Preserving Co. which processed and shipped produce in 1919. He opened a tomato packing plant in Fairview.

He had been in the scrap metal business in Franklin until he sold the firm last year to Bobby Gentry.

Mr. Tohrner was a member of the Franklin Lions Club, and was named "Lion of the Year" in 1959. He faithfully attended every meeting of the club and participated in its various functions as long as his health would permit. He also had the distinction of being a charter member of Franklin's first civic club, the Kiwanis Club.

He served two terms as director of the Williamson County Chamber of Commerce and was one of that organizations strong promoters for many years.

His father, the late Abraham Tohrner, came to America in 1883 from Poland.

Survivors are his wife, Mrs. Peggy Shatz Tohrner; daughter, *[Marion Belle Tohrner]* Mrs. Robert Eichbert *[Eichberg]* of Denver, Colorado; two sisters, Mrs. Ellis Dodson of Hickman, Kentucky, and Mrs. Joe Posnack of Franklin; three grandchildren and two great grandchildren.

Pallbearers were Fred Fine, Albert Posnack, David Shatz, Julius Falkoff, Mark Shatz, James Cannon, Col. Hensley Williams, Robert Gentry and nephews.

Honorary pallbearers were John Henry Neal and members of the Franklin Lions Club.

— The Williamson Leader, November 10, 1974

"Martin was a fine member of one of Franklin's good families whose history goes back beyond the beginning of the 1900's. He was a descendant of an émigré who started his dry goods business as a "back peddler." ... Mr. Tohrner did not have to start his business this way. ... Martin ... was an entrepreneur himself, and was soon branching out into a flourishing salvage business and eventually into a large produce business that was known over a wide range of the country. ... Mr. Tohrner was not just a good businessman, he was active in all civic organizations and community activities. He was always strictly honest in his settlements and progressive with new ideas. Martin Tohrner was, indeed, a credit to Williamson County and a fond memory to all who knew him personally."

— W. C. Yates, *Tales of a Tennessee Yeoman.* 1991.

Mrs. Martin Tohrner

It is significant that the first portrait for the New Year shows one of Williamson County's most civic-minded citizens. Mrs. Martin Tohrner is the new president of the Friends of the Williamson County Public Library and has served as a member of the Board of Directors of the Library for a number of years. She is one of the hostesses for the Newcomers Club, sponsored by the Williamson County Chamber of Commerce. Treasurer of the American Legion Auxiliary, she helped with the Big Brothers Paper Sale in December. She has served in a number of official capacities the Allied Arts Club here and the Book Study Club of Nashville. She is affiliated with the Temple in Nashville and is on the board of the Temple Sisterhood. She is past president of the Hadassah and is a member of Brandeis Women, the Council of Jewish Women, and the Jewish Community Center. In 1965 she was chosen "Woman of the Year" by the Franklin Business and Professional Women's Club. She is the former Miss Peggy Shatz of Kenton, Tennessee, and she and Mr. Tohrner reside on Nashville Pike.

As Published in *The Review-Appeal* on January 4, 1968

PEGGY SHATZ TOHRNER
1900 - 1998

Tohrner, Mrs. Peggy Shatz, age 97 years.

April 14, 1998 at her residence. She was a long time resident of Franklin, Tennessee.

Preceded in death by her husband, Martin Tohrner, who died in 1974, and will be remembered as the owner of Martin Tohrner Metal Company, Franklin, Tennessee.

Mrs. Tohrner was a Member of The Nashville Hadassah as well as the Past President, Member of The National Council of Jewish Women, Chairman of the Israel Bonds Campaign, Member of The Temple Ohabai Shalom, The Temple Sisterhood, The Jewish Community Center and The Nashville Jewish Federation. She was a Sergeant in the U.S. Army during World War II. She was named Lady of the Year in 1965 by the Franklin, Tennessee, Business and Professional Women's Club and a Philanthropist.

Mrs. Tohrner was faithfully attended by her companion of eight years, Dorothy Ramsey.

Survived by nieces, Jo Ann Fine, Elinor Posnack both of Nashville and Ellise Falkoff of Union City, Tennessee; nephews, Albert Posnack of Nashville, Sylvain Shatz of Union City, Tennessee; Sol Shatz of Florida and Albert Lax of California; step daughter, Marion Eichberg of Denver, Colorado.

Graveside services will be held 11 a.m., Thursday at The Temple Cemetery, 18th Avenue North and Clay Street conducted by Rabbi Randall Falk, Rabbi David Davis and Cantor Bernard Gutcheon.

Pallbearers: Julius Falkoff, Dr. Fred Fine, Albert Posnack, Sylvain Shatz, Dr. Herman Kaplan, Bob Altman, Sol Shatz and Albert Lax.

Memorials may be made to The Temple, 5015 Harding Road, Nashville, Tennessee 37205 or The Nashville Hadassah, 801 Percy Warner Blvd., Nashville, Tennessee 37205.

Marshall Donnelly Combs, 327-1111.

— The Tennessean, April 15, 1998

"Graciousness, enthusiasm, energy and ability are certain qualities to be considered in the selection of the 'Woman of the Year' by the Business and Professional Women's club. A perfect choice this year is Mrs. Martin Tohrner who not only has these characteristics — and in large proportion — but puts them to use and to most effective use at that. ... Mrs. Tohrner does not accept a task that she does not do well, and her interests run the gamut — religious, civic, educational, political and social."

— Derry Carlisle, *Who's Who in Williamson County*, Rick Warwick, ed., originally published in *The Review-Appeal*, March 10, 1966.

Felix Wesley Truett

Born and reared in Williamson County, Felix Wesley Truett is now owner and manager of Truett Realty Company, Williamson County's oldest real estate firm. He received his education at Battle Ground Academy, Montgomery Bell Academy and the University of Tennessee. Before entering the real estate business he was with the Federal Land Bank of Louisville, Kentucky. He is also co-owner of the Truett-Barker Insurance Company.

Mr. Truett is past president of the Franklin Real Estate Board, a former member of the Lions Club, and is at present a member of the Williamson County Court. He and Mrs. Truett reside on the Murfreesboro Road. They attend the Franklin First Methodist Church.

As Published in *The Review-Appeal* on May 16, 1968

FELIX WESLEY TRUETT, JR.
1903 - 1976

Felix Truett dies, rites Wednesday

Felix Wesley Truett, Jr., 73, prominent Franklin real estate agent for more than 40 years, died Monday night at a home on Ewingville Drive. He had been in declining health for several years.

Funeral services were held Wednesday afternoon at 3:30 at the Franklin Memorial Chapel. The Rev. Stuart Nunnally and the Rev. Bruce Strother officiated. Burial was in Mt. Hope Cemetery.

Mr. Truett was a native of Williamson County and was the son of the late Felix Wesley [Sr.] and Mary Kate Allen Truett. He was a graduate of Battle Ground Academy, Montgomery Bell Academy in Nashville, and the University of Tennessee in Knoxville.

As a young man he farmed with his father who had extensive farming operations. He started his business career with the Federal Land Bank in Louisville where he worked as an appraiser and salesman for several years.

When he returned to Franklin, he established his own real estate firm and insurance company. For a number of years he and Roy E. Barker were partners in the insurance business.

Mr. Truett was an organizer and past president of the Franklin Board of Realtors. He was also a former member of the Franklin Lions Club and was a member of the First United Methodist Church.

His wife, the former Fay Wright, died in 1972.

Survivors include two sisters, Mrs. Nelson (Thelma) Griswold, Sr., and Mrs. Katherine Culbert, both of Nashville; one niece, Mrs. Caroline Culbert Osborn of Austin, Texas, and one nephew, Nelson (Nero) Griswold of Nashville.

Honorary pallbearers were members of the Williamson County Board of Realtors.

Serving as active pallbearers were Jesse Short, Joe Bowman, Fuller Arnold, M. P. Maxwell, John Jewell, Joe Pinkerton, Dr. N. A. Wenning, Col. Fulton Beasley, Jack Whitfield, Rusty Wilkerson, Stewart Campbell, Dr. Harry Guffee, Tom West, Tyler Berry, Jr., Stanley Holtman, Judge Frank Gray, Jr., Dr. Harper Wright, and Joe Cline.

Franklin Memorial Chapel was in charge of arrangements.

— The Review-Appeal, May 13, 1976

"Only recently, William Moss Wilson, better known as Billy Wilson, formed a partnership with popular Felix Truett, Jr., of Truett Realty Company and the firm is now known as Truett-Wilson Insurance Company, with offices on East Main Street. When Felix first learned to lisp he would stand on a stool to answer his parents' telephone — the kind which hung on the wall and had to be cranked to gain central's attention — and say 'This is 107,' and when he answers today ... he still says 'This is 107.' ... Felix would put up a fight before he would allow to be taken from him that number which followed him through childhood, boyhood, young manhood until the present and hopes to still be saying 'This is 107' when old age bends his form and dims his sight."

— Jane Bowman Owen, *Who's Who in Williamson County*, Rick Warwick, ed., originally published in *The Review-Appeal*, October 19, 1950.

Joe Turk

Joseph Hale Turk, 81, died June 23, 2013

Joe was a resident of San Jose Shores since 1969, and was a long time member of Epping Forest and the Gate Governor's Club. Joe attended the University of Miami, where he was president of Kappa Alpha, and graduated from FSU *[Florida State University]* in 1953. He served in the Army in Kentucky for two years and was an executive with Southern Bell for more than 30 years, before his retirement.

Joe was pre-deceased by his parents, Clarence and Margaret Turk of Jacksonville, and his wife Marilyn Moore Turk.

Joe is survived by his sister, Nancy Falta (Bill), Jacksonville; niece Lee Falta, Bellingham, Washington; nephews Steve Falta, Jacksonville; and Ronald Falta (Debbie), and great nieces Sarah and Lisa Falta, all of Seneca, South Carolina.

A private family service will be held at a later time.

— The Florida Times-Union (Jacksonville), June 30, 2013

Portrait Published in *The Review-Appeal* on April 14, 1966

Mrs. Joe Turk Dies; Rites At Humboldt

Mrs. Joe Turk, wife of the manager of the Franklin business office of Southern Bell Telephone Company, died unexpectedly Friday morning about 8:30 at her home on Murfreesboro Road. She had been ill with pneumonia for about two weeks, but her death was apparently the result of a heart attack.

She was formerly Miss Marilyn Moore of Humboldt, Tennessee, and was the daughter of Mrs. Allen B. Moore and the late Mr. Moore of Humboldt.

She was graduated from Sophie Newcomb College in New Orleans, where she studied art, and later taught art in a high school in Memphis. An artist of considerable talent, she participated in all local exhibits and displays.

Since moving to Franklin in 1960, Mrs. Turk had been active in many civic and social organizations. She was a communicant of St. Paul's Episcopal Church and worked devotedly with the Women of St. Paul's.

She was a member of the Carter House Chapter of the Association for the Preservation of Tennessee Antiquities, the Friends of the Library, and the Town and Country Garden Club.

Her husband and her mother are her only immediate survivors.

Funeral services were held Sunday afternoon at the First Presbyterian Church in Humboldt with the Rev. William James officiating. Burial was in Rose Hill Cemetery there.

Honorary pallbearers were Dr. Joe Willoughby, Dr. William Ewers, Hugh Dallas, Livingfield More, Sam Ewin, Joe Eggleston, Bill Stewart, Ross Gillespie, Col. R. L. Duncan, Frank Green, R. O. Williams, Jr., Paul Ogilvie, Gale Ford, and employees of Southern Bell Telephone Company.

Active were Harry Love, Thurman Crim, Perry Day Crim, Jack Albright, Jr., Lloyd Adams, Jr., Jesse Hill Ford, Walter Ketchum, and Dr. Herbert Crockett.

In lieu of flowers the family requested that donations be made to the Carter House Chapter of the APTA, the Memorial Fund of St. Paul's Church here or the Memorial Fund of the First Presbyterian Church of Humboldt.

Franklin Memorial Chapel was in charge of arrangements.

— The Review-Appeal, June 16, 1966

Portrait of An Excellent Citizen

Rev. James Edward Underwood

Mr. Underwood is pastor of the Nolensville Methodist Church in Nolensville. He is married to the former Miss Nellie Kinzer and they live in the parsonage with their three children, Edward 13, David 9, and Timothy 5. Mr. Underwood is a member of the Nolensville Lions Club, the Nolensville PTA and is a director in the Community Center. He is attending Vanderbilt Divinity School.

As Published in *The Review-Appeal* on December 15, 1966

JAMES EDWARD UNDERWOOD
1933 - 1981

Funeral services for minister

Funeral services were held in Columbia, Sunday, March 23, 1981, for Rev. James Underwood, Sr., 47, of Arno Road. He died at his home, Friday, March 20 after a long illness.

He served as pastor of the Epworth United Methodist Church from 1962 to 1965 and pastor of the Nolensville United Methodist Church from 1965 until 1969 when he retired due to ill health.

Mr. Underwood was a graduate of Columbia Central High School, Martin College, Scarritt College and Vanderbilt Divinity School. Before going into the ministry, he was employed by Union Carbide Corporation.

He is survived by his wife, Mrs. Nellie Kinzer Underwood; sons, James Edward, Jr., of Bellevue, David and Timothy Ray, both of Franklin; and his parents, Mr. and Mrs. Ronald Underwood of the Williamsport Community.

Afternoon services were conducted at the Mt. Nebo United Methodist Church. Burial was in the Mt. Nebo Cemetery.

Memorial donations can be made to Martin College in Pulaski, Tennessee.

— The Review-Appeal, March 26, 1981

"It would take a tremendous power to influence a man with a wife and children to give up his job, go back to school, and enter the ministry. ... Friends had been telling him for a long time that he should be a minister, but he couldn't quite bring himself to make the change. One Sunday when he was attending the Craft Memorial Methodist Church in Columbia, the church bulletin gave some figures on how many workers are needed in full-time Christian service. Mr. Underwood read these figures over and over many times to reduce the statistics by one anyway.

"That was the fall of 1960. He enrolled in Martin College in Pulaski and moved his wife and children. ... His grades were such that upon finishing the junior college he was given a full scholarship at Scarritt College in Nashville, which he will attend while serving the Epworth Church.

"[James Edward Underwood is] the son of Mr. and Mrs. Ronald Underwood who live between Columbia and Williamsport."

— Derry Carlisle, *Who's Who in Williamson County*, Rick Warwick, ed., originally published in *The Review-Appeal*, July 19, 1962.

Excellent Citizens and Notable Partings

Dr. J. O. Walker

Dr. J. O. Walker has practiced medicine for 54 years and is known and loved throughout Williamson County as the dean of physicians here.

A native of Williamsport in Maury County, he was graduated from the first class at Columbia Military Academy and from Vanderbilt School of Medicine in 1913. In 1964 he was honored by the Tennessee Medical Association as the "Outstanding Physician of the Year." In May of this year, the Middle Tennessee Medical Association presented a plaque to him in recognition of his "continued outstanding service."

During World War I he served as a medical officer in naval aviation and was one of the first physicians to conduct research in the field of aviation medicine.

Dr. Walker served three consecutive terms as direct representative from Williamson County in the Tennessee Legislature, 1955-57-59, and in 1961 he was elected to the State Senate. He sponsored a number of bills for improvement of medical conditions and initiated legislation for the extension of hospital services and for rabies control.

Continued on next page

As Published in *The Review-Appeal* on July 18, 1968

JAMES OTEY WALKER
1888 - 1977

He was made the first chief of staff of the Williamson County Hospital which he helped found in 1958 and was honored for this service by the Williamson County Chamber of Commerce in 1960.

Always vitally interested in the work of the Tennessee Medical Association he served in the TMA House of Delegates for 35 years.

He is a director of the Williamson County Bank and is a member of the First Presbyterian Church.

His wife, the former Miss Annie Baker Jones of Williamsport, died in 1962. He has three children, J. O. Walker, Jr., and Mrs. Oliver Kittrell of Franklin and Mrs. Will Dale of Columbia and nine grandchildren.

Dr. J. O. Walker,
physician here over 50 years, dies

Dr. J. O. Walker, beloved physician in Williamson County for more than a half century, died Tuesday afternoon at Harpeth Terrace Convalescent Home where he had been a patient for several years. He was 89 years of age.

Funeral services were held Wednesday afternoon, Feb. 23, at 3 p.m. at First Presbyterian Church. The Rev. Edward K. Beckes, minister of the church, officiated, and burial was in Williamson Memorial Gardens.

Dr. Walker practiced medicine for 58 years and was known and loved throughout Williamson County as the dean of physicians here.

A native of Williamsport in Maury County, he was the son of James Rucker and Izora Moore Walker.

He was graduated in the first class at Columbia Military Academy and from Vanderbilt School of Medicine in 1913. In 1964, he was honored by the Tennessee Medical Association as the "Outstanding Physician of the Year." In May, 1968, the Middle Tennessee Medical Association presented a plaque to him in recognition of his "continued outstanding service." During World War I, he served as a medical officer in naval aviation and was one of the first physicians to conduct research in the field of aviation medicine.

Dr. Walker served three consecutive terms as direct representative from Williamson County in the Tennessee Legislature, 1955-57-59, and in 1961, he was elected to the State Senate. He sponsored a number of bills for improvement of medical conditions and initiated legislation for the extension of hospital services and for rabies control.

He was made the first chief of staff of the Williamson County Hospital which he helped found in 1958 and was honored for this service by the Williamson County Chamber of Commerce in 1960.

Always vitally interested in the work of the Tennessee Medical Association he served in the TMA House of Delegates for 35 years.

He was a director of the Williamson County Bank and was a member of the First Presbyterian Church.

Dr. Walker's first wife, Mrs. Jennie Williams Walker, died in 1918 during the flu epidemic.

His second wife, the former Miss Annie Baker Jones of Williamsport, died in 1962.

Survivors include two daughters, Mrs. William House Dale of Columbia and Mrs. Oliver Kittrell, Jr., of Franklin; one son, James Walker, Jr., also of Franklin; nine grandchildren, James Otey Walker, III, of Atlanta, John W. Walker, Mrs. Donald (Jennie Ann) Harris, Mrs. John E. (Roberta) Rodgers of Nashville, Mrs. William P. (Lillias) Johnston of Nashville, William House Dale, Jr., James Walker Dale, Andrew McLean Dale, and Frank Kittrell Dale, all of Columbia; and three great grandchildren.

Grandsons served as active pallbearers.

Honorary pallbearers were members of the Williamson County Medical Society and directors of Williamson County Bank. In lieu of flowers the family suggested donations to a favorite charity. Franklin Memorial Chapel was in charge of arrangements.

– The Review-Appeal, February 24, 1977

Excellent Citizens and Notable Partings

Portrait of An Excellent Citizen

William H. Walker

"Walker Chevrolet is still owned by the Walker family. I have purchased cars from them for as long as I can remember. They have always treated me with honesty and integrity, and with great service. I remember trading for a new car with Billy Walker, Sr. When I was getting ready to drive it out, he told me if he hadn't found two quarters under the back seat, he would have lost money on the deal."

– Leonard Isaacs, *Franklin, Tennessee, the Jewel of the Harpeth*

Portrait Published in *The Review-Appeal* on March 17, 1966

WILLIAM HELM WALKER, SR.
1928 - 2018

Franklin - William Helm "Billy" Walker, Sr., age 89 of Franklin, Tennessee, passed away July 12, 2018.

Veteran of the US Air Force during the Korean Conflict. Graduate of Battle Ground Academy. He attended David Lipscomb College then graduated from the Bowling Green Business University. He was a former elder at Fourth Avenue Church of Christ. Owner and operator for many years with Walker Chevrolet. He received his 50-year dealer recognition from General Motors and he served on various local and national committees in the automotive dealership industry. He was also a dedicated Boy Scout leader for several years. He was an Eagle Scout Honoree and recipient of the Silver Beaver Award. At the Boxwell Boy Scout Reservation, Billy was instrumental in establishing the COPE Course which is named in his honor.

He was active in the community and served as Past President of the Franklin Noon Rotary Club and was a recipient of the Paul Harris Fellow; Past Chairman of the Williamson County United Way; Past President of the Williamson County Chamber of Commerce where he was presented the Legends Award for his service to Williamson County.

Survived by: wife of 65 years, Louise Clay Walker; sons, William H. Walker, Jr., James Clay Walker, Robert Louis Walker and John Stewart (Kimberly) Walker, Sr.; grandchildren, Amanda (Chase) Young, William Walker III, Josh Walker, Hannah Walker, Tori Walker, Madi Walker and John Walker, Jr.; great grandchildren, Parker Benefield and Annalise Walker.

Funeral services will be 1:00 PM Sunday, July 15, 2018 at Williamson Memorial Funeral Home, Perry Cotham, Jim Taylor and Steve Blackman officiating.

Interment Mt. Hope Cemetery. Active pallbearers will be Boy Scout Troop 137. Honorary pallbearers will be Employees of Walker Chevrolet and Franklin Noon Rotary Club members. Memorials may be made to the Members of Churches of Christ in Scouting, Boy Scout Troop 137 or Heritage Church of Christ.

Visitation will be 5-7 PM Saturday and one hour prior to the service on Sunday at Williamson Memorial Funeral Home.

— The Tennessean, July 13, 2018

CHEVROLET · DIAL 794-2503 FOR SERVICE · Oldsmobile
WALKER
"A Quality General Motors Service Center Since 1926"

Ed B. Warren

Ed B. Warren has been a funeral director in Franklin for 31 years and is presently a member of the firm of Franklin Memorial Chapel. He served for two years on the Board of Governors of Tennessee Funeral Directors and is also president of Williamson Memorial Gardens.

Mr. Warren has been a member of the Franklin Lions Club since 1945 and has held positions of president and secretary. He was selected "Lion of the Year" in 1960 and was presented a 20-year membership pin in 1965. While serving as president, he appointed the first industrial committee in Franklin which later developed in to the Chamber of Commerce. He organized the hospital committee and as president of the Lions Club served on it. This committee was able to work with the County Court in securing a referendum which made Williamson County Hospital possible.

He was president of the Chamber of Commerce for two terms and on the Board of Directors for six years.

A member of the First Methodist Church, Mr. Warren has been on the official board since 1945 and was treasurer of the church for four years. He was chairman of the Finance Committee for four years and is presently president of the Hal Peoples Bible Class. He was delegate to the Annual Conference for seven

---

As Published in *The Review-Appeal* on May 9, 1968

years and was a delegate to the Southeastern Jurisdictional Conference in 1964 and will serve as a delegate for 1968. He has been a member of the Board of McKendree Manor, the Methodist home for retired individuals, since it was first organized.

During World War II he served in the U.S. Navy for four years with two years in the South Pacific theatre and has been in the Naval Reserve since 1941.

Mr. Warren is a graduate of Middle Tennessee State University and of Gupton-Jones School of Embalming in Nashville.

He served as president of the Franklin High School Men's Club and was chairman of the Rebel Bowl committee for three years. He was awarded the PTA Life Membership Pin. He is also a Mason.

Mr. Warren is married to the former Miss Marian Grigsby and they have two daughters, Kay and Lynn, students at the University of Tennessee.

Ed Warren, Civic, Church, and Business Leader, Dies

Edward Blythe Warren, one of Williamson County's most active businessmen and civic and church leaders, died unexpectedly Monday morning while at work at Franklin Memorial Chapel after suffering a heart attack.

Funeral services were held Tuesday afternoon at First United Methodist Church. The Rev. C. H. Hunt officiated and burial was in Williamson Memorial Gardens.

Mr. Warren, 58, was born and reared in Bethesda and was the son of the late John Blythe and Florence E. Warren. He was educated in Williamson County schools and was graduated from Middle Tennessee State University in Murfreesboro and from Gupton – Jones School of Embalming in Nashville. He had been a funeral director here for 35 years and was vice-president and a partner in Franklin Memorial Chapel. He was president of Williamson Memorial Gardens.

He was an active member of the Williamson County Chamber of Commerce, had served as president on two different occasions, in 1956 and again in 1959, and at the time of his death was chairman of the public relations committee to finance the brochure to promote the county.

As a member of the Franklin Lions Club for many years he had also served as president of this organization and was interested in all its work and projects.

A lifelong member of the Methodist Church, he was lay leader for many years of the First United Methodist Church of Franklin and had been a member of the official board a number of years. He was also a member of the Men's Choir of the church. He had represented the local congregations at the Tennessee Annual Conference frequently and had been an official representative at the national conference.

During World War II he served in the U.S. Navy with two years of his duty in the South Pacific.

He served for two years on the Board of Governors of the Tennessee Funeral Directors.

Survivors include his wife, Mrs. Marian Grigsby Warren of Franklin; two daughters, Misses Kay and Lyn Warren of Memphis; and one brother, the Rev. Fenton Warren of Nashville.

Serving as pallbearers were H. A. Robinson, Truman Harper, James Pewitt, Richard Morrison III, Clyde Stephens, Tim Akin, Jr., Hugh Williams, Jr., Coy Peach, and Jimmy Taylor.

Franklin Memorial Chapel was in charge of arrangements.

— *The Review-Appeal, February 3, 1972*

Judge James W. Warren

Portrait Published in *The Review-Appeal* on May 19, 1966

Graveside services held for former Judge Warren

Graveside services for former Williamson County Judge James Wilson Warren were last Saturday at Mount Hope Cemetery, with Father Julien Gunn officiating. Franklin Memorial Chapel was in charge of all arrangements.

Mr. Warren, who served eight years as county judge (the office is now county executive), died July 22 at Williamson County Hospital after an extended illness at the age of 87. He was a resident of Winstead Court.

Judge Warren was a highly respected citizen of Franklin as a businessman, public office holder, church and civic leader.

The Jim Warren Park on Boyd Mill Pike is named for him.

Warren was instrumental in organizing the Franklin Rotary Club and served as its first president. He was also active as an adult leader in Boy Scouts and organized the first Wolf Cub Pack in Memphis following World War I. He also was an elder in First Presbyterian Church of Franklin.

Warren operated a farm implement company for nearly 25 years, during which time he was the county's authorized John Deere tractor dealer.

A native of Lincoln County, Warren grew up in Memphis. He attended Wallace Preparatory School in Nashville and enrolled in Hamden-Sydney College in Virginia. He left college after his junior year to enlist in the Vanderbilt Hospital Unit [S] during World War I.

Survivors include his wife, Mrs. Mariclare Scruggs Warren of Franklin; one daughter, Mrs. Warren (Lenore) Taylor of Nashville; granddaughter, Mrs. R. S. Brown Jr., also of Nashville; two great grandchildren, also of Nashville and one sister, Miss Margaret Warren of Jackson.

— *The Williamson Leader, July 29, 1983*

Portrait of An Excellent Citizen

James B. White

The Review-Appeal could not play favorites with an exceptional couple as the James B. Whites and is thus featuring Mr. White as an excellent citizen this week after featuring Mrs. White last week.

Mr. White, a native of Smyrna, came to Franklin 18 years ago to work with McGee Parts Company. When that firm was sold to R. H. Chilton Co. a short time later, he remained with Chilton as branch manager of the local operation. Seven years ago he became manager of all the branch stores in the Middle Tennessee area and is now manager of the automotive warehouse for the company in Nashville.

He is a past president of the Williamson County Jaycees and was chairman of the County Center Recreation Program. This past year he was president of the Franklin High School Men's Club. He is a member of the Williamson County Rescue Squad and a former member of the CB Club. He has been a volunteer fireman for a number of years. He is a member of Fourth Avenue Church of Christ.

The Whites live on Everbright and have three daughters, Patsy, Amy, and Cindy. They are a sports loving family, particularly water sports, and spend much time at Center Hill with their boat for water skiing.

As Published in *The Review-Appeal* on July 4, 1968

James B. "Jim" White, 73, died Wednesday, September 25, while vacationing in Ennis, Montana.

He was born in Rutherford County, but made his home in Franklin. He was a veteran of World War II serving in the U.S. Navy. He worked for R. H. Chilton Company and Mid-State Steel. He was a member of Fourth Avenue Church of Christ, past president of the Williamson County Jaycees, past captain of the Williamson County Rescue Squad where he was a charter member as well as a life-time member, and a captain of the Franklin Fire Department.

Survivors include his wife, Virginia Perry White of Franklin; three daughters, Mrs. Patrick (Pat) Springer, Mrs. Dale (Amy) Pewitt and Mrs. Allen (Cindy) Gentry, all of Franklin; and 10 grandchildren.

Services will be Saturday, September 28, at Williamson Memorial Funeral Home with Tom Riley, Perry Cotham and Myron Keith officiating. Burial will follow in Williamson Memorial Gardens.

Visitation with the family will begin at 3 p.m. Friday at the funeral home.

Active pallbearers will be Jerry White, Butch White, Perry Holley, Bill Holley, Kyle Williams, Larry Inman, Jim Inman, Keith Butler, Hubert Young, and Tom Gore.

Memorials may be made to The Middle Tennessee Diabetes Association, The American Heart Association or your favorite charity.

— The Review-Appeal, September 27, 1996

***

In 1969, Jim went to work for Mid State Steel in Nashville and retired in 1987 from Carolina Steel (former Mid State Steel). Jim was a resourceful man with a quick wit, but will be most remembered for his servant heart. He loved his three daughters and their families: Pat (Patrick) Springer, Amy (Dale) Pewitt and Cindy (Allen) Gentry. His servant heart failed him in 1996 and he went to be with the Lord.

— Cindy White Gentry
December 2019

Portrait of An Excellent Citizen

Mrs. James B. White

Mrs. James B. White, the former Miss Virginia Perry of Huntingdon, Tennessee, manages a household for her husband and three children, works full time at Williamson County Bank, and finds time to accomplish many tasks for other organizations.

She is the wife of James B. White, who is with the R. H. Chilton Co. in Nashville and the mother of three children, Patsy, 18, who is now a freshman at Middle Tennessee State University in Murfreesboro, Amy, 12, in Franklin Junior High, and Cindy, 6, in Franklin Elementary School. The Whites live on Everbright Avenue.

She has been employed for the past 16 years at Williamson County Bank and is now chief teller.

Mrs. White has been active in Girl Scout work as assistant troop leader and as publicity chairman for the entire county. She has also worked extensively in PTA organizations for several years. This last year she was second vice-president and finance chairman for the Franklin High organization, and in that capacity was chairman for the concessions stand at the Harlinsdale Colt Show and at the Rodeo. Next year she will be treasurer for the Franklin Elementary-Junior High PTA.

She is a member of the Fourth Avenue Church of Christ and the 200 Bible Class.

As Published in _The Review-Appeal_ on June 27, 1968

Virginia White retired from the Bank of America (former Williamson County Bank) in 1990 where she climbed the ladder and eventually became a Senior VP with a specialty in marketing. During this time, she would greet most newcomers to Franklin with a loaf of Merridee's Bakery bread at the door of their new home.

Throughout her career, she also served in the community as Franklin Elementary PTA president as well as several years as the president of the Williamson County Chamber of Commerce where she was instrumental in bringing Columbia State Community College to the area.

She also served as the regional president of the National Association of Banking and Professional Women. Virginia loves spending time with her children, grandchildren and great-grandchildren: Pat (Patrick) Springer, Amy (Dale) Pewitt and Cindy (Allen) Gentry. Jenny has seen many changes through the years and her enduring legacy has helped shape Franklin.

– Cindy White Gentry
December 2019

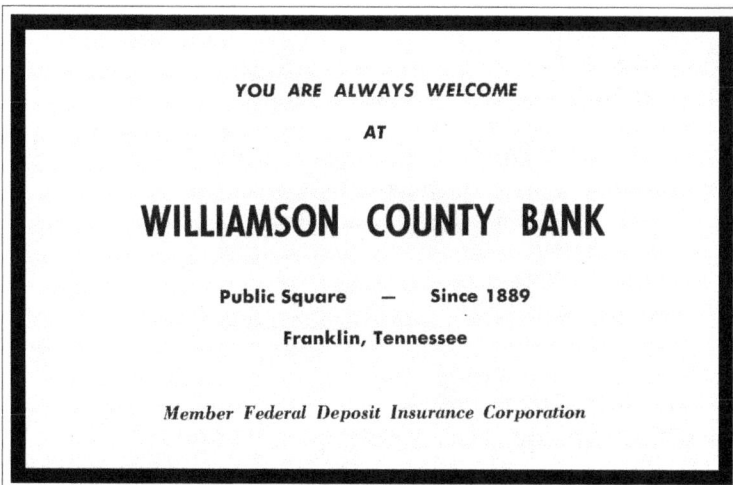

Melvin White

Melvin White who was born and reared in the Flat Creek community of Williamson County has been a farmer since he was a young man, but for the past several years has owned and operated the White Dairy Supply in College Grove.

He is married to the former Miss Zelma Creswell and they have three children. Their daughters are Mrs. Harvey Isom, of Allisona, and Mrs. William Eudailey of Memphis and their son, Tony, is a freshman at Tennessee Tech, majoring in Agriculture. Tony, a member of the Future Farmers of America, just recently was named American Farmer by FFA.

Mr. White and his family attend the Allisona Church of Christ where he is treasurer and teaches a Bible class of teenagers. He also serves as vice president of the Bank of College Grove.

As Published in *The Review-Appeal* on November 30, 1967

Melvin B. White, Age 91, Williamson County, March 16, 2007, of the Flat Creek community of College Grove, Tennessee, departed this life on March 16, 2007, at Baptist Hospital in Nashville, Tennessee, following an extended illness.

He was the son of the late Wiley B. White and Cora Reed White. He was preceded in death by a brother, Alvin R. White.

Survived by his wife of 73 years, Zelma Lee Creswell White; daughters, Harriette Jane Isom (Harvey) and Faye Eudailey of College Grove, Tennessee; a son, Tony White (Diane) of College Grove, Tennessee; four grandchildren, Brent Isom (Jamie), Amy Isom Ham (Tim), Jason Eudailey (Melissa), Jennifer Miller (Andy); 5 great-grandchildren, Clay and Jacob Isom, Tanner Ham, Judson and Foster Eudailey.

Mr. White served as an elder of the Allisona Church of Christ and was past owner and operator of White's Dairy Supply for 40 years. He served 9 years on the Board of Directors of Williamson Medical Center, helped organize the Williamson Co-op serving as Vice-President, served on the Board of Directors of the Bank of College Grove for 33 years, was a life member of and served on the Board of Directors of David Lipscomb University, and was a member of the American Dairy Association.

Funeral services will be conducted at Lawrence Funeral Home Sunday, March 18, 2007 at 2 p.m., with Brother Roy Arnold and Brother Tom Holland officiating.

Interment will follow at Mt. Hope Cemetery in Franklin, Tennessee.

Visitation will be held Saturday, March 17, 2007 from 3 p.m. until 8 p.m..

Active Pallbearers are Brent Isom, Jason Eudailey, Andy Miller, Tim Ham, Milan White and Leon Robinson. Honorary Pallbearers are Ennis Wallace, Charles Meek, Jr., Mike Moorehead, Board of Directors of Lipscomb University, H. A. Threet, George Graham, Randall Hagwood, James Anglin, James (Monk) White, Dwayne Keefer, Jim Smith, Walter Ogilvie, Charles Meek, Sr., Robert Newcomb, Russell Pulley, Brian Carter and Fred Cunningham.

LAWRENCE FUNERAL HOME AND CREMATION SERVICES, Chapel Hill, TN (931) 364-2233.

– The Tennessean, March 17, 2007

* * *

Portrait of An Excellent Citizen

Dr. Joseph L. Willoughby

Dr. Joseph L. Willoughby has practiced medicine here since 1960. Originally from Mt. Juliet, Tennessee, Dr. Willoughby was graduated from the University of Tennessee School of Medicine in Memphis and served for three years in the U.S. Navy. He is an elder of the First Presbyterian Church and has served as an adult adviser for the Youth Fellowship of the church. He is a member of the Tennessee Medical Association and other professional organizations. Dr. Willoughby is married to the former Miss Betty Chastain and they have two children, Andrew, four and a half years old, and Mary Beth, three. They live on Hillsboro Road.

As Published in *The Review-Appeal* on December 21, 1967

JOSEPH LEEPER WILLOUGHBY
1934 - 2018

Joseph Leeper Willoughby, MD, born October 15, 1934, died December 15, 2018.

Mr. Willoughby was born in Morristown, Tennessee. A graduate of Mt. Juliet High School, he attended George Peabody College and Memphis State University, graduating from The University of Tennessee College of Medicine in Memphis in 1957.

Following his graduation, he served as a medical officer in the U.S. Navy for three years. He moved to Franklin in 1960 and began a medical career lasting 53 years.

Dr. Willoughby recognized a need for more geriatric care facilities soon after moving to Franklin. In response to the need, he envisioned and was responsible for the creation of Harpeth Terrace Convalescent Center (now Grace Healthcare) and Claiborne Hughes Convalescent Center (now Claiborne and Hughes Nursing and Rehabilitation Center).

In addition to his medical practice, Dr. Willoughby was an astute businessman and was active in a variety of organizations, including the American Medical Association, the American Academy of Family Practice and Williamson County Medical Society.

He served 45 years in the House of Delegates on the Long-Term Care Committee of the Tennessee Medical Association and received the TMA's "Outstanding Physician of the Year" in 2007. He was also active in The Heritage Foundation of Williamson County, elder of First Presbyterian Church, Franklin Noon Rotary Club, founding member and president of the Carnton Association (now part of Battle of Franklin Trust).

Dr. Willoughby was also active in the Williamson County Chamber of Commerce and co-founder of Harpeth Academy (now BGA Lower School). He was the founding secretary for State Volunteer Mutual Insurance Company and a member of the SVMIC Board of Directors from 1975-2007.

He will be remembered as a kind and caring physician whose desire was to do the best for his patients and remain current with medical advances. He loved living in Williamson County and truly embodied the four quadrants of the county seal: agriculture, education, religion and history. Dr. Willoughby spent many recreational hours either on a tractor at his farm or hunting in a duck blind.

He was preceded in death by his parents, Rev. A. H. and Edna Pennington Willoughby, and brothers, Col. J. David Willoughby, Charles E. Willoughby and Dr. William E. Willoughby.

He is survived by his wife of 62 years, Betty Chastain Willoughby; son and daughter-in-law, J. Andrew (Andy) and Donna O'Neill Willoughby of Franklin; daughter and son-in-law, Beth W. and Jeff Beutel of Calhoun, Georgia; grandchildren, Amanda W. (Tommy) Holler, David A. Beutel and Scott T. Beutel; great-grandchildren, Hannah Michelle Ballow and Haven Grace Thompson; and nieces and nephews.

The family thanks the wonderful caregivers from Senior Helpers who took great care of him in recent years.

In lieu of flowers, please consider a memorial gift to Williamson Medical Center Foundation, Battle of Franklin Trust or First Presbyterian Church in Franklin.

Pallbearers will be John W. Jones, grandsons, nephews and friends.

Honorary pallbearers include Ronald S. Ligon, Dr Kenneth Dodge, Dewees Berry IV, Dan Parsons, Calvin Lehew, Embree Blackwell, Dr. Grant Hensley, James T. Oglesby and members of the Franklin Noon Rotary Club.

Visitation will be Tuesday, Dec. 18 from 4 p.m. to 8 p.m. at Williamson Memorial Funeral Home. The service will be Wednesday, Dec. 19 at 11 a.m. at First Presbyterian Church, 101 Legends Club Lane in Franklin, with visitation one hour prior to the service. Williamson Memorial Funeral Home is in charge of arrangements.

– The Williamson Herald, December 16, 2018

Portrait of An Excellent Citizen

Mrs. Franklin D. Wilson

Mrs. Franklin D. Wilson is working in the community where she was born and reared. She is the Teller at the Nolensville Branch of the Harpeth National Bank. She was before her marriage, Miss Peggy Stephenson. Mrs. Wilson received her grammar school education at Nolensville and graduated from Franklin High School in 1952. She is the mother of two children. Jackie, 13, attends Nolensville School and Marianne, a young lady of 5, is a kindergarten student at Tusculum. Mrs. Wilson is a member of the Nolensville Methodist Church and is president of the Wesleyan Service Guild. She also serves as treasurer of the Nolensville Community Center.

As Published in The Review-Appeal on October 12, 1967

PEGGY STEPHENSON WILSON
1934 –

Beyond the 1960s

My husband Frank and I have continued living in the town of Nolensville all these years. I retired from First Tennessee Bank after 27 years. Frank was postmaster of Nolensville for 30 years. Both of our children and our four grandchildren were involved in sports which kept us very active. We now have five great-grandchildren.

During Homecoming '86, the Nolensville Recreation Center Board of Directors approached me to be chairman of collecting the history of Nolensville and possibly publish a book, since it was an old, historic town. Blindfolded, I thought maybe we could staple a few pages together. Thanks to all the newspaper clippings from the Nolensville News, Review-Appeal, etc., it became a community effort of volunteers, families sharing information, pictures and a few stories of yesteryear and today. Later, a 357 page, 11" x 14" hardback book, *Nolensville 1797 – 1987, Reflections of a Tennessee Town*, was published. This big red book was the product of our efforts and is used in libraries and schools across Williamson County.

Frank and I have traveled with Tennessee Postmasters to State and National League of Postmaster Conventions several years, including Hawaii and Puerto Rico. We have continued to be members of Nolensville First United Methodist Church, spanning sixty-five years, serving on various committees. We are charter members of the Nolensville Historical Society.

We, along with other interested residents, met with the Williamson County Recreation Department Directors to help save the old Nolensville school building from demolition. Even though it was a school from 1937 – 1972, the building was used for community activities, scouts, youth sports, etc., even Nolensville's first library. The Nolensville Historical Society now has a home of longevity. The building has been completely restored. It not only houses the society but Nolensville's Museum. It remains active with wrestling and other sports activities, meetings, church and many more activities and rentals. This was my school from 1942 until I graduated 8th grade in 1948.

Growing up on a farm, wading in the Bittick Creek, climbing fences, drawing water from a well, starting to school in a one room school building, living in a small quaint community where we know most everyone, and meeting others as they move to Nolensville, has given me memories and opportunities that I will always cherish.

– Peggy S. Wilson
Nolensville, Tennessee 37135
February 2020

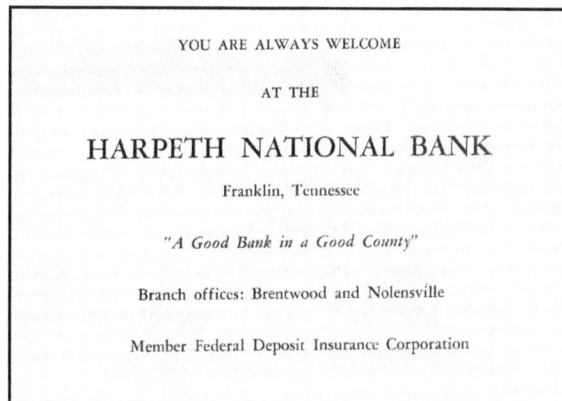

YOU ARE ALWAYS WELCOME

AT THE

HARPETH NATIONAL BANK

Franklin, Tennessee

"A Good Bank in a Good County"

Branch offices: Brentwood and Nolensville

Member Federal Deposit Insurance Corporation

Portrait of An Excellent Citizen

W. C. Yates

"W. C. was full of energy and ideas and always had some new project going to improve the school and community affairs. He organized Franklin High's first P.T.A. He formed a Men's Club to promote the athletic program. He set up a guidance counselor service. He initiated the formation of the "County Center" that transformed the high school back campus into a community recreational park. ... He was constantly busy carrying the message of the school into the community, and bringing the community leaders into the program of the school."

— W. C. Yates, *Tales of a Tennessee Yeoman, 1991.*

Portrait Published in *The Review-Appeal* on May 12, 1966

WILLIAM CLAUDE YATES
1903-1992

Yates' Life Touched Many Individuals
By Bailey Leopard, Publisher and Editor

At one time, there was hardly an adult in Williamson County whose life had not been touched in some way by William Claude Yates, who in 88 years served as school teacher, coach, principal, superintendent of education and executive director of the Chamber of Commerce.

Scores of those who learned science, vocational agriculture, football or a better way to live under the tutelage of Mr. Yates came Saturday morning to Franklin's First United Methodist Church to pay a final tribute to the man who also created one of Franklin's most attractive residential developments, published his autobiography at age 86, and taught a Bible class.

Mr. Yates died last Thursday, June 4, at Williamson Medical Center of cancer.

Dr. Edward Crump, minister of the First United Methodist Church where Yates had served as Sunday school superintendent and taught a Bible class, characterized the funeral service as "a celebration of the tremendous life of W. C. Yates."

He described Yates as "an institution within himself," and said that his life as a Christian was visible to all [who] knew the longtime educator and civic leader.

"There are few citizens who've had as much influence on Williamson County as W. C.," he added.

Myron Keith, who served for many years as minister of Franklin's Fourth Avenue Church of Christ, described Yates as "a great man who leaves such a great heritage."

John Moran, retired banker and former student under Yates, said as he walked from the church at the close of the service, "Mr. Yates is the number one man of Williamson County, and I'd say Dr. (Harry) Guffee is the number two man. He (Yates) has touched the lives of a lot of people."

Born in a log cabin in Garrison Hollow in rural Williamson County at the turn of the century, Yates attended old Southall school, graduated from Franklin High School, enrolled at the University of Tennessee at Knoxville and was a teammate of the late U.S. Sen. Estes Kefauver on the 1922 Volunteer football team that finished with an 8-2 record.

He returned to the county where he was born and devoted 43 years to educating its children.

He spent 35 years at Franklin High School, where he taught science and vocational agriculture; coached Franklin High's Rebels to the 1930 Little 10 high school football championship, and served as principal of the school during World War II.

Yates twice ran unopposed for county superintendent of education, and headed the county school's system from 1960-1968.

His contributions to education were memorialized when the former vocational training school in Franklin was named for him, and Columbia State Community College designated its Franklin facility as the Yates campus [Claude Yates Vocational Center].

It is also fitting that he was buried in Franklin's Mt. Hope Cemetery, within sight of two of the community's schools. The cemetery is passed daily by hundreds of children making their way to and from school.

For many years, Yates served as a Sunday school superintendent and taught a Bible class at First United Methodist Church. The W. C. Yates Men's Bible Class at the church is named for him.

He participated with his son Bill and Franklin developer Calvin Lehew in creating Charlton Green, a distinctive residential community near his home on Murfreesboro Road.

Two years ago, Yates wrote his memories of family, friends and acquaintances in his autobiography, *Tales of a Tennessee Yeoman*.

Survivors include his wife, Mrs. Floy Geiger Yates; son, Bill Yates of Franklin; stepdaughter, Mrs. Betty Massey of Lake Forest, Illinois; stepson, William Randolph of Franklin; and four grandchildren, Mrs. Polly Yates Stanfield, Mrs. Cindy Yates Webb, Both of Atlanta, Georgia, Mrs. Louise Randolph Jenrath of Winston-Salem, North Carolina, and Mrs. Elizabeth Randolph Giglio of Germany.

Active pallbearers were C. C. Brown, Tom Stoddard, Elmer Pewitt, Ernest Doughtey, Wilson Herbert, Jimmy Gentry, Charles Grigsby and Calvin Lehew.

Honorary pallbearers were members of the W. C. Yates Men's Bible Class of First United Methodist Church and members of the 1930 Little 10 championship football team.

Franklin Memorial Chapel was in charge of arrangements.

— *The Williamson Leader, June 11, 1992*

A Few Pointers About This Book

Names in the Table of Contents were entered as they appeared in the series.

Some of the first portraits originally published in *The Review-Appeal's* "Portrait of an Excellent Citizen" series were printed without a biographical entry. We have noted those portraits at the bottom of the page with the attribution, "Portrait Published in *the Review-Appeal* on [date]." Portraits printed with their original biographical entry, are noted in the attribution, "As Published in *the Review-Appeal* on [date]."

In this book, we have used the term *[sic]* to indicate that a word or phrase in question is printed as originally published.

[Brackets] were used to indicate omissions, corrections, or explanations that were not part of the original text.

Headings without death dates indicate the person featured was still living at the time of publication.

We made every effort to include all names that appear in the book in the Name Index. Surnames and entries in bold point to each of the Excellent Citizens.

The Subject Index contains names of businesses, churches, cemeteries, schools and universities, events and local attractions, organizations, communities, military service, governmental departments, and more.

The period advertisements placed throughout the book are actual ads which ran during the 1960s, or prior. They were used not only for the valuable content they provide, but to give the reader a more comprehensive look at the Franklin business community.

Period Advertisements

Name Index

Excellent Citizens and Notable Partings

BRAY,
Jane Pinkerton,
see "Pinkerton, Jane"
Norman, 249
BRENT
Alex, 53
Caroline, 53
Catherine Hardison, 52, 53
Catherine Leslie, 53
Craig Hardison, 52-53
Gloria, 53
Henderson Cook, 53
Louise Dudley Hassell, 53
Ransom Joseph, Jr., 52-53
Ransom Joseph, Sr., 52-53
Susan (Mrs. Craig Brent), 53
BREWER
Dempsey, 35
James, 109
BRICKNER
DeeDee, 73
Steve, 73
BRIGGS
George I., 30
Matilda Harrison, 67
BRINKLEY, Jewell, 89
BRITTAIN
Leonard (Bill), 30
Wendell, Mrs., see "Pyle, Susan"
BROOKS, Melvin, Rev., 165
BROUGHTON, Allen, 163
BROWN
Aaron V., Governor, 103
C. C., 273, 329
Charlie, 50
Daniel, 81
Martin, 271
Paul, 137
R. S., Jr., Mrs., 317
Ralph, 105, 193, 295, 299
Roy, 163
Sara, (Mrs. Danny), 81
Tom, 273
William B., 113
BROWNE, Bill, 105
BROWNING, Gordon, Gov., 147, 169
BRUMIT, C. J., 261
BRYSON
Judy, 65
Randall, 65
Randy, 65
BUCHANAN
Dave, 271
J. B., 273
Paul, 253
BUCKNER, Martha, 50
BUFORD
Bess Johnston,
(Miss Bess) 30, 31, **54-55**
James L., 121
BURCH, Bonnie, 37
BURCHETT, Lonnie, 113, 139, 173
BURKE, Sheila, 115
BURKS
Freeda (Mrs. Wayne), see
"Hunt, Freeda"
Jeffrey, 167
BURLEIGH
Marietta Eggleston, 95
Robert, 95
BURNETT, Mary Campbell, 29

BURNS
Amy, 57
Ava Anna Brandon, 57
Christine Johnson, 56, 57
Donald, 57
Edna, 57
James L. (Jim), 56, 57
James Roy, 57
James William, 56-57
Jerry, 57
Lois, 57
Melvin, 57
Milton, 57
Pattie (Mrs. Steve Dunning),
56, 57
Renee, 57
Sybil, see "Hickman, Sybil Burns"
Vickie (Mrs. Jeff Pittenger),
56, 57
BURROW
Doug, 137
Evelyn, see
"Hagerty, Evelyn Burrow"
Jean Petway, 137
Jean, 137
Jim, 137
BURTON, Byrd, Mrs., 21
BUTNER, Goldie Gertrude, see
"Gentry, Goldie Gertrude
Butner"
BUTTERFIELD, Mary Ann Liggett
(Mrs. John R. Butterfield),
see "Liggett, Mary Ann"
BUTTS
Paul, 273
Tommy, 247
BYARS
Elizabeth, 59
Elmer Ernest, 58-59
Lillian Shaw, 58, 59
P. N., 59
CABOT, Christopher, 193
CAIN
Byrd Douglas III, 61
Byrd Douglas, Jr., 60, 61
Leslie Ann, 61
Sarah Ann Drinkard, 61
Scott, 61
CALDWELL
Cecil, 32
Emmie, 32
CALLAWAY, Dr. James, 137
CALLICOTT, Clint, 35, 151
CALLIHAN, Margaret, 50
CAMERON
Ann, 65
Billy, 209, see also
"Cameron, James William"
Billy, Jr., 64, 65
Blanche (Mrs. William Moss),
61, 62
Don, 63, 65
Don, Jr., 63
Douglas, 65
Douglas, Mr. and Mrs., 62
George M., 62, 63
Iva Billington, 63
Iva Jane
(Mrs. Douglas Harmon), 62-63
J. W. III, 65
J. W., Jr., 65

CAMERON, cont.
James William (Bill), 64-65
Jean, 65
Jessie Louise Grigsby Huff,
64, 65
June, 65
Michael Stuart, 65
Mike, 65
Olie Cornelia Edgmon, 62-63
Robert M., Dr. (Bobby), 64, 65
Tim, 65
Tom, 65
William, 63
CAMPBELL
Anne James Briggs, 67
Brandon, 167
Carolyn, 201
Dana L., 167
Jacob, 167
Kaleigh, 167
Louise Farnsworth, 67
Louise Winder, 67
Patrick, 67
Rebecca, see
"Kinnard, Rebecca Campbell"
Stewart, Jr., 67
Stewart, Sr., 55, 66-67, 137, 187,
235, 247, 277, 305
William Winder, (1st), 67
William Winder, (2nd), 67
CANNON
Brown, 129, 193, 239
Cynthia Graham,
see "Fleming, Cynthia
Graham Cannon"
Henry, 113
James, 301
Newton, Governor, 103
CARBONNE, David, Dr., 213
CARLISLE
Derry, 72, 76, 85, 101, 152, 202,
213, 248, 255, 303, 309
Walter O., 83, 121, 213, 235, 275
CARPENTER
Doug, 95
Stephen, 95
CARTER
Brian, 323
Lucille, see
"Henderson, Lucille Carter"
CATHEY, Betty Regen, see
"Regen, Betty"
CATO, Jack, 297
CAVENDAR, G. W. F., 38
CAYWOOD, Hannah Meadows,
see "Meadows, Hannah"
CHAPMAN
Dan, 69
Effie Cotton, 68, 69
James H., Jr., 68, 69
James Henry, 68-69
Jim, 148
Ruth (Ruth Chapman Newman),
68, 69
CHARRON, Patricia, 50
CHASTAIN, Betty, see
"Willoughby, Betty Chastain"
CHERRY
Bill, 50
Charles, 95
Ruth, 95
William E., 217, 275

Excellent Citizens and Notable Partings

EUBANKS, Ed, 109
EUDAILEY
    Faye (Mrs. William Eudailey),
        see "White, Faye"
    Foster, 323
    Jason, 323
    Judson, 323
    Melissa, 323
EVANS
    Bill, 45
    Bobby, 113
    Lemech W., 149
    Leon, 21
    Virginia, (Mrs. L. W. Evans),
        see "Hendricks, Virginia"
EWERS, William, Dr., 307
EWIN
    Ben, 31
    Bob, 111
    Connie, 31
    Dee, 31
    John, 82, 83
    Kathryn, 31
    Marge, 30, 31
    Mason, 31
    Mildred, 31
    Sam, 30, 307
    William W., 193
EWING
    Andrew McGavock, 149
    Baxter, Mrs., see
        "Gentry, Dorothy"
    John Frank, Jr., 149
    Kathryn (Mrs. J. Frank Ewing),
        see "Hendricks, Kathryn"
FAGAN, Pat, 225
FAIR, Fairfax, Rev., 261
FALK
    Janice, see "Akin, Janice"
    Randall, Rabbi, 301, 303
FALKOFF
    Ellise, 303
    Julius, 301, 303
FALTA
    Lee, 306
    Lisa, 306
    Nancy, (Mrs. Bill Falta), 306
    Ronald, 306
    Sarah, 306
    Steve, 306
FANN, Margaret, 163
FARNSWORTH
    Louise, see
        "Campbell, Louise Farnsworth"
    Russ, ix, 66
    S. E., 29, 257, 261
FARRAR, Rudolph, Mrs., 102, 103
FARRELL, Bernadene Beasley, see
    "Beasley, Bernadene"
FARRIS, J. D., Mrs., 55
FAW, Elizabeth, see
    "Regen, Elizabeth Faw"
FAXON, Mrs., see
        "Small, Fannie Park"
FAY, Will, 207
FERGUSON, Herbert, 137
FERRELL, William B., 67
FEWELL, Gary, 57
FINCH
    Dan, Mrs., see
        "Thompson, [Sara Evelyn]"

FINCH, cont.
    Mike, 299
    Pat, 299
FINE
    Fred, Dr., 301, 303
    Jo Ann, 303
FINLEY
    Ashley, 101
    Bob, 35
    Effie Wheeler, 101
    Gerry Pentecost, 100, 101
    Jim 100, 101
    Robert Chester, Jr., 100-101
    Robert Chester, Sr., 101
    Taylor, 101
FINNEY, Ellen, 50
FISHER
    Doug, 137
    Douglas and Julie, 50
    Gerald, 149
    John, 89
    Morton, 283
    Steve, 207
    Susan McCall, see
        "McCall, Susan"
FITZGERALD
    Bolin, Lt., 163
    Charles, Sgt., 163
    Scott, 89
FIVEASH, James, 89, 225
FLATT, Carlton, 113
FLAUGHER, John T., 67
FLEMING
    Cynthia Graham Cannon,
    29, **102-103**
    G. M., Rev., 183
    Fleming, Ken, 201
    Sam M., Jr., 29, 45, 102, 103
    Sam M., Sr., 32, 102, 103
    Sam, 247
    Sheila, 50
FLETCHER, Beverly Johnston,
    see "Johnston, Beverly"
FLIPPEN
    Jerry R., 143
    Oden, 273
FLOWERS, Mattie/Mattye C.
    (Mrs. W. A. Flowers), 291
FLOYD, Page, 195
FLY
    Jerre/Jerry, 45
    Jerre/Jerry, Jr., 35, 38, 222, 273
    Jerre/Jerry, III, 38
FLYNT, Mary Lou Clinard, see
        "Clinard, Mary Lou"
FOLEY
    Red, 294
    Shirley (Mrs. Pat Boone), 294
FOOTE, Robert, Dr., 50
FORD
    Bettye, see "Ragan, Bettye
        (Mrs. Dennis Ford)"
    Elizabeth, see
        "Hutcheson, Elizabeth Ford"
    Gale, 307
    [Gerald R.], Pres., 107
    Jesse Hill, 307
FORREST, Nathan B., General, 103
FORTE
    David, 202
    Michael, 202

FOSTER
    Alison, 163
    Anne Clark, 50
    Barry, 163
    Christopher, 163
    Diane, see "Hood, Susan Diane"
    Donald, Rev., 253
    Morgan, 163
FOWLKE, Janet, 269
FOX
    Annie Elizabeth, see
        "Beasley, Annie Elizabeth Fox"
    Charlie III, 149, 235
    Charlie, Jr., 35, 129, 149
    Elizabeth (Mrs. Charlie Fox),
        see "Hendricks, Elizabeth"
    Hendricks, 35
    Joe Hendricks, 149
    T. C., 35
    Tom, 35, 149
FRANK, Jesse, 79
FRANKLIN, Linda Sue Strickland,
    see "Strickland, Linda Sue"
FRENCH
    Catherine, 79
    Imogene, 105
    Jimmy, 295
FRENSLEY
    Albert Clifton (Cliff),
    xiii, **104-105**, 113, 271
    Ann, 104-105
    Betty Dye, 104, 105
    Bill, 105
    David, 104, 105
    Grant, 105
    John Wallace, 105
    Tiffany, 105
    Walker, 107
FRIST, Thomas, Sr., Dr., 193, 247
FROST, C. Kenneth, Mrs., 91
FRYER
    Betty, 65
    Bill, 35
    Christopher, 35, 107
    Edward Allen, 106, 107
    Elizabeth Leslie Zerfoss
    (Libby), 106-107
    Geoffrey, 35, 107
    Martha Leslie Hailey, 106, 107
    Sue Beasley, see "Beasley, Sue"
    William S. (Bill), 106, 107
    Fulcher, Phillip, 233
FULLER, Dan, 189
FULTON
    Charles, Rev., 147
    Richard, U.S. Rep., 155
GALAVIN, Martha Ann Isaacs, see
    "Isaacs, Martha Ann"
GAMBLE, Howard, 89
GARDNER
    Amelia Jameson, 108, 109
    Clifford Leroy, xiii, **108-109**
    David A., 109
    Emerson, 109
    Grady, 109
    Herman, 109
    Hester Hill, see "Hill, Hester"
    Rosa, 109
    W. H., 109
GARNER, Bob, 173

HAGAN, Keith, Dr., 275
HAGERTY
    Dan, 127, **136-137**, 193
    Evelyn Burrow, 136, 137
HAGWOOD, Randall, 323
HAILEY, Ceacy, 95
HALEY
    Eula Lee, see
        "Jaqueth, Eula Lee Haley"
    Fred, Dr., 65
    Jeff, 213
HALL
    David, 139
    David, Dr., 38
    Henry W., xiii
HALLIBURTON, Margaret, see
    "Hinson, Margaret Halliburton"
HAM
    Amy Isom, see "Isom, Amy"
    Tanner, 323
    Tim, 323
HAMBLEN, Martha Belle, see
    "Strickland, Martha Belle
        Hamblen"
HAMILTON, Dorothy Clinard, see
    "Clinard, Dorothy"
HAMM, Thomas, 81
HAMMAND, Mark, 149
HANNAH, Bob, 187
HARALSON, Ivie, 229
HARDCASTLE
    Alice, 139
    B. D. (Dock), 139
    Cheryl, 139
    Cora Alice, 139
    Loy G., Jr. 138, 139
    Loy George, Sr., 91, **138-139**, 229
    Marjorie Andrews, 139
    Stan, 139
    Thomas Luther, 139
HARDIN, Brenda, 117
HARDISON
    Bob, 89
    Catherine,
        see "Brent, Catherine
        Hardison"
    Clarence, 141
    Fanny Hughes, 141
    Henry L., Prof., 140-141
    Rebecca, see
        "McCall, Rebecca Hardison"
HARDY, Bob, Dr., 21
HARGROVE, Sam A., 63
HARKREADER, Mike, 105
HARLIN
    Thomas C., 235
    Tom, 89, 213, 275
HARMON
    C. B., 113
    Douglas, 62, 63
    Eddie, 113
    Iva Jane Cameron, see
        "Cameron, Iva Jane"
HARPER
    Brownie W., 255
    Edna, see "Ragan, Edna Harper"
    Hyde III, 137, 255
    Hyde S., Jr., 137, 255
    Hyde S., Mr. and Mrs., 255
    John, 269
    Truman, 225, 269, 315

HARRIS
    Frank, 231
    George, 129
    Jennie Ann (Mrs. Donald
        Harris), 311
    Mary Moore, 231
    Paula Marie Ehresman,
        see "Ehresman, Paula Marie"
HARRISON
    Anne Briggs, 67
    James, 67
    William H., 67
HART
    Judy (Mrs. Edwin), 269
    Susan Sneed Pyle, see
        "Pyle, Susan"
HARTLEY
    Emmeline, 207
    Laban, 207
HARWELL
    Ina Blankenship, 142, 143
    Mary Ann (Mrs. Briggs Smith),
        142, 143
    Matthew Thomas, 81, **142-143**
    Merritt M., 143
    Wilma Beasley, 143
    Wyatt L., Rev., 143
HASSELL
    Amanda, 189
    Charles Berry, 53
    Clint, 189
    Louise Dudley, see
        "Brent, Louise Dudley Hassell"
HATCHER
    Blythe, 129
    John, 195
HAWKS
    Brandt, 233
    Mary North, see "North, Mary
        (Mrs. Gary Hawks)"
HAYES
    J. Michael, Mrs., 67
    Jim, 275
    Leon, 89
    Martyn, Mrs., 131
    Pat, 131
HAYNES, Fanny, 31
HAYS
    Jim, 259
    John, 259
HAZELWOOD
    Larry, 81, 143
    Martha Ann, 207
HEITHCOCK
    Dorris, 57
    Elbert, 105, 113, 271
    Elizabeth, see
        "Smith, Elizabeth Heithcock"
HENDERSON
    John H. III, 145
    John H., 145
    John H., Jr., 144, 145
    John Hughes, Judge, 144-145
    John, 147
    Lloyd T., 145
    Lucille Carter (Mrs. Thomas P.),
       146-147
    Margaret B. Heron, 144, 145
    Margaret H. (Peggy), 144, 145
    Samuel, Rev., 291
    Thomas P., III, (Tom), 145, 147

HENDERSON, cont.
    Thomas P., Jr., (Tom), 145, 147
    Thomas Perkins, ("Captain
        Tom"), 145, 146, 147
HENDRICKS
    Amanda Overbey, 149
    Elizabeth, 149
    James, 157
    Joe Rucker, 69, **148-149**
    John, 157
    John, Sr., 157
    Joseph G., 148, 149
    Kathryn, 149
    Kevin Scott, 149
    Mary Ellen, 29, 148, 149
    Robert Herman, Jr., 149
    Rosa, 149
    Scott, 149
    Virginia, 149
HENRICH, John C., Rev., 283
HENRY, W. L., xiii, 203, 269
HENSLEY, Grant, Dr., 325
HEPPER, Cliff, 153
    Hepper, Jean Hight, see
        "Hight, Jean"
HERBERT
    Ann Ruffin, 150
    Bill, 21, 99, 187
    Jan Buckner, 50
    Joseph Erwin (Joe), xiii, 150, 151,
        187, 273
    Marianne, 150
    Mary Wilson, 150, 151
    Shedie Wilson,
        24, 69, 81, 125, **150-151**, 187,
        273, 329
    Robert, 187
    Thomas, 273
    Tom, 69
    Wilson, Jr., (Shac), 38, 150
HERON, Margaret B., see
    "Henderson, Margaret B. Heron"
HICKLEN, Larry, 149
HICKMAN
    James, 21
    Sybil Burns, 57
HIGHT
    Betty Robinson, 153
    Clarice, 153
    Elizabeth, 153
    Jack, 153
    James, 153
    James A., Sr., 153
    Jami, 153
    Jean, 153
    John Chester, Rev., 91, 152-153
    John Philip, 153
    Judy, 153
    Mary White, 153
    Nancy, 153
HILL
    Ann, 155
    Claude E., 263
    Davis C., Dr., 261
    Davis, Dr., 263
    Fannie Carothers, 263
    Hazel, 155
    Heidi, 155
    Helen, 155
    Hester Sewell, 275
    Hester, 155

MCCALL, cont.
    Lycurgus, 207
    Maude Wells, 209
    Mildred Creswell, 206, 207
    Nick, 50
    Rebecca Hardison, 209
    Susan, 207
    Thomas Luther, 21, **208-209**
MCCOMBS, Estelle, see
        "Pinkerton, Estelle McCombs"
MCCORD
    Annie Millard, 210
    Billy, 273
    Dianne, 211
    E. D., 210
    James (Bubba), 211
    Jim, Gov., 169, 265
    John Millard, Sr., 113, **210-211**
    John, Jr., 89, 211
    Katherine Northcross, 210, 211
    Newt, 273
    Randall (Kip), 211
    W. H., Jr., 273
MCCORMICK, Terry,
        see "Meadows, Terry
        McCormick, Rev."
MCCOY
    Eleana, 50
    Robert, 81
MCCRACKIN, Robert, Dr., 253
MCDONALD
    Bill, 173
    LaRue, see
        "Hughes, LaRue McDonald"
MCELROY, Larry, 50
MCEWEN
    Jennie B., 103
    John B., Col., 103
MCFARLIN
    Ellis, 81
    Polly Ann Covington,
        see "Covington, Polly Ann"
MCGAVOCK
    Carrie Winder, 67
    Van, Mrs., 125
MCGEE, Kirk, 273
MCGHEE
    Jennifer, 229
    Lisa, 229
    Sandra Moody, see
        "Moody, Sandra"
MCGILL, Lois, see "Keith, Lois McGill"
MCGINNESS, Paul H., 137
MCGLOTHLEN, Gaye, Dr., 79
MCGLOTHLIN
    Bill, 79
    Jim, 79
    Lena, see "Dickerson, Lena"
MCGUGIN, Dan, 134
MCKAY
    Clifford A., Rev., 47
    Herb, 297
    Robert, 89
MCKEAND, Leonard, Jr., 187, 235
MCKEE
    Irwin, 50
    Tom, 50
MCLEMORE, C. K., 235
MCMEEN, Charles, 109
MCMILLAN, Bryant, 89

MCNAMEE
    David Bragg, 50
    Elizabeth, 50
    Jane Crane, 50
    Marc Raymond, 50
    Marc, 50
    Rebecca Bragg, see
        "Bragg, Rebecca (Becky)"
MCPEAK, Lanny, 89
MCPHERSON
    Doug, 38
    Houston, 38
MCWHERTER, Ned Ray, Gov., 49
MCWILLIAMS
    Cletus W., xiii, 121, 157, **212-213**
    Donna Jean Sanders, 212, 213
    John Cletus, 212, 213
    Melanie, 212, 213
    Sandra Louise, 212, 213
MEACHAM
    H. C., 273
    Harold, 299
    Virginia, 245
MEACHEAM, Margherita, 199
MEADE, C. B., Mrs., 55
MEADOWS
    Amy, 219
    Benjamin, 219
    [Meadows], Charlotte, see
        "Jolly, Charlotte"
    Emily, 219
    Hannah, 219
    Laura, 219
    Terry McCormick, Rev., 219
    Thomas A., Rev., 218, 219
MEDICK, Erin Marie, 219
MEDLIN
KELLER, 289
    Meredith, 289
MEEK
    Charles, Jr., 323
    Charles, Sr., 323
MEYRING
    Inge, see "Smith, Inge"
    Walter, 284, 285
MILLER
    Andy, 105, 323
    Bill, 289
    Henry North, 222
    Henry Ross, 222
    Inez, see "Hood, Inez"
    Jennifer, 323
    Laura May Tyer,
        (Mrs. William Hart Miller),
        29, 220-222
    Leah, 93
    Louise, 163
    Margaret, Mrs., 67
    Nancy (Mrs. Lester Miller)
        127, 129
    Sallie Stockett, 221
    Samuel G., Jr., Rev., 281
    William E., Judge, 119
    William H., 91, 121, 123
    William Hart., 220-222
    William W., 221
    William, 113, 173, 193, 209, 247, 257
    Winston, 149

MILLS
    Alma Jean Weatherly, 224, 225
    Ben, 259
    Craig, 259
    Eliza, 259
    L. I. III (Buddy), 222, 224, 225
    Latham, Jr., 184
    Latham, Sr., 183, 184
    Lilbourne Irby, Jr. (Buddy,
        Buddie), 79, 89, **224-225**
    Mary Johnson Knowles, 141,
        183, 184, 185
    Paige, 259
    Peter, 224, 225
    Russell, 259
MINTON
    H. P., Jr., 147
    H. P., Mrs., 146, 147
    Thomas, 147
MITCHAM
    Brenda Smith,
        see "Smith, Brenda"
    Laura Kate, 283
MITCHUM, Millard, 273
MIZELL, Andrew, Mrs., 102-103
MOBLEY, Henry P., Jr., Rev., 63
MOFFET, Claudia, 291
MONTAGUE
    Jane McCall (Mrs. Van Montague),
        see "McCall, Jane"
    Leila, 209, 226, 227
    Leila Bettis, 227
    Rebecca (Becky), 226, 227
    Thomas Larimore, 227
    William Larimore, 227
    Van Bettis, 209, **226-227**, 275
MOODY
    Charles, 229
    Connie Neal Carr, 229
    D. E., 229
    David, 229
    Denville, Sr., 229
    Ed, 24, 35, 38, 79, 91, 127, 137,
        225, 275
    Ed, Jr., 229
    Eileen, 24
    Isabelle Wiggs, 228, 229
    Jack, 229
    James, 229
    John, 229
    Sandra, 228, 229
    Thomas Calvin (Tom),
        91, **228, 229**
    Tom C. II, 228, 229
    Tommy III, 229
MOON, Tom, 35
MOORE
    Allen B., Mr. and Mrs., 307
    Catherine Morrow, 230, 231
    Izora, see
        "Walker, Izora Moore"
    J. D., 263
    Jerry, 170
    Johnnie, 245
    Marilyn, see
        "Turk, Marilyn Moore"
    Maurice, Rev., 293
    Robert N., Jr., 230, 231
    Robert Nathaniel, xiii, **230-231**
    Virgil H., Jr., 231
MOOREHEAD, Mike, 323

SCHIAVELLO
 Michael, 197
 Rachael Lawrence, 197
SCHKLAR
 Gerson, 213
 Lillian, 213
SCHMIDT
 Jack, Dr., 95
 Joan, 95
SCHULER, Beth, 35
SCIVALLY, Elsie Green, 125
SCRUGGS
 Mariclare, see
  "Warren, Mariclare Scruggs"
 William F., Elder, 291
SELPH, Frances Liggett
 (Mrs. W. R.), 198-199
SENSING, Carol, 50
SEWELL
 Barbara (Mrs. David S. Jones), 275
 Barry, 189
 Christy (Mrs. Lloyd), 269
 Cynthia, (Mrs. Robert A.
 Sewell), 275
 Daisy Beasley, 275
 J. M., 55, 113
 Malcolm L., 275
 Nathan A., Dr., 275
 R. Ernest, 275
 Robert A., Dr., 275
 Robert and Harriet, 50
 Robert Ewell (Bob), 45, 55, 91,
 113, 127, 129, 209, 222, 229, 235,
 247, 257, **274-275**
 Ruth Alexander, 274, 275
SEXTON, Alice, see
  "Liggett, Alice Sexton"
SHAFFER, Gilbert, 97
SHARBER, Jerry, Mayor, 151
SHATZ
 David, 301
 Mark, 301
 Peggy, see "Tohrner, Peggy Shatz"
 Sol, 303
 Sylvain, 303
SHAW
 Elynor, see
  "Bellenfant, Elynor Shaw"
 Eva Mai, see
  "Robinson, Eva Mai Shaw"
 Lillian, see
  "Byars, Lillian"
SHERWOOD, Betty Sue Pinkerton,
  see "Pinkerton, Betty Sue"
SHORT
 Alma Bennett, 276, 277
 Barbara, 191
 James C., Judge, xiii, 229, 277
 James, Sr., 79
 Jesse E. [Sr.], 277
 Jesse E. III, 222, 276, 277
 Jesse Edelin, Jr. 276-277
 Jesse, 305
 Lucille (Lucille Short Bennett),
 277
 Lucille Cotton, 277
 Mary Anne (Mrs. James E.
 Warren), 276, 277
 Walter B., 276, 277
 William Miller ("Bilbo"),
  222, 276, 277

SICKLER, Cletus, 175
SIMMONS
 Clifton, 215
 J. B., 257
 John, 137
 Lynn, 215
SIMMS, Janice, see "Akin, Janice"
SIMS
 Belton Wayne, 278-279
 Beth, 278, 279
 Chris, 278, 279
 John, 89
 Martha Roberts, 278, 279
SINGLETON, Josie, 271
SKELLEY, Skyler, 295
SLATER, Nancy R., 265
SLAYTON, Edward, 271
SLOAN
 Anne Joy, 281
 Elizabeth (Elizabeth Sloan
 Bainum), 281
 George Arthur II, 280, 281
 John Elliott, 280, 281
 John Elliott, Jr., 280, 281
 Katherine (Katherine Sloan
 Thomas), 281
 Margaret Howe, 280, 281
 Paul [Sr.], 280, 281
 Paul Lowe III, 280, 281
 Paul Lowe, Jr., 281
 Thomas Howe, 280, 281
SLUSHER, Jan, 251
SMALL
 Fannie Park, 29
 John Parkes, 45
SMITH
 Al, 120
 Arch, Dr., 213
 Arlie, 85
 Billy, 295
 Brenda (Mrs. Tom Mitcham),
 282, 283
 Briggs, Mrs. (Mary Ann Harwell),
  see "Harwell, Mary Ann"
 Charles B., 143
 Devan Elizabeth Swain, 45
 Donald, 38
 E. F., 39, 203
 Edith, see "Little, Edith Smith"
 Elizabeth Heithcock, 282, 283
 Erich, 38
 Frank, Jr., 38
 Inge Meyring, 284-286
 Ingelein, 284
 Jessie, (Mrs. Coy Smith), see
  "Price, Jessie"
 Jim, 323
 John Lewis (Johnny), 282, 283
 Kathleen, see
  "Ogilvie, Kathleen Smith"
 Kevin, 50
 Mark J., 297
 Mont, 284
 Norman, 21
 Paul, 284, 286
 Phoebe Fly, 38
 Pleas, 145
 Roscoe, 237
 Stefan, 284
 T. Wyatt, 143

SMITH, cont.
 Thelma Beasley, see
  "Beasley, Thelma"
 Tom, Rev. 293
 Wallace, Judge, 127, 145
SMITHSON
 Carl, 99
 Charles, 35
 Don, 27
 Howard, 81
 Jackie, 163
 Ronnie, 163
 Rosie Hood, see "Hood, Rosie"
 Waldon, 27, 89
 Waldron [Waldon], 113
SMOTHERMAN
 Eddie, Rev., 38
 Wilma Harwell, 143
SNEED, Cara, see "Pyle, Cara Sneed"
SNELL
 Brandon, 57
 Jessica, 57
SOUTH
 Sara Cogswell, see
  "Cogswell, Sara"
 Will, 76
SOUTHGATE, Royland, 21
SOWELL, Mary Z., 27
SPARKMAN
 Christine O'Bryan, 288, 289
 Jan, 289
 Judith Sue, (Mrs. Judy Travirca),
 288, 289
 Patricia Ann (Mrs. Patsy Morel),
 288, 289
 Richard Hanes, Jr., 125, 288, 289
 Richard Hanes, Sr., 288, 289
 Seth, 109
 Tom, 289
 Tripp, 289
SPEAKMAN, Jim, 38
SPENCER
 Addie, 291
 Anne V. Wilson, 291
 Billie, 117
 Charles B., 290, 291
 J. E., 27
 James, 291
 Jessie, 291
 Mae Frances, 291
 Patricia Diane (Mrs. Sherman
 Williams), 291
 William, Rev., 291
SPRINGER,
 Pat White, see "White, Pat"
 Patrick, 319, 321
STAFFORD
 Clay, 285, 286
 Faye, 163
 Jim/Jimmy, 163
STAMMER, Sarah Harwell, 143
STANFIELD, Polly Yates, 329
STANFILL, James, 157
STEAKLEY, Glen, 27
STEELE
 Alex, 47
 Alex, Mrs., 29
 Allen, 29
 Edward T., 145
 Lewis M., 145
 Lewis, 47

Excellent Citizens and Notable Partings

Subject Index

Excellent Citizens and Notable Partings

Excellent Citizens and Notable Partings

www.ingramcontent.com/pod-product-compliance
Lightning Source LLC
Chambersburg PA
CBHW061758260326
41914CB00006B/1156